MW00685213

PACEMAKER®

Careers

GLOBE FEARON

Pearson Learning Group

Pacemaker® Careers, Second Edition

We would like to thank the following educators, who provided valuable comments and suggestions during the development of this book:

Consultants

Content Consultants:

Laura Norris, Occupational Course of Study Support Teacher, Charlotte Mecklenburg Schools, Charlotte, North Carolina

Robert Havas, Career Development Instructor and Adjunct Assistant Professor, Psychology, County College of Morris, Randolph, New Jersey

Kathryn McNally, School Counselor, North Shore High School, Glen Head, New York

ESL/ELL Consultant:

Elizabeth Jimenez, GEMAS Consulting, Pomona, California

Reviewers

Teacher Reviewer:

Melissa Canet, High School Vocational Skills Teacher, La Vega High School, Waco, Texas

Project Staff

Art and Design: Tricia Battipede, Evelyn Bauer, Eileen Brantner, Susan Brorein, Bernadette Hruby, Heather Kemp, Daniel Trush

Editorial: Stephanie Cahill, Elaine Fay, Monica Glina, Maury Solomon, Tara Walters, Shirley White

Manufacturing and Production: Irene Belinsky, Karen Edmonds, Jennifer McCormack, Sonia Pap, Cathy Pawlowski

Marketing: Maureen Christensen, Douglas Falk, Linda Hoffman

Publishing Operations: Kate Matracia, Debi Schlott

Technology: Joanne Saito

About the Cover: A career is a chosen occupation. There are many kinds of careers that people choose to follow. Some people choose to work in the construction field as building contractors. Part of their responsibility is to look at blueprints. Other people choose to work in the field of technology because it allows them to work with computers. The medical field offers a lot of different careers, too. Those people who choose a career in healthcare often use instruments that help them take care of others. A blood pressure gauge and cuff are used by many healthcare professionals to take a person's blood pressure. A career in the field of transportation is great for people who like to travel. Pilots who fly airplanes and helicopters can travel over great distances.

Photography Credits appear on page 373.

Copyright © 2005 by Pearson Education, Inc., publishing as Globe Fearon®, an imprint of Pearson Learning Group, 299 Jefferson Road, Parsippany, New Jersey 07054. All rights reserved. No part of this book may be transmitted in any form or by any means, electronic or mechanical, including photocopying, recording, or by any information storage and retrieval system, without permission in writing from the publisher. For information regarding permission(s), write to Rights and Permissions Department.

Globe Fearon® and Pacemaker® are registered trademarks of Globe Fearon, Inc.

ISBN 0-13-024676-X

Printed in the United States of America
2 3 4 5 6 7 8 9 10   08 07 06 05

Globe Fearon
Pearson Learning Group

1-800-321-3106
www.pearsonlearning.com

Contents

Charts

Letters and Forms

A Note to the Student

In this book, you will read about how to choose a career and achieve your career goals. You will find out how to identify your strengths, interests, and abilities. You will also explore your personality traits and values. You will see how these things relate to a career choice and how a career choice relates to jobs. In addition, you will find important information about many different careers in education, transportation, computers and technology, sales, healthcare, law, and much more.

After you have identified a career that matches your interests, you will need to prepare for that career. How much education or training will you need? How do you apply for jobs? How do you successfully interview for jobs? This book will help you to answer those questions.

Finally, you will need to know what happens after you begin a job. What will your paycheck look like? How can you grow in the job? How can you reshape your career plan when your life changes? Answers to these questions are also found in this book.

Several parts of this book will help you learn the things you need to be successful in your career. The photographs and **Learning Objectives** that are found at the beginning of each chapter will focus on the chapter's main ideas and career topics presented. Each chapter ends with a **Career Portfolio Project**. The Career Portfolio Project is a way to help you use what you have learned in the chapter.

Each chapter also contains a **Job Description** that you may want to know more about. Other features, such as **Learn More About It** and **Career Path**, provide interesting information related to topics discussed in each chapter.

We hope that you find the information in this book helpful and interesting. We also wish you success in your school studies and in achieving your career goals.

Unit 1

Careers and You

Before You Read

In this unit, you will learn what a career is and why it is important to plan your career.

Before you start reading, ask yourself these questions:

1. What is the difference between a career and a job?

2. Why is it important to have a career that I like?

3. Do I know what my personal strengths are?

There are many different resources to help you plan your work life. These resources include books found in resource centers in schools.

Learning Objectives

- Explain the difference between a career and a job.
- List three reasons for working and for having a career.
- Outline the seven steps used to plan a career.
- List three reasons why you should plan your career.

Chapter ▷ **1** ▷ **Planning a Career**

Words to Know

career	a chosen field of work in which you try to advance over time
occupation	another term for career
job	any activity done in exchange for money or other payment
employment	having a job
job application	a form that a worker fills out when applying for a job
resource	something that can be used for support or help
salary	the payment a person regularly receives for work
retirement	when someone leaves a job or career after many years
pension	a regular payment given to a retired person for work that he or she performed; usually given by a former employer
working conditions	how things are at a job, such as the number of hours worked in a week
technology	the use of science to create new or better products
production	the act of making something
promotion	a job change that moves a person to a higher position or level in a company
career ladder	a series of related jobs within a career that leads to greater responsibility and a higher position or level

It is a hot summer afternoon in the year 1800. Antonio, who is 16, works beside his father picking grapes on their farm in Italy. The father's arms ache from the hard work. Read the brief conversation between Antonio and his father, which follows on page 4.

"Antonio. This work is for the young. Soon, I will turn the farm over to you."

Antonio takes a deep breath. He must now tell his father the truth. "Father, I don't want to be a farmer. I find the work boring."

The father scowls. "Nonsense. It is tradition for a son to take over the work of his father. You will be a farmer, like me."

Career Choices and Responsibility

Career Trend

In 1900, women made up about 18 percent of the workforce in the United States. By 2001, that figure had risen to about 47 percent. By 2010, that figure is predicted to be about 48 percent.

Career Fact

There are expected to be about 22 million job openings between now and the year 2010. These jobs will range from clearing tables and managing offices to running large companies.

Life has changed since the 1800s. A young man is no longer expected to make a living the same way his father did. He may work as a carpenter, a writer, or even a singer. The role of women has changed, too. Many more women work outside the home now. The number of women who are doctors and lawyers increases each year.

A **career** is a chosen field of work in which you try to advance over time. An **occupation** is another term for *career*, or a chosen field of work. A **job** is any activity done in exchange for money or other payment. Another word for having a job is **employment**.

No one in the United States is assured of having a job. People often compete for jobs. Employers sometimes receive hundreds of applications for a single job. A **job application** is a form that a worker fills out when applying for a job.

Schools and job training programs help people prepare for work. Guidance and career counselors, government agencies, and many other career resources are available. A **resource** is something that can be used for support or help. The Internet is a resource. This book is also a resource. It will help you make career choices and get started in a career.

✓ Check Your Understanding

Write your answers in complete sentences.

1. How has choosing a career changed since the 1800s?

2. What is a job application?

3. What are three resources that can help you choose a good career for yourself?

Understanding What a Career Is

As a child, you might have been asked what you wanted to be when you grew up. You may have answered that you wanted to be a police officer, a firefighter, a teacher, or some other occupation that you admired or understood. These are good careers. However, they are not the right careers for everyone.

Before you can make a good career choice, you need to understand better what a career is.

> **Did You Know** ❓
>
> The word *career* first appeared in the middle 1500s. Its original meaning was "road" or "race course."

1. A career brings some rewards, such as money and satisfaction.

Most adults work because they need money to buy food, clothes, and shelter. Some people choose their careers based on how much money they can earn on the job. The money received on a regular basis for work performed is called a **salary**.

However, people often choose their careers based on other reasons. A woman who starts a small business may enjoy being the owner. A social worker who helps homeless people believes she is making the world a better place. An artist may feel he is making the world more beautiful by what he paints. The small business owner, the social worker, and the artist all get satisfaction from their careers.

Follow your interests and talents when you choose a career, such as working with young people.

Some of these careers may not pay very well. Yet people choose them because they fit their values, talents, or interests.

A good career helps you discover who you are. Many jobs allow us to connect with the people around us and contribute to the world. Work should offer a sense of satisfaction and accomplishment.

2. **A chosen career is a long-term—but not always a lifetime—activity.**

People in earlier generations may have chosen a career early in life. They may have followed a career path, or an outline of how to move or advance in a company or business. Many people stayed in that business until retirement. **Retirement** is when someone leaves a job or career after many years and does not return to a paid job.

For some of these people, the biggest reward was job security, or protection against losing their job. They felt that they would always have a steady paycheck. They would have a pension when they retired. A **pension** is a regular payment given to a retired person by a former employer.

Today, workers are more flexible, or more willing to make changes. A television news reporter might move from station to station to find the best salary and working conditions. **Working conditions** are how things are at a job. The number of hours a person must work and the comfort of the work area are examples of working conditions.

People today often have more than one career and more than one career path. A computer programmer may decide to start her own restaurant. A teacher may sell real estate when his children grow up. A factory worker may decide to become a nursing aide.

As you will learn in Chapter 2, technology has changed the nature of many jobs. **Technology** is the use of science to create new or better products. Many office tasks, such as writing letters, are now done with the help of a computer. Robots in some factories now do much of the work that people once did.

People today often have to move to where the best jobs are found. Companies often move from state to state. For example, they may move to lower their labor or production costs. **Production** involves the act of making something.

For these reasons, a "long-term" career in today's world might last for only 3 to 5 years. In modern times, career success comes from being flexible.

3. **A career gives you a chance to discover and develop your talents.**

   Selena Gonzales has been a nursing home aide for 30 years. She takes care of people who are too sick or weak to live on their own. Selena treats her patients with affection and respect. Because of this, Selena is the most respected aide in the nursing home. She is the person always chosen to train all the new aides.

   Selena's daughter Anne is the manager of a discount clothing store. The store is part of a nationwide chain. Anne worked her way up from sales clerk to store manager. She is now trying to get a promotion to manage several stores. A **promotion** is a job change that moves a person to a higher position or level in a company. In 5 years, Anne hopes to be at an even higher level. Anne is working her way up a career ladder. A **career ladder** is a series of related jobs. These jobs usually lead to more responsibility and a larger salary.

   Which of these women has a career? They both do, and they are both successful. A career does not necessarily mean you are always being promoted or making more money. It does mean staying in a particular field and trying to do your best in it.

✓ Check Your Understanding

Write your answers in complete sentences.

1. What are some of the rewards you can get from a career?

2. Give one reason why workers today must be flexible.

3. What is a career ladder?

How to Plan a Career

A career, if it is the right one for you, can be very rewarding. However, finding the right career is a challenge. How do you find the right career? Here are some key steps in planning for a career. You will learn more about these steps in this book.

STEP 1   Look at the big picture.

Which job areas are the fastest-growing in the United States? What kind of education and training will workers need for these jobs? Unit 1 of this book helps answer these questions.

STEP 2   Ask yourself questions about your talents and the way you want to live.

What are your talents and interests? What rewards, including salary and job satisfaction, do you want from a career? Unit 1 will also help you find out.

STEP 3   Explore different careers.

People often accept jobs without really knowing much about them. They do not know what it will be like to work at them day after day. Once they begin working, they may be surprised or disappointed. Units 2 and 3 of this book will introduce some careers. They will provide information on popular and growing career areas.

STEP 4   Create a plan for your career.

What do you do after you have chosen a career? In Unit 4, you will learn how to make a career plan. That plan includes how to get the education and experience you will need to succeed in your career. The chapters in this unit will also show you how to follow through with your plan.

> **Using Technology**
> Use the Internet to find Web sites about careers in demand. The information found at these sites is often more recent than information found in books. Find career Web sites that end in *.org*, *.edu*, or *.gov* for the most useful information.

STEP 5   **Get hired.**

Starting a career does not always mean getting a job that pays a salary. Some people do volunteer work to get started in a career. A volunteer is a person who works for free, usually for a good cause. Many jobs, whether they include a salary or not, are in demand. Unit 4 will also show you how to get a job. It includes information on how and where to apply for jobs.

STEP 6   **Be successful.**

Many things can affect how well you succeed in your career. These include your outlook on life, your feelings about yourself, and your feelings about the people with whom you work. Unit 5 will show you how to avoid problems in these areas.

STEP 7   **Continue planning.**

Career planning usually takes place throughout a person's life. As you change and jobs change, you will want to rethink your career plans. It is up to you to keep active in terms of managing your career. This is explained in Unit 5.

Career Fact

Most people will change careers, or their field of work, two or three times in their lives. They will change jobs, or the actual activity they do for a salary, at least six or seven times.

Why You Should Plan a Career

Planning your career takes time, energy, and careful managing. So why do it?

Ask Janice. Janice did not make any serious career plans. She entered a trade school to become an electrician. She had heard that electricians make a good salary. There was a training school near Janice's home. She took the entrance test, passed it, and thought she was on her way to a great career.

Halfway through the course, Janice discovered that she did not like doing electrical work. She missed talking with people. It seemed like all she did was connect wires. Yet, she had spent many months and thousands of dollars on the training.

A small amount of career planning might have saved Janice time, money, and energy. If she had spoken to electricians she would have learned what they do on the job. She might have discovered that this was not the career for her. She could have seen that a career involving contact with people would be more rewarding to her.

Geraldo just turned 50. He also just opened his second store. Geraldo buys and sells used sports equipment and clothing. His stores are packed with tents, backpacks, skis, down jackets, and more.

In the past, Geraldo worked at repairing shoes. "Now," says Geraldo, "for the first time in my life, I feel that I have a real career. I have always liked sports. I am very glad to be running my own business. I do not mind working long hours, because I am doing what I like."

Geraldo's only regret is that he did not start his business sooner. "Perhaps if I had done some thinking about my interests 10 years ago, I could have been doing this all along."

Making career plans can be an exciting process of discovery. You can learn about yourself and the world you live in. If you plan, you are less likely to spend your time doing work you do not like. By taking control, you will more quickly earn the rewards that work can bring.

Write About It

Fold a sheet of paper in half. On the left side of the paper, write the rewards you would like to get from a career. On the right side, write your interests and talents. Then, write a paragraph about how a career that makes use of your interests and talents can help you earn the rewards you listed.

✓ **Check Your Understanding**

Write your answers in complete sentences.

1. Why is it important to explore different careers?

2. What do you do after you choose a career?

3. What are two ways to start a career?

Learn More About It

JOB RATINGS

The Jobs Rated Almanac is a useful book for career planning. This book rates, or ranks, jobs in the United States. It also provides lists related to jobs. One such list is of the fastest-growing jobs. Another is of the fastest-declining jobs.

The Jobs Rated Almanac uses six topics to rate jobs. As you work on your career plan, keep these six rating topics in mind.

Rating Topic	Explanation
Salary	How much money does the job pay?
Stress level	How much pressure is there on the job?
Physical demands	How many hours will there be in a workday? Will the work be dangerous? Will physical activities be required?
Environment	Will the work area be clean, well lit, and quiet?
Outlook	Are the number of jobs in this field growing or decreasing?
Security	How secure is the company with its finances?

CRITICAL THINKING What other rating topics can you think of to add to this list?

JOB DESCRIPTION
Home Health Aide

Job Summary
A home health aide cares for sick, injured, or older people in their homes. The patients that a home health aide works with need more care than their families can usually provide.

Most home health aides visit several different patients on the same day. Work hours can vary. Full-time and part-time positions are usually available. Some home health aides work evenings, nights, and weekends.

Work Activities
A home health aide may do any or all of the following activities:

- Pick up medications from a drug store.

- Give patients medications.

- Help patients exercise.

- Help patients to bathe and dress.

- Change bedding, do laundry, and clean patients' rooms.

- Keep records of each patient's condition and progress.

- Make telephone calls for patients.

- Read to patients.

Education/Training Requirements
Some employers do not require a home health aide to have a high school diploma or previous work experience. However, many other employers require the completion of a training program in home care. At the end of the program, the students must pass an exam. Other requirements may include training in cardiopulmonary resuscitation (CPR) and first aid training.

Think About It

What kind of person would make a good home health aide?

Summary

- Today, we have both the freedom and responsibility to choose our own careers. We also must prepare to compete for jobs. We should use available resources to become our own career managers.

- A career is your chosen field of work. A job is an activity done in exchange for pay. You do not have to stay with one career or one job your entire life. A career should give you the chance to develop your talents.

- Rewards come in many forms. Money is one reward. However, it is not always the most important one. Job and personal satisfaction are other rewards.

- There are seven important steps in planning a career: 1) Look at the big picture in the job market. 2) Get to know yourself and your talents. 3) Explore different careers. 4) Create a plan for your career that includes education and experience. 5) Get hired. 6) Work at being a success. 7) Make career planning part of your life.

- Plan and manage your career to save yourself time, energy, and money. Find the work that is most rewarding to you.

career
job
promotion
salary
technology

Vocabulary Review

Complete each sentence with a term from the list.

1. A job change that moves a person to a higher position or level in a company is a _____.

2. A _____ is a chosen field of work.

3. You receive a _____ for doing work on a regular basis.

4. An activity done in exchange for money or other payment is a _____.

5. The making of new or better products using science is called _____.

Chapter Quiz

Write your answers in complete sentences.

1. How do people choose careers today?

2. What are three different career resources?

3. What is the difference between a job and a career?

4. What are three basic needs money can help us meet?

5. What rewards other than money might a career offer?

6. What is a promotion?

CRITICAL THINKING

7. How has technology changed the workplace?

8. Why is career planning important throughout your life?

Career Portfolio Project

Make a list of five tasks you have completed in the past of which you are very proud. Maybe you did a great art project or important volunteer work. Maybe you helped out a friend or trained your pet. After each item on your list, write down what made doing this task so satisfying. What were the rewards? What were the challenges? Did any of these tasks take special talents? Did they use your personal interests? Write a paragraph describing what these tasks have in common and how completing them might help you pick a career.

The number of jobs in some careers depends on the economy. Construction work is an example. In good economic times, there are many jobs in construction. In bad economic times, there are fewer jobs.

Learning Objectives

- List and explain four things that affect employment.
- Name two areas in which career opportunities are increasing.
- Name two areas in which career opportunities are decreasing.
- Describe the relationship between employment and education.

Chapter 2 — Looking at Career Trends

Words to Know

unemployment rate	the percentage, or fraction, of people in the labor force who are looking for work but who have not found jobs
goods	things that can be seen, touched, bought, and sold
services	paid work done to help others, such as teaching or waiting on tables
cyclical unemployment	what happens when people are out of work due to a slowdown in the economy
recession	a period when the production of goods and services decreases for 6 months or more
depression	a very long, severe period of recession
manufacture	to make goods with machines, usually in a factory
demographics	certain facts about a population

Grace and Michael were sophomores in high school. As they walked home one day from school, they began to talk about their futures.

Neither had chosen a career yet. However, they were not too concerned about that. They knew they had time to make choices. Still, the news about the economy was worrying both of them. Their conversation, which follows on page 18, explains their concerns.

Chapter 2 • Looking at Career Trends   17

"I don't know," Grace said. "All I hear on the news are stories about high unemployment. The future doesn't look too good to me."

"I know what you mean," Michael replied. "My brother managed to get a pretty good job after high school, though."

"What does he do?" Grace asked.

"Something with computers," Michael said. "He always liked learning new things about them. Anyway, he says working with computers is a growing career field."

"A growing career field! Everybody keeps telling me there are no jobs in any career."

"The next time he's home, I'll ask him how he knew where the jobs were. Maybe he can help us choose our own career fields."

The Big Picture of Employment

Newspapers often contain stories about companies closing and people being let go from work. These stories can be very discouraging. In the story above, Michael's brother looked beyond the bad news. He did some research and learned where the jobs were. He was then able to match his interests to a career field in which there were a growing number of jobs.

This chapter takes a look at "the big picture" of employment in the United States. In this chapter, you will learn about employment trends. A trend is a direction in which something is going. You will also learn about the kinds of things that affect these trends. As Michael's brother did, you can use this information to become informed about careers. This information can help you to prepare yourself for the future.

What Affects Unemployment?

The **unemployment rate** is the percentage, or fraction, of unemployed people in the labor force looking for jobs. Labor force is all the people who are working or looking for work. If the unemployment rate is low, the country's economy is good. If this rate is high, then the economy is not doing too well. In this chapter, you will learn about four things that strongly affect unemployment rates and trends. These are:

- demand for goods and services

- world events

- technology

- population

Career Fact

The labor force is made up of people 16 years old or older. These people must either be working or be looking for work. The labor force does not usually include students who are in high school.

The Demand for Goods and Services

Every country produces goods and services. **Goods** are things you can see, touch, buy, and sell. Clothing and food items are examples of goods. **Services** are types of work that a person does for others, usually for money. Salespeople, doctors, and hair stylists all provide services.

Most goods and services are produced by businesses, or companies. Businesses produce what they think people will buy. The charge for an item or a service is based on how much a company thinks people will pay for it. The "demand" for goods and services directly affects the number and types of jobs there are.

Here is an example. New products that use the latest technologies are very popular today. Many people want goods such as cellular phones, plasma-screen televisions, and flat-panel computer monitors. As the demand for these products grows, more of the products are made. This often means that more people are hired to make, sell, and transport the products to where they will be bought.

Remember
Production is the act of making something.

In the United States and elsewhere, the economy goes through periods of time called cycles. During a certain part of the cycle, the economy grows. Then, the economy slows down, or shrinks, for a period of time. Here is how the economy works:

When people are employed, they can spend more money. Companies then produce more goods for people to buy. To increase production, companies employ more workers. The economy grows. Over time, demand for goods starts to slow. People spend less. Production of goods slows down, so fewer workers are needed. The unemployment rate increases. This increase is called **cyclical unemployment**.

Cyclical unemployment occurs during slowdowns in the economy. A slowdown may last 6 months or more. If it does, the economy is said to be in a **recession**. A long, severe recession is called a **depression**.

The highest unemployment rate in the United States was in 1932. This was during a time known as the Great Depression. Unemployment rose to almost 25 percent.

The Great Depression began in 1929. Many people in the United States were left poor and hungry. They waited in long lines for food.

✓ Check Your Understanding

Write your answers in complete sentences.

1. Explain the difference between goods and services.

2. Suppose you hear on the news that production of goods is slowing down. How does this affect the unemployment rate?

3. When does a recession become a depression?

How World Events Affect the Economy

World events can also affect the production of goods and unemployment rates in the United States. One example is World War II. This world event led to the lowest-ever unemployment rate in the United States.

During the years of World War II, from 1939 to 1945, the manufacture of war goods, such as planes and weapons, in the United States increased. To **manufacture** a product means to make it using machines. Manufacturing is usually done in a factory. The demand for war supplies led to this increase. The unemployment rate was also very low during World War II. That was because many young male workers were in the armed forces.

Trade agreements and competition from other countries can also affect employment rates. Changes in the price of oil from the Middle East, for example, have often affected the U.S. economy.

One trade agreement that may affect future employment rates is the North American Free Trade Agreement, or NAFTA. NAFTA is a trade agreement between the United States, Mexico, and Canada. It was signed in 1994. Studies on how NAFTA affects the U.S. employment rate are still underway.

Did You Know ?

Other events that can affect the U.S. economy include wars in other countries and presidential elections.

Technology and Jobs

Technology has made it possible to produce goods and services faster. Technology has improved healthcare. It has allowed us to keep in touch with people far away in seconds. However, technology has also changed the job market. The number of jobs in some fields has decreased or disappeared altogether.

At the same time, technology has also created jobs. The fields of medical technology and computer networking, for example, have grown rapidly in the last 10 years. Workers must often learn new things to do these new jobs.

How Population Affects Jobs

Population is the number of people in a country or area. Certain facts about a population are called **demographics**. These facts include age, sex, and employment patterns of people in the population. By studying a population's demographics, we can better predict where future jobs will be.

For example, in 1946, after World War II, the number of children born in the United States went up 50 percent. A large part of the U.S. population today was born in the 1950s. As these people age, they will need more healthcare services. This is one reason why jobs in the healthcare industry are growing.

Career Fact

In 2004, Asians made up one of the fastest-growing parts of the workforce in the United States.

The workforce of the future will include more women and people with different cultural backgrounds. By 2010, Hispanics will make up more of the U.S. labor force than will African Americans. About 30 percent of the American workforce will be made up of African Americans and Hispanics.

✓ Check Your Understanding

Write your answers in complete sentences.

1. How did World War II affect the U.S. economy?

2. What is an example of technology creating new jobs?

3. How will an aging U.S. population affect jobs?

Learn More About It

THE TRANSISTOR

Are you thinking about working in the computer industry? Maybe you would like to design robots for a living. Perhaps you would like to work as a computer crime detective. This person tracks down people who use computers to steal information or money.

If you are considering a career in computers, you can thank the transistor. The transistor is a very small device that acts like a switch. It controls the flow of electric current. It was first used widely in radios and televisions in the 1950s. Today, transistors can be found in many different products. These products include computers.

Personal computers run on tiny chips called microprocessors. Microprocessors are the brains of the computer. A single microprocessor can contain millions of transistors. Together, these transistors can perform hundreds of millions of calculations each second!

The transistor and the microprocessor have changed the way people work all over the world. Together, they are responsible for many new jobs in the computer industry.

CRITICAL THINKING What are some possible careers for someone interested in how computers work?

Five Major Employment Trends

Every few years, the U.S. Department of Labor looks at trends in employment. These trends are best guesses about what will happen. They help to predict how the demand for certain goods and services will change. They also predict whether certain jobs and careers will increase or decrease.

Knowing trends can help you to be realistic about job competition. Trends can also help you prepare yourself with needed training and education to get a job. However, do not choose a career based only on trends. Your interests, talents, and abilities are also important.

Here are five of the major trends expected to continue between now and the year 2010:

1. **In general, the U.S. economy is expected to grow slowly in the twenty-first century.**

    Total U.S. employment is expected to grow from 146 million jobs in the year 2000 to 168 million jobs in 2010. This is an increase of about 22 million jobs, or 15.2 percent. However, these jobs will not be evenly divided over all industries.

2. **In the future, there will be more demand to produce services than to produce goods. In other words, the greatest number of jobs will be in service occupations.**

    Dental assistants, insurance salespeople, fast-food workers, and gas, electric, and water workers are all examples of people with service jobs.

    Service industries are expected to account for about 20 million of the 22 million new jobs added between 2000 and 2010. About four out of every five new jobs will be service jobs or jobs in sales. Most of these new jobs will be in the business, health, and social services areas. Computer and data processing services will account for most of the business jobs.

3. **Technology is continuing to change the workplace.**

Some of the fastest-growing occupations today are computer-related. These kinds of occupations are usually referred to as information technology occupations.

Many of the technical jobs will be health-related. For example, emergency medical technicians will be in high demand. These people will have to know how to operate the latest lifesaving equipment in ambulances. Hospitals and doctors are relying more and more on emergency medical technicians.

People with technical jobs do not always operate complex machines. For example, medical records technicians and health information technicians handle health information. The only machines they operate are computers. Paralegals work with lawyers. They do research on the Internet and elsewhere and complete legal forms. Lawyers are relying more and more on paralegals.

4. **There will be fewer jobs in agriculture, forestry, fishing, and mining.**

Farmers in the United States will continue to grow more food. However, with improved equipment, it will take fewer people to produce more food. The same thing is happening in mining and ranching.

5. **Workers of the future will need to be better educated.**

Professionals are people with jobs that require higher education. They include doctors, lawyers, dentists, and pharmacists. These professional service occupations will grow faster than most others. They will add 7 million of the 22 million new jobs by 2010. This adds more jobs than in most other career fields except for service jobs. Generally, workers who have the most education will earn the most money per year.

Using Technology

Use an online search engine to find out about technical careers in the medical or law fields. Many hospitals and large law firms have their own Web sites that can provide information on career opportunities.

Write About It

A friend who lives in another city writes to tell you that he is thinking about dropping out of school to go to work. He wants to be able to buy a new car. What could you write to your friend about trends in education and in employment? Use facts to support your statements.

This does not mean that everyone must have 4 or more years of college to get a job. High school graduates with a solid background in computers, math, language, and problem-solving should be able to find jobs that pay well. There will be service jobs for those who do not have any special training, too. However, these jobs will pay less, on average, than jobs in other fields.

✓ Check Your Understanding

Use the graph below to answer the questions.

1. What is the subject of this graph?

2. What is the average lifetime pay of a person who did not graduate from high school?

3. What can you say about education and salary based on this graph?

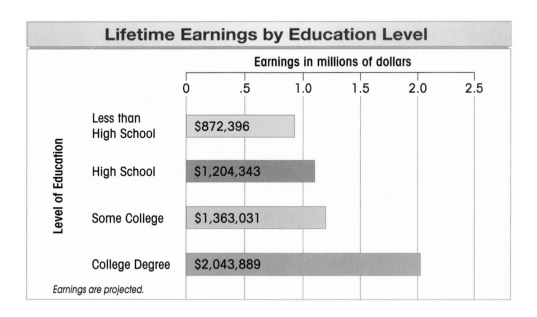

Lifetime Earnings by Education Level

Earnings in millions of dollars

Level of Education	Earnings
Less than High School	$872,396
High School	$1,204,343
Some College	$1,363,031
College Degree	$2,043,889

Earnings are projected.

JOB DESCRIPTION
Fitness Trainer

Job Summary

A fitness trainer helps people to reach their physical fitness goals. A fitness trainer also shows individuals or small groups of people how to perform physical exercises. They help people use equipment and weights properly. Fitness trainers usually specialize in certain areas, such as weight lifting, aerobics, jazz dancing, or yoga.

Fitness trainers work mostly indoors at gyms, fitness centers, or health clubs. Fitness trainers may also work in the homes of their clients. Work hours can vary. The schedule depends on when the trainer is needed. Most fitness trainers work about 40 hours a week. Many work on weekends and in the evenings.

Work Activities

A fitness trainer may do any or all of the following activities:

- Measure the fitness level of individuals.

- Plan exercise programs.

- Show individuals how to use equipment.

- Explain the importance of safety in a gym.

- Keep records of his or her clients' progress in reaching their goals.

Education/Training Requirements

Education requirements range from a high school diploma to a college degree. A person wanting to become a fitness trainer must show that he or she has the ability and training. A number of different organizations offer certification. Other requirements may include training in cardiopulmonary resuscitation (CPR) and first aid.

Think About It

Why might someone decide to become a fitness trainer?

2 ▷ Review

Summary

- Employment and employment trends are affected by four major factors. These are the demand for goods and services, world events, technology, and population.

- When the demand for goods and services is high, the economy is growing. Employment usually goes up. When the demand for goods and services decreases, so does production. Employment then goes down.

- World events that affect U.S. employment include war, trade agreements, and foreign competition.

- Demographics, or certain facts about the population, help shape employment trends.

- Overall, the U.S. economy is expected to continue to grow slowly. The greatest number of new jobs will be in service occupations and technical fields.

- Workers of the future will need to be better trained and better educated. This need will largely be due to new and better technology in the workplace.

cyclical unemployment
demographics
goods
recession
unemployment rate

Vocabulary Quiz
Complete each sentence with a term from the list.

1. The percentage of people in the labor force who are looking for work but have not found jobs is the _____.

2. Things that can be seen, touched, bought, and sold are called _____.

3. Certain facts about a population are called _____.

4. When people are out of work due to a slowdown in the economy, it is called _____.

5. A _____ occurs when the production of goods and services decreases for 6 months or more.

Chapter Quiz

Write your answers in complete sentences.

1. If people have little money to spend, is demand for goods and services likely to be high or low?

2. If the demand for goods and services rises, what is likely to happen to the number of available jobs?

3. What is a recession that lasts a very long time called?

4. What are two jobs created by technology?

5. What are service occupations?

6. What are some of the demographics of a population?

CRITICAL THINKING

7. The world today is well connected due to cell phones and e-mail. Modern companies often operate in several countries. How do you think this might affect employment trends?

8. Explain why you think people who have more years of education earn higher salaries overall.

Career Portfolio Project

You are a reporter for your local newspaper. You are assigned to write an article on career trends in your town or city. How many people in your area are unemployed? What are the most common jobs? Write a list of sources you could use to find this kind of information. Then, choose two items from your list, and use these sources to find information for your article.

Personal strengths, such as having good speaking skills, are important in many careers.

Learning Objectives

- Explain why it is important to know your strengths.
- List four resources for finding out what your strengths and interests are.
- Explain the differences between interests, skills, and personality traits.
- Describe a personal accomplishment and the strengths related to it.

Chapter 3 — Identifying Your Strengths

Words to Know

skill	an ability to do something well, usually because you have practiced it
self-esteem	self-respect
self-assessment	figuring out your strengths and interests
career counselor	a trained professional who helps people with their career searches
aptitude	a natural ability to learn something or to do something well
personality traits	the different ways a person behaves; characteristics
data	information

Toward the end of his junior year of high school, Devon decided to look for a summer job. Before beginning his job search, he spoke with his friend Mark. Here is their conversation:

"I could apply for a job at the mall," Devon said, "but I don't want just any job. I want to enjoy the work. I suppose that I should think about what I like doing and what I'm good at."

Mark thought for a moment. "Maybe you should try getting a job in a sports equipment store. You know a lot about sports, and people are comfortable around you. The customers would like you. You would be good at selling things. Plus, you're good at math. You would have no trouble adding up the prices of things."

Devon smiled. "I think a good job for you is helping people find jobs!"

Why Identify Your Strengths?

You are unique. You were born being different from everyone else. The person you are is made up of all of your ideas, abilities, talents, likes and dislikes, dreams, and more. Understanding yourself—who you are and what qualities you are made up of—will help you in your search for the right career.

Self-knowledge is a key ingredient in any career search. You cannot believe in yourself unless you know what it is that you believe in. You cannot set smart and realistic goals for yourself without knowing where your talents and strengths lie. You cannot find the right career for you if you do not know who the "you" is.

Your actions and words send a message about who you are to other people. Other people respond to these messages by treating you in certain ways. If you feel that you are worth people's attention and respect, you will act that way. If you care about and respect yourself, others will feel that way about you, too.

The more you know yourself, the better you will be at finding your ideal job and ideal lifestyle. By knowing who you are, you can then build up your self-respect.

Part of getting to know yourself is getting to know your strengths and abilities. Devon, as we saw, was taking a look at the things he likes to do and the things he does well. He is exploring his interests and his skills. A **skill** is an ability to do something well, usually because you have practiced it. Devon is trying to identify, or assess, his strengths and match these to a job. Successful people choose work that allows them to put their strengths to good use. You may find that the things you like to do and the things you do best are often the same.

Career Fact

Are you a thinking type of person or a feeling type? Thinking types decide things based on facts and figures. Feeling types decide things based on emotions. Each of these types of people should choose a career based on how they most often decide things.

Identifying your strengths can help you in another way. Employers hire workers because their strengths will help their companies. People who can talk about their strengths during job interviews have a better chance of being hired.

Looking at your strengths is also a good way to boost your **self-esteem**, or self-respect. People with high self-esteem are confident. They feel good about themselves. Self-esteem comes across in job interviews. Employers see it as a positive trait.

People with a high level of self-esteem do not always get the jobs they want right away. However, they do recover quickly from disappointment. Then, they get on with their job search.

Resources to Help You Identify Strengths

Taking a long, hard look at who you are may be new for you. There are several good resources to help you identify your strengths.

Remember
A resource is something that can be used for support or help.

Books

Later in this chapter, you will do a self-assessment. A **self-assessment** will help you identify your strengths and weaknesses. This textbook and other career books are important tools that can help you do this activity. They can guide you through the steps of self-assessment. Completing these steps takes some time and energy. However, it is often a satisfying process of self-discovery.

One of the most popular career books of all time is *What Color Is Your Parachute?* by Richard Nelson Bolles. This book contains many self-assessment exercises for career seekers. You should be able to find this book in your local library.

Family and Friends

To do a good assessment of your strengths, you must be honest with yourself. However, even if you are trying to be honest, you may underestimate yourself and what you do well. On the other hand, you may think you are better at something than you really are. For these reasons, family members and friends are also good resources. They can point out strengths you may not be aware of. Mark pointed out Devon's strengths at the beginning of this chapter.

Career Counselors

Career counselors help match people with the right careers. A **career counselor** is a trained professional who helps people with their career searches. Career counselors are trained to identify a person's strengths. They can suggest different career areas where these strengths can be used.

If you do work with a counselor, remember that the two of you form a team. The counselor can ask good questions and give you helpful information. However, your time, energy, and honesty are still required.

Where do you find a career counselor? Most high schools have guidance counselors who are trained to give career advice. If there is no such counselor in your school, a teacher may be able to direct you to career counselors in your community. Try to get a recommendation or the name of a counselor from someone you trust.

You can also look in a telephone book under the heading *careers*. Be sure to ask any counselors you contact outside of school about fees they may charge for their services.

Assessment Tests

Career counselors often use assessment tests to help people determine their strengths. Such tests are not the kind you pass or fail. Their purpose is to help identify your interests and strengths.

> ### Career Trend
>
> Many counselors today advise young people to start a "career portfolio." This is a collection of items that reflect a person's talents and accomplishments. The portfolio is "proof" of your qualifications and can include items, such as writing samples, newspaper stories, and samples of artwork.

One series of 12 short assessment tests is the General Aptitude Test Battery (GATB). The GATB measures a person's **aptitude**, or natural ability to learn something or do well in certain areas. For example, some people have an aptitude in math. They add, subtract, and perform other math activities more easily than most people do. Another test assesses personality. Yet another test helps a person to examine his or her work-related interests and skills. This test will also provide a list of possible occupations that might suit a person's skills and interests.

A career counselor or some other trained person may have to show you how to complete some of these tests. A trained person will also help you understand your test results.

Using Technology

There are many free assessment tests offered on the Internet. They test everything from your personality type to your strengths and interests. These tests can be fun to do as well as helpful. Use a search engine to help you locate Internet sites that have these tests.

Music, art, writing, and sports are just a few areas in which some people may have great aptitude.

✓ Check Your Understanding

Write your answers in complete sentences.

1. Give one reason for assessing your strengths.

2. How are your family and friends important assessment resources?

3. What does the word *aptitude* mean?

How to Begin a Self-Assessment

When young people begin self-assessments, they often say, "I have never held a job. I do not have any real strengths."

All of us do have strengths, though. We just have to know how to recognize them. As you read earlier, there are many career books that can help guide you through the steps of self-assessment. Here, however, is a way to help you get started right now:

Begin by listing your accomplishments. An accomplishment is something you have done well. Here are some examples:

- won a tennis match

- wrote a poem

- received an *A* on a world history project

- decorated my bedroom

- got a large part in a school play

- worked as a recreation assistant with the local parks department

It does not matter how small the accomplishment was. List as many accomplishments as you can think of. A list of 10 is a good start.

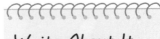

Write About It

Pick an accomplishment that was difficult for you to do and write about it. Tell why you decided to try it in the first place and the steps you took to make the accomplishment happen. Tell about any obstacles you overcame. Finally, describe any rewards you received from accomplishing the task.

Interests Are Also Strengths

Look at your list of accomplishments. It should give you clues about what your interests are. An interest is something you are curious about or like to do. You might have an interest in sports, music, art, computers, animals, children, clothes, books, or food.

List your interests and then think carefully about them. Which do you feel strongly about? If you had to make choices, which ones would you choose? Ranking your interests can help you decide what you would like to spend the most time doing.

Later, you can match these interests to possible careers. For example, you may have an interest in animal care and an interest in computers. Computers are fun to use. However, you might not want a career involving computers if your interest in animal care is stronger. You should take this into account when choosing a career.

Did You Know ?

Early in the year 2002, many people in the United States were unemployed. A large employment agency asked job seekers whether they cared about finding work that helped make the world a better place. More than 29 percent of these people described this goal as very important.

Hard and Soft Skills

As you read earlier, a skill is the ability to do a task well. Skills can generally be placed into one of two groups: hard skills and soft skills.

Hard skills are those that are related to specific jobs or tasks. For example, operating a keyboard is a hard skill. Operating a cash register is a hard skill. So is operating a forklift. Employers often look for people with hard skills to fill certain jobs.

Think back to Devon's situation at the beginning of this chapter. Suppose one of his accomplishments had been to win a city tennis tournament. Devon could list tennis strokes as hard skills.

Soft skills are those skills that can be used on almost any job. For example, some people find it easy to talk to other people. Such people have spoken, also called verbal, communications skills. Soft skills can help a person do just about any job. As a result, soft skills are sometimes called transferable skills.

✓ **Check Your Understanding**

Write your answers in complete sentences.

1. What is meant by self-assessment?

2. What is the difference between an interest and a strength?

3. Suppose you write a story using a word processor on a personal computer. What are the soft and hard skills you have used?

Your Personality Traits

Your **personality traits**, or the different ways you behave, are also important in choosing a career. Some examples of personality traits are loyalty, friendliness, and curiosity.

Some personality traits show up at birth. Some babies cry loudly, while others are quiet. Some smile easily, while others are shy.

Career counselors can help you define your personality traits. You can also match your personality traits to your accomplishments. For example, when Devon entered and won the tennis tournament, he showed that he was competitive. Being competitive could serve him well as a salesperson or in another, similar career.

Did You Know ❓

Many of our personality traits are determined by our genes. However, certain personality traits are determined by what happens to us after we are born.

Read this list of personality traits. Which traits could you use to describe yourself?

Some Personality Traits		
• pays attention to details	• outspoken	• predictable
• adventurous	• emotional	• supportive
• likes to analyze	• forceful	• risk-taker
• calm	• loyal	• team player
• friendly	• outgoing	• unselfish
• dependable	• sensitive	• patient
• talkative	• thoughtful	• shy
• moody	• cheerful	• fun-loving

Strengths and Accomplishments

By now you should be developing an idea of what your own strengths are. If you have not already done so, begin listing them. Add to the list as you think of new strengths. Think, too, about which skills you want to continue using. In many chapters of this book, you will see how to match your strengths to a career. You will also see how to use your strengths when applying for jobs and going on job interviews.

Become more aware of your accomplishments. Write them all in your career portfolio. Some accomplishments might not have taken much time to learn or do, such as learning to operate a copy machine. Other accomplishments, such as writing a term paper, will be the result of long, hard work.

With each new accomplishment, think about the interests, skills, and personality traits that went into accomplishing your goal. By doing so, you will learn more about yourself. Remember that knowing yourself is the most important part of your career search.

Learn More About It

THE DICTIONARY OF OCCUPATIONAL TITLES

The Dictionary of Occupational Titles (DOT) is a book published by the U.S. Department of Labor. The DOT includes descriptions of many different jobs and the skills needed for each job. The DOT is also available online at online.onetcenter.org. A database called O*Net provides similar information.

The DOT divides all skills into three categories: data, people, and things. **Data** is information. Data skills involve working with numbers and information, such as statistics or reports.

People skills can be used with anyone you may have contact with. These people include coworkers, bosses, and customers.

The third category, *things*, relates to machines and materials. Here are examples of some skills in each of the three categories:

Data	People	Things
• analyzing	• instructing	• driving
• computing	• serving	• handling
• comparing	• speaking	• operating
• coordinating	• persuading	• setting up

CRITICAL THINKING Think about your own accomplishments. Then, think about the skills you have used in these accomplishments. Have you worked more with data, people, or things? Explain your answer.

JOB DESCRIPTION
Childcare Worker

Job Summary
A childcare worker takes care of children of all ages. He or she may care for children when parents are at work or away. A childcare worker plays an important role in a child's development.

Childcare workers may look after children at a school, a private home, or a daycare center. Some childcare workers live in the home of the child's family. Work hours can vary. There is usually full-time and part-time work available.

Work Activities
A childcare worker may do any or all of the following activities:

- Dress, feed, and play with children.

- Organize activities to help children learn.

- Help children with their homework.

- Take children to and from school.

- Help children explore their interests and interact with others.

Education/Training Requirements
Education requirements for a childcare worker can vary. Some childcare workers have a high school diploma, have taken community college courses, or have a college degree in early-childhood education. Some employers require previous experience in a childcare-related field. Some will hire employees who have little or no related experience. Other requirements may include a driver's license, certification in cardiopulmonary resuscitation (CPR), and first aid training.

Think About It
Name one way in which childcare workers play an important role in the development of children.

Summary

- To find a career that is right for you, first identify your strengths. Knowing your strengths will help improve your self-esteem. Employers like job seekers who show high self-esteem.

- There are many resources to help you identify your strengths. These resources include career books, your family and friends, career counselors, and assessment tests.

- Start a self-assessment by listing your accomplishments. Then, identify the interests, skills, and personality traits that have made your accomplishments possible.

- Hard skills help a person do specific jobs. Typing and operating a computer are examples of hard skills. Soft skills include speaking and writing. Some soft skills are transferable from one job to another.

- Knowing which strengths you want to continue to use and develop will help steer you toward a rewarding career.

aptitude
career counselor
data
self-assessment
skill

Vocabulary Review
Complete each sentence with a term from the list.

1. Having an _____ means having a natural ability to learn something or to do something well.

2. Another term for information is _____.

3. A _____ can be used to figure out your strengths and interests.

4. A _____ is a trained professional who helps people with their career searches.

5. A _____ is an ability to do something well, usually because you have practiced it.

Chapter Quiz

Write your answers in complete sentences.

1. Why is it important to identify your strengths?

2. Where can you find assessment tests?

3. Why do people with self-esteem do well on job interviews?

4. What could an assessment test tell you?

5. What are two ways you can find a career counselor?

6. What is a common first step in doing a self-assessment?

CRITICAL THINKING

7. Jean lists baking a cake from scratch as an accomplishment. She uses an electric mixer to make the batter and follows a recipe. What are her interests and some of her hard and soft skills?

8. What are three personality traits that could be considered strengths?

Career Portfolio Project

Use the information about self-assessment that you worked on for this chapter to think of several job possibilities that might suit you. Then, make up an advertisement, or ad, for one of these jobs.

Your ad will appear in a newspaper's help-wanted section of the classified ads. The classified ads advertise jobs that need to be filled and items for sale. What is the job title found in your ad? What experience would be needed for the job? What personal qualities would be needed? What other information might be included in the ad? If you wish, design the help-wanted ad on a computer.

Flight attendants work in the service industry. They should enjoy traveling and working with people.

Learning Objectives

- Explain how lifestyle choices are linked to career choices.
- Identify personal values and list these in order of importance.
- Name five lifestyle factors.
- Describe how trade-offs work when making lifestyle choices.

Chapter 4

Lifestyles and Career Choices

Words to Know

attendant	a person who serves or helps another
prioritize	to rank in order of importance, or priority
work environment	all the things that surround and affect a person at work
leisure	free time used for rest or recreation
personnel agency	a business that helps people find either temporary work, staff jobs, or both
apprenticeship	an on-the-job training program in which a skilled worker teaches someone, called an apprentice, a trade or craft
vocational school	a school in which students are trained in specific jobs or trades
executive	a person who helps run a business
job sharing	a situation in which two people share the responsibilities of a single job

Sometimes, the career you choose can make a big difference in your lifestyle, or the way you live. For example, having a career as an airline pilot, a flight attendant, or as a traveling salesperson will affect your lifestyle. Such careers offer a very different lifestyle from people who have careers as restaurant chefs or office workers.

In the conversation on page 46, read about the lifestyle choices made by Mr. D'Angelo. Mr. D'Angelo is a flight attendant. An **attendant** is a person who serves or helps another. A flight attendant is a person who helps others while traveling by airplane.

"I have the cross-country route," Mr. D'Angelo explained to a group of students during Career Day. "That means I fly from New York to Los Angeles, California, several times each week. I share an apartment in each city with friends. On the airplane, I spend a lot of my time serving food and drinks to the passengers. Often, I have to calm people who are nervous about flying.

"I enjoy my work," the speaker continued, "because I like meeting new people, and I like to travel. Because I work for an airline, I can get discounts on plane tickets, too. On my vacation, I can fly almost anywhere in the world for a very low cost—sometimes, even for free!"

Later, Julia and Luke talked about what they had heard. "It sounds like a great job," Julia said. "Living in different cities and meeting new people all the time is exciting!"

Luke looked doubtful. "Maybe," he said. "But I wouldn't like having to be in an airplane all the time and having to serve food. Being an airline attendant wouldn't really fit the lifestyle I want."

Finding a Suitable Lifestyle

Remember
In Chapter 3, you read about how important it is to assess your strengths when thinking about a career choice.

By matching interests, skills, and personality traits to a career, you can increase your chances of enjoying your job. Another factor to consider is lifestyle. Think about the lifestyle you want. Lifestyle choices and career choices go hand in hand. Luke did not want a job that required him to travel. Julia, on the other hand, found the flight attendant's lifestyle appealing. She liked to travel and meet new people.

Values and a Balanced Lifestyle

Making lifestyle choices begins with looking closely at your work-related values. In Chapter 1, you learned that values are the principles, or standards and beliefs, a person holds to be important. Work-related values are those values that are related to, or affect, your work life.

For example, Jen is a young mother who has a three-year-old son. Jen's most important value is being a good mother. However, she also wants to have a career in fashion design. Jen has a part-time sales job in a clothing store. There, she can keep up on the latest clothing designs. She spends most of her free time raising her son. In the evenings, she tries to take at least 30 minutes to do something for herself, such as reading. Jen feels her life has balance.

There are many values and lifestyle choices. Your best friend's idea of a balanced lifestyle may be very different from your own. Values and lifestyle choices change over time, as well. Ask your teacher how he or she spent Saturday nights as a teenager. Does your teacher spend Saturday nights the same way now?

The following chart will help you to identify some of your work-related values. You may wish to prioritize these values. When you **prioritize**, you rank items in order of importance. By ranking your values, some lifestyle choices may become clearer to you.

Career Fact

You should continue to review your values and lifestyle choices as you grow older.

Work-Related Values			
• Being a leader	• Working with my hands	• A good education	• Learning new things
• Being creative	• A good sense of humor	• Working with tools	• Being part of a team
• Making money	• Having lots of free time	• Challenges at work	• Being respected
• Helping others	• Being part of a community	• Working outdoors	• Working by myself
• Feeling secure	• Living in a healthy manner	• Working with others	• Being honest

Rating Your Values

Use the chart on page 47 to do the following activity on a separate sheet of paper:

- Write all of the work-related values from the chart that apply to you. If you like, add more values to your list.

- Rank the values in order of their importance to you. The most important value will be number 1, the second most important number 2, and so on.

- Look at your most important value. How might it affect your career decision? Give an example.

Exploring Lifestyle Choices

Perhaps you are asking the question, "How can I choose a lifestyle? I still live at home. I am just beginning to think about a career."

For now, all you need is a little knowledge, interest, and imagination to explore lifestyle choices. Have you thought about where you would like to live in the future? Are you planning to have a family of your own someday? If so, you are already exploring lifestyle choices. The more you know what it is you want, the better chance you have of choosing a career that will help you get it.

✓ Check Your Understanding

Write your answers in complete sentences.

1. What are work-related values?

2. Why is a balanced lifestyle important?

3. How do values affect lifestyle choices?

Did You Know ?

Your accomplishments, interests, skills, and personality traits are most likely linked to your values.

Lifestyle Factors

Following are five lifestyle factors to consider when thinking about careers. As you study them, recall your interests, skills, personality traits, and values. You may find that making lifestyle choices is a fun exercise.

Factor 1: Location

Some people want to live near their families. Others cannot wait to move away. People who like to windsurf want to live near an ocean or other body of water. They usually do not want to live in the mountains.

Career Trend

Today, about 80 percent of the U.S. population lives and works in cities. The other 20 percent lives in small towns or in rural areas.

Right now, you may want to apply for jobs close to where you live. As you grow older and become more independent, you may wish to explore other parts of the country. It is also possible that your career will require you to move away.

Think carefully about where you live. How will that affect *how* you live? Ask yourself these questions to help you determine where you might like to live:

- Do I prefer to live in a big city, a small town, the suburbs, or a rural area?

- Am I willing to commute, or travel a long distance, to work each day? If so, how many miles am I willing to travel?

- Do I want to be close to mountains, oceans, rivers, or forests?

- What climates do I prefer?

- Do I want to live near my family and friends?

- Would I like to live where there is a different culture?

- What kinds of cultural or athletic resources do I want to be near?

Factor 2: The Work Environment

A **work environment** is all the things that surround and affect a person at work. It includes the space you work in, the people you work with, the type of work you do, and more. Quite often, people choose jobs or careers based on the work environment.

Sarah, for example, took a summer job selling snacks at a ballpark. She actually enjoyed the noise, the crowds, and the fresh air. Juan preferred to take a summer job putting books back on shelves in a library. He liked the quiet atmosphere, the books, and working by himself. Sarah and Juan each found a work environment that suited his or her personality.

Take a moment to think about your ideal work environment by asking yourself the following questions:

- Would I like sitting at a desk all day?

- Would I like working with a computer for several hours each day?

- Does it matter to me if there are windows where I work?

- Can I work where it is noisy?

- How would I feel about working outside in cold or rainy weather?

- Would I like a job that would require me to wear a uniform or a suit every day?

- Would I like attending meetings and being asked to speak in front of others?

- Would I enjoy helping people to solve work-related problems?

- Which work environment appeals to me more, a ballpark or a library? Why?

Using Technology

Explore online Web sites that will give you more information about work environments. Use a search engine and key search terms, such as *office jobs* and *work environments* to help you find this information.

Factor 3: Time Requirements

At the start of the twentieth century, it was common for many people in the United States to work 6 days a week, 12 hours each day. There was less time for outside interests, family matters, and **leisure**, or free-time, activities. Many workers today look for careers that will allow them time to enjoy other interests.

Today, people have more choices than ever before about fitting their lifestyles to their careers. There are full-time and part-time jobs. **Personnel agencies**, or employment agencies, are places that specialize in helping people find full-time or part-time jobs. Temporary personnel agencies help people find jobs that last only a certain number of days, weeks, or months. To have more control of their time, people sometimes start their own businesses. Working for yourself, however, often means working longer and harder than when you work for others.

Think about the following questions when considering time factors in a career:

- Would I be willing to work night shifts?

- Would I be willing to work weekends?

- Would I mind being available any time for emergencies at work?

- Do I want full-time or part-time work?

- Do I want to work for a temporary agency?

- Would I be willing to spend long hours running my own business?

Factor 4: Training and Education

In Chapter 2, you read that getting an education can increase your chances of finding a job. Usually, the more education a person has, the more money he or she will earn.

Career Fact

Working overtime is increasing in the United States. In the year 2003, 1 in 6 employees said they worked more than 60 hours a week. Only two years earlier, this number was 1 in 8 employees. The number of women working more than 60 hours doubled in that same time period.

Students may learn auto repair skills at a vocational school.

However, after high school, not everyone wants to or is able to attend a four-year college. Some people will want to take part in **apprenticeships**, or on-the-job training programs. Other people will want to go to **vocational schools**, or schools that train people in certain skills or for specific jobs or trades. Community colleges sometimes offer the lowest-priced job training.

Before choosing a career, ask yourself the following questions:

- Am I willing to spend time in training or in college?

- Would I be willing to take college classes in the evening if I have to work during the day?

- Am I willing to do on-the-job training if it means lower pay while I am being trained?

- Am I willing to give up leisure time while developing my skills?

Factor 5: Salary

Just about everyone wants to earn a lot of money. Not everyone, however, can achieve that. An **executive** is a person who helps run a business. A highly paid executive may work 80 hours a week and worry constantly about business. Sometimes, people work hard for many years before earning large salaries. Be realistic about salary. Ask yourself the following questions:

- What is the minimum amount of money I would need to make?

- What is my ideal salary?

- Would I be willing to work at a job in which the top pay is not much more than the starting pay?

Making Choices: A Question of Trade-offs

Shelly, a high school student, thought carefully about her values and lifestyle. She then decided that she might like a career as a lifeguard in Hawaii. She also wanted to live in a large house, own an expensive entertainment system, and earn about $80,000 per year.

When Shelly looked into a career as a lifeguard, she found that she would make about $20 per hour. Because housing in Hawaii is quite costly, Shelly would need to share an apartment with friends. As for the entertainment system, she might have to settle for a portable CD player and a set of earphones.

Shelly will have to trade one thing to get another. She may decide that being a lifeguard in Hawaii is more important to her than earning a salary of $80,000 per year. She may decide to explore a career that would allow her to earn that much. Whatever decision Shelly makes, she will know what she must give up to get what she wants most.

Write About It

Start a journal in which you record your career possibilities. One section should be for careers you would most like to have. Another section should be for careers that would be second choices. A final section should be for careers you might consider. Under each career or job title, write what attracts you most to that kind of work.

In Units 2 and 3, you will explore different careers. It may be that you will find the ideal career to suit your strengths, values, and chosen lifestyle. More likely, you will find that you have to make some trade-offs. Like Shelly, you should try to make career decisions based on what matters most to you.

✓ **Check Your Understanding**

Write your answers in complete sentences.

1. What are five factors that affect lifestyle choices?
2. What are some different ways to get education or training for a job?
3. What is an example of a career trade-off?

Learn More About It

JOB SHARING

In 2002, about 60 percent of mothers in the workforce had children under the age of 6. How did they balance the need for a career and income with the responsibilities of being a mother of young children?

One way was through job sharing. **Job sharing** means that two or more employees share the responsibilities of a single job. They meet regularly to discuss their shared tasks.

More and more companies are allowing working parents to job share. One survey showed that employees who shared jobs had higher overall job satisfaction. However, the actual numbers of people who share jobs remains small. Also, job sharing is not right for everyone. It requires flexibility and the ability to communicate well.

CRITICAL THINKING What is one way that job sharing can help meet a person's lifestyle needs?

Job Summary

On an airline flight in the United States, there must be at least 1 flight attendant for every 50 passengers. A flight attendant's most important responsibility is to help passengers in the event of an emergency.

Because flight attendants are required to travel, they spend a lot of time away from home. They usually have to work some nights, weekends, and holidays. Flight attendants spend between 75 and 85 hours of each month flying. They stand during most of the flight. They must be able to lift relatively heavy luggage into overhead bins. In addition to flying, flight attendants spend time on the ground preparing for flights and waiting for arriving planes.

Work Activities

A flight attendant may do any or all of the following activities:

- Greet passengers when they board the plane and check tickets.

- Review safety and emergency features of the airplane.

- Give out pillows, blankets, magazines, and earphones.

- Check that passengers are wearing their seat belts.

- Serve drinks, meals, or snacks to passengers.

Education/Training Requirements

All airlines require a high school diploma. Some require college courses, too. There are usually height requirements and minimum age requirements. Those flight attendants working for international airlines must speak a foreign language. Flight attendants must go through a training program that may last from three to seven weeks.

Think About It

What do you think would make the job of a flight attendant difficult?

Summary

- Lifestyles and career choices go hand in hand. One greatly affects the other. Deciding on the type of lifestyle you want to lead will help you select a rewarding career for yourself.

- Identifying your work-related values will help you to make more realistic lifestyle choices.

- Reviewing and revising your lifestyle choices is a lifelong process, just as career planning is.

- There are at least five important lifestyle factors to consider when thinking about a career. They are location, work environment, time requirements, education and training, and salary. Each factor requires careful thought.

- It is rare for people to find careers that match all of their requirements. Often, they trade one thing, such as a large salary, for another, such as a pleasant work environment.

attendant

leisure

prioritize

vocational school

work environment

Vocabulary Review

Complete each sentence with a term from the list.

1. A school that trains people to do specific jobs or trades is called a _____.

2. To _____ is to rank items in order of importance.

3. All of the things that surround and affect a person at work make up what is called the _____.

4. An _____ is a person who serves or helps another.

5. Some people spend their _____ time on hobbies.

Chapter Quiz

Write your answers in complete sentences.

1. What does an attendant do?

2. What does it mean to prioritize values?

3. What are five factors to consider in making career and lifestyle choices?

4. What is one thing to consider when choosing a location in which to work and live?

5. What are two ways to get education or training for a career or job?

6. What is an example of a lifestyle choice that will require a trade-off?

CRITICAL THINKING

7. You enjoy teaching children. However, you do not like the fact that school classrooms can be noisy places. What might be some other career choices that you can look into?

8. Suppose you are offered on-the-job training to learn the job of a builder's assistant. However, you enjoy mountains and trees. You had always hoped to become a forest ranger. What factors will you consider in making your career choice?

Career Portfolio Project

Select one of the five lifestyle factors described in this chapter. Answer all of the questions that are listed under that factor. Then, write a one-page paper in which you explain how these lifestyle factors will help you to choose a particular career.

Photographers use cameras, screens, special lights, and other equipment to take photographs.

Learning Objectives

- Describe how careers are divided into different groups.

- Define some job titles.

- Describe how to explore careers.

- Explain how to take part in an informational interview.

Chapter 5 ▷ Exploring a Career

Words to Know

career cluster	groups of careers that are related to each other based on a similar industry or business
technician	a person who has training in technology in a certain field
assistant	a person who helps another person who holds a higher-level job
specialist	a person who works in and knows a lot about one field
research	to carefully read and study facts about a certain subject
informational interview	a question-and-answer session between a person who is interested in a career or job and a person who has that career or job
professional association	an organization whose members all have the same career or occupation

Read about how Luke, a high school student, is exploring a career as a photographer in the story below.

Luke and Tasha walked to their lockers. "Why are you going to see Mr. Greene, the guidance counselor?" Tasha asked.

"I told Mr. Greene that I might like a career as a photographer," answered Luke. "Mr. Greene is going to give me information on that career. He also has a friend who is a photographer. Mr. Greene is going to ask his friend to come to the school so that I can ask him questions about his career."

Tasha watched her friend walk away. She thought it was about time for her to begin exploring careers, too.

Different Types of Careers

Luke is exploring a career as a photographer because he likes taking pictures. He has taken pictures for his high school newspaper and yearbook. Because Luke is interested in taking pictures, he wants to learn about being a photographer. Then, he can decide if it is the right career for him.

In Chapter 2, you identified your strengths and interests. You have also considered lifestyle factors. Now you, too, are ready to explore careers. First, you need to find out what kinds of careers there are.

There are many different kinds of careers. Some careers can be related to each other because they are in the same type of industry, or business. For example, careers in baseball, sculpture, dance, and music are all related careers in the sports and arts industry.

The U.S. Department of Education has divided the many kinds of careers into 16 groups. Each group is called a career cluster. Within each **career cluster**, the careers are related to each other based on a similar industry. For example, marketing, sales, and services careers make up one cluster. These careers are in the sales industry.

Did You Know ?

Marketing is the business of moving goods and services from a producer to a customer. It includes planning and selling the good or service.

Different Types of Jobs

Just as there are different types of careers, there are also different types of jobs. Certain jobs can have titles that describe the type of work being done. For example, a **technician** has training in technology in a certain field. A technician usually works with computers or other machinery. There are different types of technicians, such as computer service technicians and medical laboratory technicians.

An **assistant** is a person who helps another person who holds a higher-level job. An administrative assistant to a manager helps the manager to perform his or her duties. Other types of assistants include dental assistants, medical assistants, veterinary assistants, and library assistants.

A **specialist** is a person who works in and knows a lot about one field. A fire prevention specialist may speak in schools about fire safety. Other types of specialists include purchasing specialists, environmental specialists, and skin care specialists.

The Career Cluster Chart on page 62 shows different industries and the career cluster or clusters that are related to them. The chart also lists careers or jobs that can be found in those career clusters. Many career sources and agencies have created their own lists of career clusters.

Career Fact

The titles of some other types of jobs include *clerk*, *worker*, *aide*, and *technologist*. You can find out more about these job titles by looking through career books and magazines and at career Web sites on the Internet.

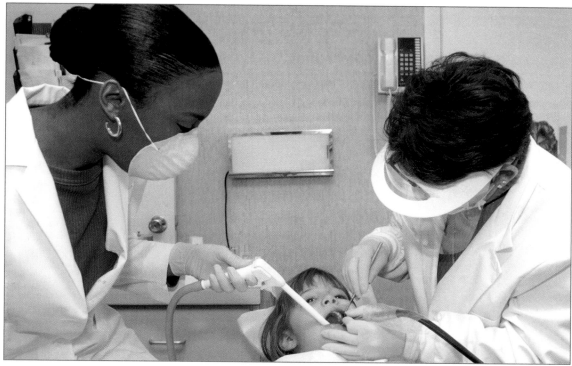

A dental assistant helps a dentist treat patients.

Career Cluster Chart

Industry	Career Cluster	Examples of Careers and Jobs
Agriculture and the Environment	Agriculture, Food, and Natural Resources	Agricultural inspector, environmental activist, farmer, fisher, forester, logger
Construction Trades	Architecture and Construction	Architect, bricklayer, carpenter, construction worker, electrician, plumber
	Manufacturing	Assembler, machine setter, machinist, tool-and-die maker
Office	Business, Management, and Administration	Administrative assistant, clerical supervisor, information clerk, receptionist
	Finance	Account collector, bank teller, bookkeeper, loan officer, payroll clerk
Education and Training	Education and Training	Curator, library technician, museum technician, teacher, teacher assistant
Government	Government and Public Administration	Air Force mechanic, Coast Guard seaman, government accountant, postal service worker
Healthcare	Health Science	Emergency medical technician, licensed practical nurse, nurse aide, pharmacy technician
Human Services	Hospitality and Tourism	Chef, host, hostess, hotel clerk, transportation ticket agent, travel agent
	Human Services	Childcare worker, cosmetologist, dietitian, minister, social worker
Law and Public Safety	Law, Public Safety, and Security	Court reporter, firefighter, hearing officer, legal assistant, paralegal, police officer, security guard
Sales	Marketing, Sales, and Services	Cashier, counter and rental clerk, customer service representative, marketing manager, real estate agent
Sports and the Arts	Arts, Audiovisual Technology, and Communications	Camera operator, cartoonist, coach, dancer, fashion designer, musician, photographer, referee
Technology	Information Technology	Computer programmer, computer support specialist, database administrator
	Science, Technology, Engineering, and Mathematics	Automotive service technician, clinical laboratory technician, line installer, office machine repairer, science technician
Transportation	Transportation, Distribution, and Logistics	Aircraft pilot, bus driver, railroad conductor, sailor, taxi driver, truck driver

Many kinds of careers can be grouped into career clusters based on similar industries.

✓ **Check Your Understanding**

Write your answers in complete sentences.

1. What is a career cluster?

2. What is a technician?

3. According to the Career Cluster Chart on page 62, which industry is manufacturing listed in?

4. Give an example of a career or job in the healthcare industry.

Ways to Explore a Career

A good way to start exploring a career is to read the Career Cluster Chart on page 62. First, read the left column of the chart. Ask yourself, "Do any of these industries interest me?" Once you find an industry of interest, read the list of careers and jobs in the right column of the chart. Then, choose a career or job to explore further. Here are some more ways in which you can explore a career:

- Talk to a career counselor.

- **Research**, or carefully read about and study, the career.

- Set up an informational interview. During an **informational interview**, you ask someone whose career or job you are interested in, questions about that career or job.

Researching a Career

Career counselors can suggest jobs that may match your interests, skills, and personality traits. However, career counselors can only direct you. They cannot make decisions for you. It is a good idea for you to do research on your own about a career and what it offers.

Using Technology

There are government agencies that give online career information. You can go to www.bls.gov or www.census.gov to get salary information and descriptions for different occupations.

Career centers and most libraries have career information. They have books, magazine articles, CDs, and sometimes videos or DVDs about different careers and jobs. They may also have computers that can be used to connect to Web sites that offer career information.

A very useful book for career information is the *Guide for Occupational Exploration* (*GOE*). The *GOE* is published by the U.S. Department of Labor. It lists 14 major interest areas and the occupations that match those interests. For example, *repairing computers* is an interest. *Computer technician* is a suggested occupation under that interest.

The *Occupational Outlook Handbook* (*OOH*) is another helpful book with career information. The Bureau of Labor Statistics publishes this book every 2 years. You can find up-to-date information about trends in more than 250 jobs in the *OOH*.

Information about careers and occupations can also be found online. A helpful Web site is run by the U.S. Department of Labor. It gives information about the skills, tasks, knowledge, and work activities needed for many different occupations. This Web site is located at online.onetcenter.org.

Remember

In Chapters 1 and 2, you learned about certain career terms such as *employment* and *job trends*.

When you read about careers that you are interested in, write the important details in a notebook. List the types of jobs that are related to that career, the kind of work that is done, the salary range, the job trends, and the education or training requirements for those jobs.

✓ **Check Your Understanding**

Write your answers in complete sentences.

1. List two books that give career information.

2. What are some details about a career that are important to know?

THE *OCCUPATIONAL OUTLOOK HANDBOOK*

The *Occupational Outlook Handbook* (*OOH*) is a very useful book for people exploring careers. The *OOH* groups more than 250 occupations, or jobs, into career clusters. Each career cluster lists occupations. Information from the *OOH* table of contents is shown below. It lists some occupations under the career cluster *Service occupations.*

Service occupations

Protective service occupations
Correctional officers
Firefighting occupations
Police and detectives
Private detectives and investigators

It is a good idea to look over the entire table of contents in the *OOH* for occupations that you want to explore. Some occupations may be listed under different career clusters.

For each occupation, the *OOH* gives information about the kind of work performed, the working conditions, employment, education and training requirements, job outlook, salary information, and related occupations. The *OOH* also lists professional associations that can provide more information about each occupation. A **professional association** is an organization whose members all have the same career or occupation.

CRITICAL THINKING If you were exploring a career as a police officer, what kind of information could the *OOH* provide?

An Informational Interview

At the beginning of this chapter, you read that Luke plans to interview a photographer. The information that Luke receives may help him decide if he really wants a career as a photographer.

Informational interviews are a good way to explore careers. What you learn during an informational interview might not be found in a book. For example, a roofer can tell you what it is like to work on top of a house, 30 feet above the ground. This kind of information may help you to make a decision about a career.

Informational interviews will take up not only your time but also the time of the person you interview. That is the reason why you should only hold interviews when you are serious about a career. Follow these steps to hold an informational interview:

1. **Find a person who has the job or career that you are interested in.**

   Your family, friends, a career counselor, or a teacher may know of such a person. You can also call or write to a professional association for the name of a person who might be willing to talk to you about his or her career.

2. **Call and make an appointment with the person whom you want to talk with.**

   Politely ask if that person would be willing to share information about his or her job or career. Limit the interview to about 30 minutes.

3. **To prepare for the interview, write your interview questions ahead of time.**

   Think carefully about what you want to find out. Some questions that you might ask are, "What are your job responsibilities? What things do you like about your job? What things do you not like?"

Career Fact

Do not ask for a job during an informational interview. If you ask for a job, the person whom you are interviewing might feel that you misled him or her about the purpose of the interview.

Write About It

Make a list of five more questions that you would ask at an informational interview.

4. **Keep your appointment and arrive on time.**

   If you cannot keep the appointment, be sure to call the person and ask to reschedule the interview.

5. **Write the answers to your questions.**

   If the person whom you are interviewing gives you important information, be sure to write it down. Then, you can study your notes after the interview.

6. **At the end of the interview, thank the person with whom you interviewed.**

   A day or two after the interview, you should also send a letter thanking the person for the important information that he or she gave you.

Career Trend

More informational interviews are being held over the telephone or by e-mail than in the past. Because it is often difficult to contact some people, it is easier to use technology to hold an informational interview rather than to hold a face-to-face meeting.

After an Interview

After the interview, you should read your notes to decide if you are still interested in the career or occupation. Even if you are no longer interested, you have learned important things that can help you to decide on your career.

One informational interview may not give you enough information to make a decision about a career. Hold as many informational interviews as is necessary to get the information that you need.

Exploring Careers

The chapters in the next two units introduce many careers. It is up to you to explore careers further before you decide which one is right for you. Talk to counselors, do research, and hold informational interviews. The time and energy you spend on exploring careers can save you from considering jobs that do not match your career goals.

✓ **Check Your Understanding**

Write your answers in complete sentences.

1. About how long should an informational interview last?

2. What are some questions that you might want to ask during an informational interview?

3. What should you do at the end of an informational interview?

Additional Sources of Career Information

U.S. Industry & Trade Outlook 2000.
National Technical Information
Service

Professional Careers Sourcebook.
Gale Group, 7th Edition
(September 2002)

Professional's Job Finder:
1997–2000. Planning
Communications
(June 1997)

Specialty Occupational Outlook:
Professions. Gale Group
(January 1991)

Guide to Federal Jobs.
Jist Works; 2nd Revised Edition
(December 15, 2000)

Career Guide to America's Top
Industries.
Jist Works; 5th Edition (June 2002)

Encyclopedia of Careers and
Vocational Guidance.
Ferguson Publishing Co.
(October 2002)

Planning Job Choices.
National Association of Colleges and
Employees (2003)

JOB DESCRIPTION
Photographer

Job Summary
A photographer uses a camera to take photographs. The subjects of the photographs can be people or events. Some photographers specialize in certain areas such as portrait, scientific, or news photography. A successful photographer usually has a good imagination and is creative.

A photographer often works long, irregular hours. Some photographers must be available to work on short notice. A photographer may work in his or her studio or may travel to different locations to take photographs. He or she must be able to stand for long periods of time and carry heavy equipment.

Work Activities
A photographer may do any or all of the following activities:

- Develop and print photographs.

- Use computers and special software to work with and improve the quality of photographs.

- Take photographs of weddings or other special events.

- Take photographs of people, places, or events for books, magazines, or newspapers.

Education/Training Requirements
Many jobs for photographers require a college degree in journalism or photography. However, some people start out as assistants to experienced photographers.

Think About It

Why do you think it is important for a photographer to be creative?

Summary

- Some careers are related to each other because they are in the same type of industry or business. The U.S. Department of Education has grouped careers into 16 career clusters based on similar industry.

- Certain jobs have titles that describe the type of work being done. Some of these titles include technician, assistant, and specialist.

- Talking to a career counselor, reading about a career, and holding informational interviews are three ways to explore careers.

- Informational interviews can help you find information about a job or career that you are interested in. Friends, family, teachers, career counselors, and professional associations are good ways to find people to interview.

- Steps in the informational interview include: 1) Finding the person who has a job or career you are interested in. 2) Making an appointment. 3) Preparing interview questions. 4) Keeping the appointment. 5) Writing answers to your questions. 6) Thanking the person with whom you interviewed.

career cluster
professional association
research
specialist
technician

Vocabulary Review

Complete each sentence with a term from the list.

1. An organization whose members all have the same career or occupation is called a _____.

2. Groups of careers that are related to each other based on similar industry, or business, are called a _____.

3. Carefully reading and studying facts is called _____.

4. A person who works in and knows a lot about one field is called a _____.

5. A person who has training in technology in a certain field is called a _____.

Chapter Quiz

Write your answers in complete sentences.

1. Why are some careers grouped together in clusters?

2. What are three job titles that describe types of work being done?

3. How can a career counselor help you to explore careers?

4. What important details should you research in order to find out more about a career?

5. Why is it a good idea to hold an informational interview if you are really interested in a career?

6. What are two questions you might ask during an informational interview?

CRITICAL THINKING

7. Why is it helpful to know the trends for a job that you are interested in?

8. After an informational interview, you decide that the career no longer interests you. Was the informational interview a waste of time?

Career Portfolio Project

Use a source for career information, such as the *Guide for Occupational Exploration* (*GOE*) or the *Occupational Outlook Handbook* (*OOH*), to look up careers that you may be interested in. Choose three occupations that you find interesting. Write the positive factors about each occupation. Then, write the negative factors about each occupation. Review what you have written about all three occupations. Are you still interested in any of them? Explain your answer.

Unit 1 **Review**

Choose the letter of the best answer to each question.

1. What happens when a worker is promoted?
   A. He or she retires.
   B. He or she is moved to a lower position in the company.
   C. He or she is moved to a higher position in the company.
   D. He or she changes careers.

2. Why should you plan a career?
   A. because your teachers tell you that you should
   B. because you want to do something that you will enjoy and are interested in
   C. because your friends are doing it
   D. because you want to be rich someday

3. What factors can affect employment rates?
   A. war
   B. trade agreements
   C. competition from other countries
   D. all of the above

4. Why is it helpful to be aware of career trends?
   A. Career trends can help you to be realistic about jobs.
   B. Career trends can tell you what salary you will earn.
   C. Career trends can tell you if you will like a particular job.
   D. Career trends can tell you how to apply for a particular job.

5. What resources can help you identify your strengths?
   A. books and magazines
   B. friends, family, and career counselors
   C. assessment tests
   D. all of the above

6. How can an informational interview be helpful?
   A. It can help you get a job.
   B. It is a good way to explore a career.
   C. It can tell you what your strengths and abilities are.
   D. It is a good way to have a balanced lifestyle.

Critical Thinking
Explain how identifying your strengths and interests can help you to choose a career.

Careers in Business and Services

Before You Read

In this unit, you will learn about different careers in business and services. You will find out what the job trends, lifestyles, and education and training requirements are for many of these types of careers.

Before you start reading, ask yourself these questions:

1. Are any of these types of careers interesting to me?
2. Do I have the right skills for these types of careers?
3. Would my personal interests match any of these careers?

Many office careers require people who can perform many tasks at the same time.

Learning Objectives

- Identify some careers in the office.
- Discuss trends in careers in the office.
- Describe strengths and lifestyles of people who have office careers.
- List ways to find out more about careers in the office.

Chapter 6 ▷ Careers in the Office

Words to Know

clerical	relating to office work
receptionist	a person who receives customers or visitors in an office
billing clerk	a person who records bills and sends them to customers
accounts receivable clerk	a person who keeps track of the bills that have or have not been paid
bookkeeper	a person who keeps records on how much money a business spends and makes
payroll clerk	a person who makes sure that paychecks are correct and delivered on time
stock clerk	a person who keeps track of the goods in stockrooms or warehouses
shipping and receiving clerk	a person who tracks goods that are received and goods that are shipped to other places

Karen, a high school senior, volunteers one hour each day in the office at her high school. Read how she describes her job to a friend.

"It isn't always easy working in this office." said Karen. "All three phones ring at the same time. While I'm writing phone messages, visitors to the office ask me questions." She continued, "I'm also responsible for making the attendance record."

Karen then said, "But I've learned to perform different tasks at the same time. Now, I can handle all kinds of situations. I really like working in the office!"

Careers in the Office

Offices can be found in almost any business setting. Many offices are located in buildings where different businesses are run. There are offices in schools, banks, factories, and department stores.

Office workers have the very important role of helping an office run smoothly. They handle mail, telephone calls, paperwork, and other office duties. Office workers are sometimes called **clerical** workers.

There are many different types of clerical jobs. For example, **receptionists** and information clerks are people who receive customers or visitors in an office. They greet these people and inform them about the services the business offers. Receptionists may also arrange appointments and determine which visitors are allowed into the office.

An office clerk may perform the duties of a receptionist in addition to other tasks. Some of these tasks include organizing paperwork, filling orders, ordering office supplies, or entering information into a computer.

Other types of office workers include financial clerks. These people keep track of money. There are different types of financial clerks. **Billing clerks** record bills and send them to customers. **Accounts receivable clerks** keep track of the bills that have or have not been paid. **Bookkeepers**, or bookkeeping clerks, record how much money a business spends and makes. **Payroll clerks** make sure that paychecks are correct and delivered on time.

Another group of clerical workers includes stock clerks. **Stock clerks** are in charge of the goods in stockrooms or warehouses. They record items that are entering and leaving. They unpack incoming goods and store them.

Using Technology

Most financial clerks use computer software programs to help them keep track of the money a business spends and makes.

Shipping and receiving clerks are clerical workers who keep track of goods that are received and goods that are shipped to other places. They make sure that orders for goods are packaged and shipped in the right way.

Secretaries and assistants are also clerical workers. They have a wide range of job duties. These duties include organizing and filing paper and electronic files, managing projects, and providing information through the mail, e-mail, and over the telephone. They also answer telephone calls, type letters and e-mails, and schedule meetings. Clerical supervisors and managers train and oversee other office workers.

Job Trends in Careers in the Office

In general, the outlook for many jobs in office careers between the years 2002 and 2012 looks good. Many of the new jobs will be for receptionists and information clerks. The number of jobs for receptionists is expected to increase between 21 and 35 percent. The number of jobs for information clerks is expected to increase 10 to 20 percent. One reason for these increases is that the number of offices for doctors, law firms, and other service-related businesses is also expected to grow. Most receptionists and information clerks are employed in these types of businesses.

At the same time, there may be little change in the number of some other clerical jobs between the years 2002 and 2012. Some of these jobs include bookkeepers and payroll clerks. Can you guess why? Technology is the reason. Office machines, such as computers and fax machines, help office workers to work at faster rates. Computers can be used to keep track of employee hours and paychecks. As a result of technology, fewer office workers may be needed to perform certain office tasks in the future.

Career Trend

More Americans have jobs in office careers than in any other career cluster. In the year 2000, about 20 million workers were employed in clerical jobs.

Write About It
Make a list of the different ways in which computers help office workers do their jobs. Share your list with the class.

Copy machines that use the latest technology can perform many tasks in a short period of time.

Write About It

Most large warehouses use robots to handle materials. Write a short paragraph explaining what benefits there are for using robots instead of humans to do this task.

Technology is also expected to cause the number of jobs to grow more slowly than the average for stock clerks and shipping and receiving clerks. The main reason for this slow growth is that robots and computers are now used to handle the duties that people in these occupations were once responsible for.

Strengths of People Who Have Careers in the Office

Do you always hang up your coat? Do you perform the same kinds of activities at the same time every day, such as brushing your teeth? Do you organize your notes? If your answer is *yes* to some of these questions, then an office career may be right for you.

People who work in offices should be careful, neat, and well organized. An office clerk who misplaces important papers will probably not be successful at a company. A payroll clerk who forgets to deliver the paychecks on payday will not be considered for a promotion.

People who enjoy working in an office share some similar personal strengths. Being able to do more than one job at a time is a strength. For example, a receptionist may answer a telephone call while also writing messages. Flexibility, or the ability to adjust to something new or different, is another personal strength. An office clerk shows flexibility when he or she handles customer orders one day and then handles travel arrangements the next day.

Remember
You learned in Chapter 3 that personal strengths can be things that you like or things that you do well.

Some office workers perform the same activities from day to day. Stock clerks, for example, sort and label all new items with certain codes. They may also have to lift these items onto shelves. Many new items are received every day. People with these careers have to be comfortable repeating daily activities. They also need to have physical strength in order to lift and place items onto shelves.

A strength that most office workers share is the ability to handle problems. Problems occur very often in an office setting. For example, a payroll clerk may notice mistakes on some paychecks. He or she will have to find ways to get new paychecks printed. A clerical supervisor may have to decide how to reassign work when two clerks are absent because of an illness. A receptionist might have to handle 20 telephone calls in 10 minutes. In such cases, knowing which calls to respond to first is important. Staying calm is also important.

✓ **Check Your Understanding**

Write your answers in complete sentences.

1. What is another name for office workers?

2. What do stock clerks do?

3. What are three personal strengths that all office workers should have?

Lifestyles of People Who Have Careers in the Office

Office workers are needed in almost every type of business. Banks need bank tellers. Health clubs and doctors' offices need receptionists. Bookstores require stock clerks. Even your school employs office workers such as receptionists and secretaries.

Most offices are clean, well-lighted spaces that are pleasant to work in. Workers dress neatly and professionally. For stock clerks, it is important to dress in clothing that allows them to do physical work. In general, office workers must have some computer skills. A typical office may have several computers, a copy machine, and a fax machine.

Most office positions are daytime jobs. The usual working hours are between 8 A.M. and 5 P.M. Workers in stockrooms, however, might have afternoon or evening shifts. Almost all offices are closed on weekends. However some people, such as receptionists and information clerks, might work evenings, weekends, or even holidays.

Career Fact

Most people who are hired as receptionists usually have good technical skills, clerical skills, and communication skills.

Many beginning clerical jobs require a person to have a high school diploma. Students should take classes in business math, technology, or bookkeeping to increase their chances of being hired in an office setting. Some businesses offer on-the-job training to help workers improve their skills and advance to higher-level jobs. Jobs for supervisors and managers usually require college degrees. However, many clerical workers can become supervisors or managers with experience and after working a certain number of years for a company.

The salaries of office workers can vary. Usually, the more education and experience a person has, the greater his or her income. In the year 2002, the average hourly rate for a stock clerk was about $10.00. In 2002, bookkeeping clerks earned an average hourly rate of $13.77. The average salary of secretaries was greater than $26,000. Clerical supervisors and managers can earn more than $30,000 a year.

Did You Know ?

The national minimum wage, or lowest wage that an employee in the United States can earn per hour, has increased over the years. In the year 1996, the national minimum wage was $4.75. In 2003, the minimum wage increased to $5.15.

Clerical supervisors and managers have more responsibilities than many other office workers.

How to Learn More About Careers in the Office

For information about office careers, you can write to the associations listed on page 84. Be sure to ask for specific information about the kind of career that you are interested in. You can also do one or more of the following:

- Volunteer to work in your school's office. Working even an hour a week will give you an idea of what office work can be like. You could also learn some useful office skills.

- Visit an office supply store. Look at the resources that businesses use to stay organized.

- Take courses in typing, word processing, business math, or bookkeeping. Take as many of these courses as possible. They can help you to gain the knowledge that you will need if you choose to work in an office.

- Look in a telephone directory under *business schools* to find schools that specialize in training people to work in offices. Write to these schools for information about training in careers that interest you. You can also write to community colleges for information on business-related courses.

- Go to the career section of a library. There are many books that describe the different kinds of careers in an office setting. Look through these books to find out about different jobs or careers that you might be interested in.

- Look up different office careers on the Internet. There are many Web sites that give information about a variety of jobs and careers. The site for the *Occupational Outlook Handbook* can be found at www.bls.gov/oco/home.htm. Visit this Web site or others to learn more about job trends and working conditions for office careers.

- Hold an informational interview with someone who works in an office setting. Prepare a list of questions for that person before the interview. Be sure to ask about working conditions, working hours, and the experience needed for that job.

- If you are a member of a club, volunteer to become the secretary or treasurer of the club. The skills that you will learn in either role might help you to get a job in an office setting.

Using Technology

O*Net OnLine gives information about different careers in the office. Visit its Web site at online.onetcenter.org to read about the tasks, knowledge, skills, and abilities required for many jobs in an office setting.

✓ Check Your Understanding

Write your answers in complete sentences.

1. Why would an office clerk need to be flexible?

2. What kinds of classes should people take if they are interested in office careers?

3. What is one thing that you can do to learn more about office careers?

Career Path

WORKING IN A BANK

In high school, Peter took classes in business math and technology. When he graduated, Peter applied for a job as a bank teller. Peter did not get the job. However, the manager of the bank did mention that there was a position open as a bank clerk. He offered Peter the job.

Peter took the bank clerk job. He worked all day putting bank slips and checks in the right places. He did not mind doing the same kind of work every day. However, he did wish that he could advance to a bank teller position. That job would allow him to have more contact with customers.

Finally, a teller position became available, and it was offered to Peter. The bank placed him in a training program. Peter really enjoyed his contact with the customers. More importantly, he was very careful with their money.

After several years, Peter became manager of the bank. Peter's attention to detail and his good communication skills made him a success.

CRITICAL THINKING What strengths did Peter have that led him to be successful in his career?

Associations for Careers in the Office

American Management Association
1601 Broadway
New York, NY 10019

**Communication Workers
of America**
501 Third Street, NW
Washington, DC 20001

**Educational Institute of the
American Hotel and Motel
Association**
2113 North High Street
East Lansing, MI 48906

**National Association of Executive
Secretaries and Administrative
Assistants**
900 South Washington Street
Suite G-13
Falls Church, VA 22046

National Management Association
2210 Arbor Boulevard
Dayton, OH 45439

**Office and Professional Employees
International Union**
265 West 14th Street, 6th Floor
New York, NY 10011

More Careers in the Office

Administrative assistant
Assistant treasurer
Bank teller
Budget analyst
Cost accountant
Customer service agent
Data entry clerk
Debt counselor
Human resource manager
Insurance appraiser

Loan officer
Mailroom clerk
Meeting and convention planner
Operations manager
Order clerk
Paralegal
Personal financial adviser
Personnel recruiter
Systems analyst
Tax collector

JOB DESCRIPTION
Administrative Assistant

Job Summary
An administrative assistant helps an office run smoothly. He or she provides support, or help, to people working in the office. An administrative assistant may also be responsible for organizing the daily activities of the office.

The office that an administrative assistant works in may be located in a building with other offices, or in a store, school, or hospital. Administrative assistants usually sit for long periods of time. They may also spend a lot of time working on a computer. Most administrative assistants work about 40 hours a week.

Job Activities
An administrative assistant may do any or all of the following activities:

- Schedule meetings and answer telephones.

- Prepare and write letters.

- Arrange conference calls, or telephone calls between more than two people.

- Handle travel arrangements.

- Conduct research on the Internet.

- Provide training to new staff members.

Education/Training Requirements
Many administrative assistant positions require a college education. However, some employers hire people with basic office skills. Knowledge of certain computer programs is also helpful.

Think About It
What other skills do you think an administrative assistant should have?

Summary

- Offices can be found in almost any business setting. Office workers are also called clerical workers. They perform a variety of tasks such as answering telephones, greeting customers, keeping records, or handling shipments of goods. They perform tasks that will help an office to run smoothly.

- There are many types of office jobs. Some of these jobs include receptionist, billing clerk, payroll clerk, and shipping and receiving clerk.

- While the number of some office jobs is expected to increase, technology will cause the number of some other office jobs to decrease.

- Office workers should be careful, neat, and well organized. They must also be able to do more than one task at a time and handle problems.

- The salary that an office worker earns can depend on the amount of education he or she has, the type of work performed, and the level of his or her experience. The more skills an office worker has, the more he or she is likely to earn.

accounts receivable clerk
billing clerk
clerical
payroll clerk
receptionist
shipping and receiving clerk

Vocabulary Review

Complete each sentence with a term from the list.

1. A person who receives customers or visitors in an office is called a _____.

2. A person who makes sure that paychecks are correct and that they are delivered on time is called a _____.

3. A person who tracks goods that are received and goods shipped to other places is called a _____.

4. A person who records bills and sends them to customers is called a _____.

5. The term that means "relating to office work" is _____.

6. A person who keeps track of the bills that have or have not been paid is called an _____.

Chapter Quiz

Write your answers in complete sentences.

1. Which office workers keep track of money?

2. What does a bookkeeper do?

3. How might technology affect the need for billing clerks?

4. Who needs more people skills to do their job, a receptionist or a stock clerk?

5. Who works in a stockroom, a payroll clerk or a shipping and receiving clerk?

6. If you like dressing up for work every day, should you apply for a job in an office or a stockroom?

CRITICAL THINKING

7. A large company employs 100 information clerks. In the next ten years, it will hire 10 percent more information clerks. How many new information clerks will be hired in the next ten years? Does this number support information on job trends for information clerks? Explain your answer.

8. How could a person increase his or her chances of getting a job in an office?

Career Portfolio Project

Choose an office career that interests you. Search career sites on the Internet or look through the *Occupational Outlook Handbook* for information about this career. Then, make a list of strengths needed for this career. Check off all of the strengths that apply to you. Write an essay that describes the career and why it might be right for you.

A career in education allows a person to help others, especially children, to learn.

Learning Objectives

- Identify some careers in education and training.
- Discuss trends in careers in education and training.
- Describe strengths and lifestyles of people who have careers in education and training.
- List ways to find out more about careers in education and training.

Chapter 7 ▶ Careers in Education and Training

Words to Know

teacher assistant	a person who helps a teacher
librarian	a person who works with materials and people in a library
curator	a person who works with objects in a museum or wildlife in a zoo, aquarium, or nature center
museum educator	a person who helps people to learn about a museum's objects
overtime	the amount of time worked in addition to the normal 40 hours in a business week
part-time worker	a person who works less than 35 hours in a business week

Jordan is about to find out that his cousin Tracy has a career in education. Read their conversation below:

"What are you doing?" Jordan asked Tracy.

"I'm correcting papers," Tracy answered.

"I didn't know that you were a teacher," replied Jordan.

"Actually, I'm a teacher assistant. I help a fourth grade teacher," said Tracy.

"Do you like it?" Jordan asked.

"Yes. I do. I wasn't sure what to do after I graduated from high school, but I really like children. Now that I know what it is like working in a classroom, I'm going to get my teaching degree," Tracy replied.

"I think that you will make a really good teacher," said Jordan.

Careers in Education and Training

Tracy is a teacher assistant. A **teacher assistant** helps a classroom teacher with many everyday school tasks, such as grading papers, recording the grades, and passing out books and papers. A teacher assistant is one of the many occupations in the education and training career cluster.

People who have careers in education and training help others to learn. In 2002, there were more than 7 million people who were employed in this career cluster. Careers or occupations in this cluster include teachers, teacher assistants, instructors, librarians, library educators, and museum workers.

Teachers make up the largest number of occupations in this career cluster. There are, however, many different kinds of teachers. Preschool teachers teach children between the ages of two and five. Elementary, middle, and high school teachers teach students from kindergarten through grade 12. College professors teach students who have usually completed high school. These students can range from teenagers to older adults.

There are also careers in education and training that are outside of a school setting. For example, a **librarian** works with the materials and people in a library. He or she helps library users to find information, orders and organizes library materials, and supervises the other people who work in a library.

A **curator** works with objects in a museum or wildlife in a zoo, aquarium, or nature center. He or she plans and manages the displays or exhibits. A **museum educator** is a person who helps people to learn about a museum's objects. He or she usually shows groups of people the different museum objects and explains where these objects came from.

Remember
In Chapter 1, you learned that a person's occupation can be his or her career.

Career Trend

Demand for librarians who work in corporations and businesses was rising as of 2003. Such librarians research competitors and help develop business plans.

Job Trends in Careers in Education and Training

Between the years 2002 and 2012, the expected increase in the number of new jobs in this career cluster will depend on the occupation. Employment in some jobs is expected to grow at about the average rate. The average rate is 10 to 20 percent. Some jobs are expected to grow faster than the average rate, at about 21 to 35 percent. Other jobs may grow more slowly than the average rate, at about 3 to 9 percent.

The number of teaching jobs for almost every type of teacher is expected to increase at about the average rate. One reason for this positive outlook for teachers is that a large number of teachers are expected to retire by 2012. Many new teachers will be needed to fill these teaching jobs. Another reason is the growing student population. As the number of students increases, the number of jobs for teachers will also increase. The number of jobs for teacher assistants is also expected to increase faster than the average rate.

The number of jobs for museum curators and educators is expected to increase at about the average rate. However, the number of jobs for librarians is expected to grow more slowly than the average rate. One reason for this slow growth may be due to the increasing use of computers to find and store information. Improvements in technology have reduced some responsibilities of librarians.

Write About It

Make a graph to show the three different rates at which jobs in education and training will grow or decrease.

Career Fact

There are more job opportunities for curators in art and history museums than in other kinds of museums.

✓ Check Your Understanding

Write your answers in complete sentences.

1. Name five careers in education and training.

2. What is the job trend for teacher employment?

3. What is the job trend for librarians?

Strengths of People Who Have Careers in Education and Training

Teachers of young children need to be kind and caring. They should be able to help children feel safe in new environments. Small children need to be able to trust their teachers.

Teachers of older students need to feel comfortable talking in front of large groups. They should also be able to motivate their students to learn.

People who work in museums or libraries should enjoy working in a learning environment. Because a large part of their jobs includes finding information, people who work in museums or libraries should enjoy research. Curators, museum educators, and librarians need to be careful about details and facts.

Almost all careers in education and training require the ability to keep detailed records. Patience and a helping attitude are very important, too. The ability to understand the needs of different students and different people is also needed.

A museum educator helps children to learn about art objects.

Lifestyles of People Who Have Careers in Education and Training

Most teachers work in schools, usually in classrooms. Classrooms contain desks, books, and other learning materials. Some teachers are tutors. These types of teachers work in private homes.

Museums and libraries are quiet places. Museums contain exhibits that reflect the museum's collection of objects. Exhibits can include artwork, furniture, or models of animals that lived long ago. Libraries contain books. They also have computers and other equipment to help people search for information.

Educators and trainers usually work a regular workweek. A regular workweek is usually equal to 40 hours. A normal workday is eight hours. Librarians, curators, and museum educators may work evening and weekend hours. They may also work overtime. **Overtime** is the amount of time worked in addition to the normal 40 hours in a workweek. Many teachers also work overtime. In addition to teaching students, teachers must also grade papers, prepare lessons, and meet with parents.

Some people who have jobs in education and training are part-time workers. **Part-time workers** usually work less than 35 hours in a business week.

Most people work 12 months a year with two or more weeks of vacation time. However, most teachers work 10 months a year. They do not work during the summer when students are on vacation.

Most careers in education and training require a college degree. Many jobs for teachers, librarians, and curators require additional degrees. There are some jobs for teacher assistants that only require a high school diploma. However, related experience is helpful.

Career Fact

In middle school and high school classes, teachers may not spend the entire day in only one classroom. They may move from one classroom to another to teach different students.

Did You Know

During summer months, many teachers work at other jobs, teach summer school classes, or prepare for their next year of teaching.

Most careers in education and training also require computer skills. Librarians, curators, and museum educators must be able to use computers to store information and to research information. Teachers must also have computer skills. Teachers may use computers to help them organize their work. They may also use computer programs to help students learn on their own.

The average salary for teachers, librarians, and curators can depend on the amount of training and job experience that a person has. The average salaries for these occupations in the year 2002 ranged between $40,000 and $46,000. The average salary for teacher assistants in the year 2002 was $20,000.

How to Learn More About Careers in Education and Training

There are many ways to learn more about careers in education and training. You can read descriptions for many of these jobs in career resource books and at career Web sites. You can also follow any of the suggestions listed below:

- Volunteer to help one of your teachers. You will learn what a teacher does when he or she is not teaching a class.

- Volunteer at a library. You may find out what it is like to help someone search for information.

- Spend a day at a museum. Watch how museum visitors react to the displays.

- Set up an informational interview with an educator or trainer. Be sure to make a list of questions before you interview the person.

- Write to one of the associations listed on page 96 for more information.

Using Technology

The American Association of Museums has a Web site that gives information about jobs in museums. Visit this Web site at www.aam-us.org.

✓ Check Your Understanding

Write your answers in complete sentences.

1. What kind of personal qualities should a teacher of young children have?

2. Name a skill that almost all careers in education and training require.

3. What is overtime?

4. Name one way to learn more about careers in education and training.

Learn More About It

WORKING PART TIME

A part-time worker usually works less than 35 hours per week. A full-time worker usually works 40 or more hours per week. Since the 1980s, more people are choosing to work part time. In the year 2002, four out of every ten teacher assistants worked part time.

Part-time work has many benefits. Working shorter hours can allow a person to spend time doing other things. For example, some part-time employees are students. They spend a certain number of hours attending classes and doing schoolwork. Some part-time workers spend time with their families. Many people who choose to work part time only work to earn extra money. These men and women may not have a career plan that they are following.

Part-time jobs have some disadvantages. For example, part-time workers may not earn the same salary as a worker who has the same job but who works full time. A part-time worker may not have paid vacation time. Also, part-time workers may not move ahead in their careers at the same rate as full-time workers in the same occupation.

CRITICAL THINKING If you wanted to get ahead in your career as fast as possible, would you work part time? Explain your answer.

Associations for Careers in Education and Training

American Association of Museums
1575 Eye Street, NW, Suite 400
Washington, DC 20005

American Council on Education
One Dupont Circle, NW
Washington, DC 20036

**American Federation of
Teachers, AFL-CIO**
555 New Jersey Avenue, NW
Washington, DC 20001

American Library Association
50 E. Huron
Chicago, IL 60611

Library of Congress
Human Resources Office
101 Independence Avenue, SE
Washington, DC 20540-2231

National Education Association
1201 16th Street, NW
Washington, DC 20036

Special Libraries Association
1700 18th Street, NW
Washington, DC 20009

Society of American Archivists
527 Wells Street, 5th Floor
Chicago, IL 60607

More Careers in Education and Training

Archivist
Biology teacher
Chemistry teacher
English teacher
Health educator
History teacher
Information scientist
Library assistant

Library technician
Math teacher
Media aid
Nursing instructor
School librarian
Special education teacher
Training and development manager
Training and development specialist

JOB DESCRIPTION
Teacher Assistant

Job Summary
A teacher assistant helps a classroom teacher. A teacher assistant also works with one student or small groups of students to provide extra help that students might need in learning class material. A teacher assistant is sometimes called a teacher aide or instructional aide.

Most teacher assistants work part time. However, there are some full-time jobs available. A teacher assistant may work in a preschool or elementary, middle, or high school.

Work Activities
A teacher assistant may do any or all of the following activities:

- Grade tests and papers.

- Check students' homework.

- Keep classroom attendance records.

- Listen while students read aloud in small groups.

- Type, file, and photocopy materials for use in the classroom.

- Provide personal attention to students with special needs.

Education/Training Requirements
Many jobs for teacher assistants require some college courses. A teacher assistant who performs teaching tasks generally needs more training than one who does not. Most employers require some previous teaching experience. Some schools hire teacher assistants who have only a high school diploma.

Think About It
What other career do you think a teacher assistant may be interested in?

Summary

- People who have careers in education and training provide information to others. Careers or occupations in this career cluster include teachers, teacher assistants, librarians, curators, and museum educators.

- From the year 2002 through the year 2012, the increase in the number of new jobs in this career cluster will depend on the occupation. The outlook for most teaching jobs is very good.

- Almost all careers in education and training require good computer skills and the ability to keep detailed records. Patience and a helping attitude are important strengths of those people who have careers in education and training.

- 40 hours a week is the normal number of working hours for most businesses. Some people who have jobs in education and training work part time. Part-time workers usually work less than 35 hours per week.

curator
librarian
museum educator
overtime
part-time worker
teacher assistant

Vocabulary Review

Complete each sentence with a term from the list.

1. A person who helps a teacher is called a _____.

2. A person who works with materials and people in a library is called a _____.

3. A person who usually works less than 35 hours per week is called a _____.

4. The amount of time worked in addition to the normal 40 business hours in a week is called _____.

5. A person who works with the objects in a museum or wildlife in a zoo, aquarium, or nature center is called a _____.

6. A person who helps people to learn about a museum's objects is called a _____.

Chapter Quiz

Write your answers in complete sentences.

1. Which occupation makes up the largest number of jobs in education and training?

2. What are two careers in education and training that are not in a school setting?

3. Who does a museum educator help?

4. Which type of job in education and training is expected to grow faster than the average rate?

5. How many hours do part-time workers usually work?

6. Why would volunteering at a library be helpful in learning more about a career in education and training?

CRITICAL THINKING

7. Why would a person choose to work part time?

8. Write at least two questions that you would ask during an informational interview with a museum educator.

Career Portfolio Project

Make a two-column chart. In the first column, list the personal strengths of people with careers in education and training. In the second column, write a check mark next to each personal strength that you have. Look at your chart. In a short paragraph, explain whether or not you would consider a career in education and training.

To perform their jobs, some American soldiers wear special uniforms and must follow certain directions.

Learning Objectives

- Identify some careers in government.
- Discuss trends in careers in government.
- Describe strengths and lifestyles of people who have careers in government.
- List ways to find out more about careers in government.

Chapter 8 ▷ Careers in Government

Words to Know

government	the way a country, state, or city is organized and managed
civil servant	a person who works for the government
civil service	the system that is used to hire people for government jobs
park ranger	a person who works to protect the natural resources in national or state parks
military personnel	the people who work in the armed forces
enlist	to join
recruiting specialist	a person who provides information to people about joining the armed forces

Anthony Suarez is a mail carrier for the U.S. postal service. He is the guest speaker in a high school career education class. Read what Anthony Suarez likes most about his job below.

> Anthony Suarez told the class, "There are many things that I like about my job. I like working outdoors, even in the rain or snow. Also, as long as I deliver the mail on time, I can work at my own pace."
>
> He added, "Being a postal worker offers me the chance to meet many different people. I also enjoy working for the government." Anthony Suarez went on, "My job helps me to serve my country. Delivering the mail is a service to all people."

Careers in Government

Government is the way a country, state, or city is organized and managed. In the United States, there are three levels of government: federal, state, and local.

The federal government, or national government, is based in Washington, D.C. The head of the federal government is the president of the United States. There are 50 state governments. Local governments manage counties, cities, townships, and other special districts, or parts, in each state.

At each level of government, people are employed to serve the country and its people. Government workers are called **civil servants**. The system used to hire government workers is called the **civil service**.

Career Fact

Most people who have government jobs at the state and local levels work in the field of education.

Thousands of civil service jobs are similar to jobs found in private businesses. The government employs office workers, construction workers, teachers, healthcare workers, and more. However, some careers are found only in the government. For example, the services provided by a mail carrier and a park ranger are not offered by private businesses. A mail carrier works for the U.S. Postal Service. He or she delivers and collects mail. A **park ranger** works to protect the natural resources in national or state parks.

Careers in the Armed Forces

The military, or armed forces, is run by the federal government. People who work in the armed forces are called **military personnel**. These people **enlist** in, or join, the Army, Navy, Air Force, Marines, or Coast Guard.

The main goal of military personnel is to protect and defend the country. For example, an artillery, or weapons, team leader may supervise the destroying of military targets. A special operations team member might take part in a search-and-rescue mission for missing soldiers.

There are many different military careers and jobs. For example, the job of a **recruiting specialist** is to provide information to people about joining the armed forces. A construction specialist may help build plumbing systems in aircraft or ships.

Some jobs in the military are similar to jobs found in private businesses. For example, some military jobs are for office workers. Records must be kept on military personnel, equipment, supplies, and finances. Military personnel with office careers keep track of these subjects. The military also hires office clerks, bookkeepers, secretaries, assistants, payroll clerks, and shipping and receiving clerks. Some other military jobs include computer technician, electrician, doctor, nurse, office assistant, librarian, and dental assistant.

Did You Know ?

College credit can be given to people in the armed forces for the technical training that they receive while serving in the military.

Careers for Elected People

There are some government workers who are elected, or voted in, by American citizens to fill certain jobs in government. This group of people includes the president of the United States, state governors, senators, representatives, and local mayors. These elected government workers can then appoint, or choose, people to do other jobs. For example, in September 2001, President George W. Bush appointed Governor Tom Ridge to become Secretary of the Department of Homeland Security. On a local level, a city's mayor chooses, or appoints, the city's police chief and fire chief.

✓ Check Your Understanding

Write your answers in complete sentences.

1. What are the three levels of government?

2. What are civil servants?

3. What are people who work in the armed forces called?

Job Trends in Careers in Government

The government is the largest employer in the United States. In the year 2003, there were more than 20 million government workers.

The job trend for many government careers between the years 2002 and 2012 is good. The number of jobs for government workers in the future is expected to increase between 10 and 20 percent. Many people believe that in the twenty-first century, or the years that follow the year 2000, there will be a great need for military protection. World events, especially war and the threat of violence, will increase the need for many workers at all levels of government.

The number of jobs for postal service workers, on the other hand, may decrease between the years 2002 and 2012. A reason for this decrease is the use of computer equipment to sort mail and an expected decrease in the total amount of mail to be delivered.

Strengths of People Who Have Careers in Government

The desire to serve one's country is a personal strength of many people who work for the government. If you have the same desire, then you may be interested in a career in government.

Another personal strength that many government workers share is patience. Getting a civil service job can often be a long process. To apply for a civil service job, a person must first fill out a job application form. Then, those people whose applications are accepted must take a test in the career that they are interested in. When a job position is open, the first people considered for that job are those who scored highest on the test. This hiring process can sometimes take months or even years to complete.

Career Trend

The number of people who enlist in the armed forces is usually high when the economy is doing poorly.

Remember

In Chapter 1, you learned that a job application is a form that a worker fills out when applying for a job.

A mail carrier and many other civil servants must pass an exam in order to be employed by the government.

The armed forces also requires people with special strengths. Military personnel should be able to follow rules. They should enjoy hard work. Many people in the armed forces go through hard physical training. They may face tough conditions during wartime.

Lifestyles of People Who Have Careers in Government

Working for the government has many benefits. Even when the economy is weak, government jobs are often more secure than jobs in private businesses. In addition to a salary, full-time government workers also receive fully paid medical insurance and dental insurance.

Write About It
What kind of rules do you think military personnel might have to follow? Write a list of these rules. Place an X next to the rules that you would find the most difficult to follow.

Career Fact

Active military personnel receive fully paid room and board. People in the armed forces may also receive training in skills that can be useful in jobs outside of the military.

A person who enlists in the armed forces should be prepared for a very different lifestyle. New military personnel sign contracts that require them to serve from two to six years. They leave home, family, and friends for several months of training. Once trained, they may serve anywhere in the world.

Today, the United States has an all-volunteer military force. To be accepted, a person must be between 17 and 35 years of age. A person must have at least average reading, writing, and thinking skills. People with high school diplomas or higher degrees are preferred. Good health is also important.

How to Learn More About Careers in Government

For information about government jobs, you can write to the associations listed on page 108. Be specific about the kind of career information that you are interested in. You can also follow these suggestions:

- Look through federal government job listings at a Federal Job Information Center (FJIC). Look under *federal listings* in a telephone directory to find the FJIC nearest you.

- Visit a large post office. Many post offices publish listings of job openings in the U.S. postal service.

- Most libraries have booklets to help people prepare for civil service exams. Find one for a career that you are interested in. Take the practice exams. Learn which skills you need to improve upon in order to score well on a civil service exam.

- Practice filling out an application form for civil service jobs. The SF-171 is the form that most people use to apply for civil service jobs. You can pick up several copies of this form at a post office.

Using Technology

You can visit www.militarycareers.com for information about careers in the armed forces.

✓ Check Your Understanding

Write your answers in complete sentences.

1. What is the trend for many government careers in the years between 2002 and 2012?

2. How does a person apply for a civil service job?

3. What is one benefit of working for the government?

Learn More About It

THE STAY-IN-SCHOOL PROGRAM

When Shane was a junior in high school, his parents were having a hard time finding jobs. Shane wanted to help his family. He thought about quitting school to work full time. Shane spoke to his high school counselor about his idea.

The counselor told Shane about the Stay-in-School Program. The Stay-in-School Program provides jobs with the federal and state governments to students in need of money and to students with disabilities. Students who are accepted into the program work part time while in school. In the summer and during vacation periods, they work full time. In exchange, the students must stay in school and work toward a diploma, certificate, or degree. The program is open to students who are at least 16 years old and who are in high school, vocational school, or college.

Shane applied to the program and was accepted. He worked in a local government office. He helped sort mail, answered telephone calls, and ordered office supplies. His salary helped him to support his family. Shane was also able to stay in school and earn his high school diploma.

CRITICAL THINKING What do you think would have happened to Shane if he had not applied to and been accepted in the Stay-in-School Program?

Associations for Careers in Government

American Federation of State, County, and Municipal Employees, AFL-CIO
1625 L Street, NW
Washington, DC 20036-5687

Commandant of the Marine Corps
Marine Corps Headquarters
2 Navy Annex
Washington, DC 20380-0001

Department of the Army
U.S. Army Recruiting Command
Headquarters
Fort Sheridan, IL 60037

National Association of Counties
440 First Street, NW
Washington, DC 20001

The National League of Cities
1301 Pennsylvania Avenue, NW
Suite 550
Washington, DC 20004

Navy Recruiting Command
5722 Integrity Drive
Building 784
Millington, TN 38054

United States Air Force (USAF) Recruiting Service
Public Affairs Office
550 D Street, Suite 1
Randolph Air Force Base, TX 78150

More Careers in Government

Administrative officer
Cargo inspector
Census clerk
Correction officer
County director
Court administrator
Court clerk
Economist
Federal aid coordinator
Firefighter
Forester
Immigration officer

Legislative aide
Nuclear weapons specialist
Office assistant
Police officer
Postmaster
Postal service worker
Registered nurse
Revenue agent
Submarine officer
Tax assistant
Teacher assistant
Urban planner

JOB DESCRIPTION
Mail Carrier

Job Summary

A mail carrier is a U.S. postal service worker. A mail carrier is responsible for delivering letters, bills, packages, and magazines to homes and businesses. Some mail carriers also collect outgoing mail.

A mail carrier begins work very early in the morning. He or she spends most working hours outdoors. A mail carrier must deliver mail in all kinds of weather. Overtime hours are usually required during busy times, such as the winter holidays.

Work Activities

A mail carrier may do any or all of the following activities:

- Arrange mail in a certain order.

- Deliver and pick up mail from homes and businesses.

- Collect money for postage.

- Collect money for COD (cash on delivery) packages.

- Obtain signatures on receipts for registered, certified, and insured mail.

- Provide change-of-address cards and other postal forms.

Education/Training Requirements

A mail carrier must be at least 18 years old. He or she must also be a U.S. citizen. A person applying for a mail carrier position must pass a written exam and a physical exam. Some mail carriers must be able to lift a mail sack weighing 70 pounds. Additional requirements include a driver's license and a good driving record. Employers provide on-the-job training for mail carriers.

Think About It

What are some benefits of being a mail carrier?

8 ▷ Review

Summary

- Government is the way in which a country, state, or city is organized and managed. In the United States, there are three levels of government: federal, state, and local.

- Government workers are called civil servants. The system that hires government workers is called the civil service. The government is the largest employer in the United States. Thousands of civil service jobs are similar to jobs found in private businesses.

- People who work in the armed forces are called military personnel. The main goal of military personnel is to protect and defend the country. Military personnel should be able to follow rules and should also like hard work.

- Working for the government has many benefits. Fully paid medical and dental insurance and a certain amount of job security are among the benefits.

- Government employment agencies carry listings of job openings. People who are interested in applying for a federal government job can visit a Federal Job Information Center (FJIC).

civil servant
enlist
government
military personnel
park ranger

Vocabulary Review

Complete each sentence with a term from the list.

1. A person who wants to join the armed forces must _____.

2. People who work in the armed forces are called _____.

3. A person who works for the government is called a _____.

4. A person who works to protect the country's natural resources in a national or state park is called a _____.

5. The way a country, state, or city is organized and managed is called _____.

Chapter Quiz

Write your answers in complete sentences.

1. What is the system that is used to hire government workers called?

2. Name three jobs that can be found in the government and in private business.

3. How does the mayor of a city usually get his or her job?

4. What is a personal strength that government workers usually have?

5. What is an FJIC? What will you find there?

6. What is the trend for jobs for postal workers?

CRITICAL THINKING

7. How can people in the armed forces benefit from their work experience after they have left the armed forces?

8. How can a person increase his or her chance of getting a civil service job?

Career Portfolio Project

Choose a government career that you find interesting. Then, research that career. Career exploration books and Web sites are good sources of information. Write a job description for that career. Use the Job Description on page 109 as a guide in writing your description. Read the job description that you have written. Decide if you are still interested in that career. Explain your answer in a short paragraph.

A person who cuts, styles, or colors a customer's hair usually learns these skills at a special school.

Learning Objectives

- Identify some careers in human services.
- Discuss trends in careers in human services.
- Describe strengths and lifestyles of people who have careers in human services.
- List ways to find out more about careers in human services.

Chapter 9 ▷ Careers in Human Services

Words to Know

social worker	a person who helps people to meet their needs by providing counseling and arranging other services
dietitian	a person who plans and manages food programs for healthy eating
dietetic technician	a person who helps a dietitian plan, prepare, and manage food programs
cosmetologist	a person who helps people to look neat and well-groomed
license	a legal document that gives a person permission to do something
certification	a process that shows that an individual has met certain requirements to do something

Linda is a hairdresser. She is helping a customer get ready to attend a wedding. Read about Linda's work.

"Just a few more pins in your hair and it will stay in this style for the entire wedding," Linda told her customer.

"I like how you have styled my hair!" the woman replied. "How do you know so many hairstyles?" she asked.

Linda replied, "I learned how to style hair at a special school for hairdressers."

"It must be fun working on other people's hair," the woman said.

"It can be. I like making people feel good about the way that they look!" said Linda.

Careers in Human Services

You read that Linda is a hairdresser. She cuts and styles people's hair. Hairdressers are grouped in the human services career cluster. People in this career cluster provide services to individuals or families.

There are many different careers or occupations in human services. Some of these careers or occupations fulfill basic needs of people. For example, a childcare worker cares for children of all ages. They may teach children, organize activities for them, or provide them with basic care. Basic care includes feeding and dressing children.

A **social worker** also helps people to meet their needs. A social worker may help people who are unemployed or suffering from illnesses. By counseling and arranging certain services, a social worker can help people to find jobs, housing, or solutions to problems.

A **dietitian** helps people meet their needs for healthy eating. He or she may plan food programs. A dietitian may also advise people on what foods to eat to prevent or treat illnesses. A **dietetic technician** helps a dietitian plan, prepare, and manage food programs. He or she may also advise people about food and healthy eating habits.

Other careers in the human services career cluster also provide people with personal services. A fitness trainer helps people to reach their physical fitness goals. He or she develops exercise programs and keeps track of customers' progress toward their goals.

A travel agent, also called a travel guide, helps people make arrangements to visit other places. The services that a travel agent provides save people time from having to make their own arrangements. These arrangements are usually for transportation, hotels, rental cars, or tours.

Career Fact

Childcare workers include nannies, babysitters, and workers in daycare centers and preschools.

Write About It

Dietitians plan meals for healthier eating. Write a list of foods that a dietitian might include in a food program for high school students.

A chef prepares food for people. He or she also manages other kitchen workers. A **cosmetologist** helps people to look neat and well-groomed. Other careers related to cosmetology include barbers, hairdressers, and skin care specialists.

Job Trends for Careers in Human Services

The outlook for many jobs in human services between the years 2002 and 2012 is expected to be good. One reason for this trend is the growing population of older people. Older people need many personal services.

Occupations affected by this growth include social workers and dietitians. Social workers provide older people with advice on services such as finding affordable housing and ways to pay for long-term healthcare. Dietitians provide healthy food programs in places such as hospitals and homes for the elderly. More social workers and dietitians will be needed as the size of the elderly population increases.

The number of jobs for social workers between the years 2002 and 2012 is expected to increase between 21 and 35 percent. The number of jobs for dietitians is expected to increase between 10 and 20 percent.

Jobs in human services will also increase because the population of children under five years old is expected to increase. This increase will affect the number of jobs for childcare workers. The number of jobs is expected to increase 10 to 20 percent between the years 2002 and 2012.

The number of jobs for cosmetologists is also expected to increase between 10 and 20 percent. The increasing population, higher incomes, and increasing demand to look well-groomed are expected to provide many jobs for cosmetologists.

Did You Know ?

Long-term care is care given to people who have diseases or disabilities that last for a long period of time. It does not include hospital care.

Remember
In Chapter 2, you read that world events can affect unemployment rates.

As you have read, the outlook for jobs in human services is affected by the age of the general population. However, events in the United States and throughout the world can also affect job trends in human services. These events may include uncertain economies, outbreaks of illnesses, and violent acts such as war. These events can also change the way people plan to spend their vacations. World events may also affect jobs in the travel industry. For example, in the years between 2002 and 2012, travel within the United States and to other countries is expected to decrease. As a result, the number of jobs for travel agents is expected to increase at a slower than average rate.

✓ **Check Your Understanding**

Write your answers in complete sentences.

1. How does a social worker help people meet their needs?

2. How does a fitness trainer help people?

3. What is the expected increase in the number of jobs for childcare workers between the years 2002 and 2012?

Strengths of People Who Have Careers in Human Services

Many people who have careers or jobs in human services want to help other people. Social workers want to help people improve their lives. A dietitian wants to help people eat foods that are healthy for them. A personal trainer wants to help people improve their physical fitness levels. Do you want to help others? Are you interested in providing these kinds of services to other people? If you are, you may find a career in human services rewarding.

People in this career cluster must work to satisfy the needs of others. For example, a dietitian and a dietetic technician need to satisfy the needs of people who want to eat healthy foods. A cosmetologist should try to satisfy a customer's need to look well-groomed. A travel agent must work to satisfy the travel needs of his or her customers.

In order to satisfy customers' needs, people in human services need good communication skills. Cosmetologists and fitness trainers must be able to talk to their customers in order to understand what their customers' needs are. Social workers need good communication skills in order to get information from people. They must also be able to give information to people. In order for children to feel safe, childcare workers must be able to talk to them and respond to their needs.

Some careers in human services also require special abilities. A chef must have the ability to produce food that looks good and tastes good. He or she must also be able to supervise people who work in a kitchen. In order to keep up with new hairstyles, a cosmetologist should have an understanding of art and the latest fashions. A fitness trainer should be able to motivate a customer to reach his or her fitness goals. A childcare worker should be able to comfort and care for a sick child. A travel agent must know all the travel requirements for a person visiting different countries.

Career Trend

Many chefs become the owners of their own restaurants. Some chefs become instructors at cooking schools.

In addition to providing services and satisfying the needs of others, many of these careers require a caring attitude. A person who becomes a social worker usually does so because he or she cares about helping people. A childcare worker cares about the safety and well-being of children. Dietitians and dietetic technicians care about helping people improve their health by eating the right foods.

Lifestyles of People Who Have Careers in Human Services

Lifestyles of people who have careers in human services depend on the type of occupation. Working conditions, hours of work, training requirements, and salaries also affect lifestyles.

Jobs in these careers take place in a variety of spaces. For example, childcare workers are employed in daycare centers, schools, or private homes. Travel agents and social workers usually work in offices. Social workers may also visit the houses of the people that they are trying to help. Chefs work in the kitchens of restaurants, schools, businesses, or hospitals. Dietitians and dietetic technicians usually work in the kitchens of schools, homes for the elderly, or hospitals. Most cosmetologists work in beauty salons. All of these spaces are usually clean and well-lighted.

The work schedules of people in the human services career cluster can vary. Many of these people work regular business hours. However, some of them can also work evening and weekend hours.

Training and education requirements also vary. Some occupations require a special license. A **license** is a legal document that gives a person permission to do something. To get a license of any type, a person often has to take an exam. He or she usually takes courses in order to pass the exam. Most cosmetologists, some childcare workers, and some social workers need licenses to practice their work.

Certification is a requirement that most fitness trainers must have. **Certification** is a process that shows that an individual has met certain requirements to do something. Getting certified is similar to getting a license. The individual usually takes classes and then must pass an exam. However, certification comes from a private organization. It is not a legal process.

Career Fact

Social workers can be called during emergency situations. For example, after a fire, a social worker may help people who no longer have homes find places to stay.

Some occupations in human services may only require a high school diploma. Some childcare workers and chefs may be given on-the-job training. However, advancement in these occupations often requires additional training in a vocational school, college, or community college.

There are also differences in the salaries of all the occupations in human services. In 2002, the average salary for a childcare worker was about $17,000. The average salary for a social worker was about $36,000. A cosmetologist earned about $22,000. A chef earned about $32,000, and the average salary of a travel agent was about $30,000.

Most fitness trainers work in gyms, health clubs, and fitness centers.

How to Learn More About Careers in Human Services

Using Technology

The Bureau of Labor Statistics gives employment information for many careers in human services. Visit its Web site at www.bls.gov.

There are many sources that can give you information about careers in human services. Web sites and career reference books are a good place to start your research. The *Occupational Outlook Handbook* lists some of these careers under "Community and social services occupations" and others under "Personal care and service occupations."

You can also follow any of the suggestions listed below:

- Look up travel agencies in a telephone directory. Telephone and ask to speak to a travel agent. Ask the travel agent if you can hold an informational interview with him or her.

- Try to find a job as a babysitter. You will find out if you enjoy caring for children.

- Get experience working in the kitchen of a restaurant. You can observe how a chef cooks and manages a kitchen staff.

- Visit a beauty salon. Watch how the cosmetologists cut and style hair. Observe how they communicate with their customers.

- Volunteer to help a social worker at a state or local social services office. You may be able to help people get the services that they need.

- Go to a gym that provides the services of a fitness trainer. Ask for information about those services. This information can tell you more about the job responsibilities of a fitness trainer.

✓ Check Your Understanding

Write your answers in complete sentences.

1. What are two strengths that some people in human services careers should have?
2. What is a license?
3. How can you learn more about becoming a cosmetologist?

Career Path

DIETITIAN

Claudia is a registered dietitian. She works in a hospital where she studies the nutritional needs of different patients. She gives her patients advice about eating the right foods to treat and prevent diseases. Claudia also plans menus and food programs to help her patients eat healthy diets.

Claudia always knew that she wanted to become a dietitian. When she was twelve years old, Claudia was diagnosed with celiac disease. This disease prevents her from eating many of the foods that she likes, such as chocolate, all kinds of breads, and many fruits. With the help of a dietitian, Claudia learned to stay away from those foods. Her dietitian designed a special diet for Claudia. The diet includes food products that are safe for her to eat and are similar to the foods that Claudia likes.

Claudia knew that she wanted to help people in the same way that her dietitian had helped her. To prepare for a career as a dietitian, she took college courses that included biology, anatomy, chemistry, and food service. She graduated with a degree in foods and nutrition.

Years later, Claudia still follows the diet that her dietitian designed for her. Claudia is also helping people to eat healthy foods. Many of her patients have diseases that prevent them from eating certain foods, too.

CRITICAL THINKING How did Claudia choose her career as a dietitian?

Associations for Careers in Human Services

American Council on Exercise
4851 Paramount Drive
San Diego, CA 92123

American Culinary Federation
10 San Bartola Drive
St. Augustine, FL 32085

The American Dietetic Association
120 South Riverside Plaza
Suite 2000
Chicago, IL 60606

**International Council on Hotel,
Restaurant, and Institutional
Education**
2613 North Parham Road
Richmond, VA 23294

**National Association of
Social Workers**
750 First Street, NE, Suite 700
Washington, DC 20002

National Childcare Association
1016 Rosser Street
Conyers, GA 30012

National Cosmetology Association
401 North Michigan Avenue
22nd Floor
Chicago, IL 60611

The Travel Institute
148 Linden Street
Suite 305
Wellesley, MA 02482

More Careers in Human Services

Aerobics instructor
Career counselor
Caterer
Community food-service worker
Cook
Electrologist
Food and beverage director
Food service manager
Funeral attendant
Health educator
Human services assistant
Massage therapist

Mental health counselor
Minister
Nanny
Nutritionist
Preschool teacher
Religious leader
Restaurant host
Short-order cook
Teacher assistant
Tour operator
Tourism assistant
Travel coordinator

JOB DESCRIPTION
Cosmetologist

Job Summary

A cosmetologist helps people to look well-groomed. He or she provides grooming services to customers. A cosmetologist may be trained in many areas of personal grooming including hair care, facial care, and makeup application.

Most cosmetologists work indoors. They may work in a beauty salon or spa. A cosmetologist often stands for long periods of time. He or she usually works a 40-hour week but may work longer hours during busy times of the year. Full-time and part-time positions are available. Most cosmetologists work evenings and weekends.

Work Activities

A cosmetologist may do any or all of the following activities:

- Shampoo, cut, color, and style hair.

- Give manicures, pedicures, and facials.

- Apply makeup on the faces of customers.

- Make appointments for customers.

- Keep records of services given to clients.

- Sell hair products and beauty supplies.

Education/Training Requirements

All cosmetologists must be licensed by the state in which they work. In order to be licensed, people who want to work as cosmetologists must pass an exam that shows that they have the required skills. This exam includes a written test and a demonstration of basic cosmetology skills. Some employers also require a high school diploma.

Think About It

What type of person might make a good cosmetologist?

Summary

- There are many different careers in human services. Some of these careers fulfill basic needs of people. Some careers in human services include social worker, dietitian, dietetic technician, fitness trainer, travel agent, and cosmetologist.

- Between the years 2002 and 2012, there will be an increase in the number of jobs for many occupations in this career cluster. Reasons for this increase include the growing population of older people and the growing population of children under five years old.

- People in this career cluster provide services to other people and should be able to satisfy the needs of others. Some careers in human services require good communication skills and a caring attitude.

- Lifestyles for careers in human services depend on the type of occupation. The working conditions, hours of work, training requirements, and salaries also affect lifestyles.

certification
cosmetologist
dietitian
license
social worker

Vocabulary Review

Complete each sentence with a term from the list.

1. A person who helps people to meet their needs by providing counseling and arranging other services is called a _____.

2. A person who helps people to look neat and well-groomed is called a _____.

3. A process that shows that an individual has met certain requirements to do something is called _____.

4. A legal document that gives a person permission to do something is called a _____.

5. A person who plans and manages food programs for healthy eating is called a _____.

Chapter Quiz

Write your answers in complete sentences.

1. Which human services occupation helps people to reach their physical fitness goals?

2. What does a cosmetologist do?

3. List three types of world events that can affect the number of jobs in human services.

4. What kind of special ability does a successful chef need?

5. Name a human services occupation that requires certification.

6. Describe one way in which a person can learn more about careers in human services.

CRITICAL THINKING

7. Explain how the increase in the population of older people can affect the number of jobs for social workers.

8. Name a human services occupation that requires a caring attitude. Explain your answer.

Career Portfolio Project

Choose five careers discussed in this chapter. Research each career. Then, describe the lifestyles, strengths, and training or education requirements for each. Decide if any of these careers interest you. Explain which ones interest you and which ones do not interest you.

Firefighters work to protect people and property. When fighting fires, they wear protective gear and use heavy equipment.

Learning Objectives

- Identify some careers in law and public safety.
- Discuss trends in careers in law and public safety.
- Describe strengths and lifestyles of people who have careers in law and public safety.
- List ways to find out more about careers in law and public safety.

Chapter 10

10 Careers in Law and Public Safety

Words to Know

security guard	a person who protects stores and businesses from illegal activities, such as robbery
correctional officer	a person who works in a prison as a guard
emergency dispatch operator	a person who answers and handles emergency calls
fire inspector	a person who examines buildings to make sure that they are safe from fires
fire investigator	a person who gathers facts to determine the cause of a fire

Gina thought she was just going shopping. Instead, she found herself thankful to people who work in law and public safety. Read about Gina's experience below.

Gina was so busy trying on coats in a department store that she forgot about her purse. It was in her shopping cart. At least it had been. Now it was gone.

Looking around, she saw a man carrying her purse running toward the door. "Stop that man. He has my purse!" Gina shouted.

Just then, a store security guard appeared in front of the man. "Sir," said the security guard, "this lady claims you have her purse!"

A few minutes later, police officers arrived. Soon, Gina had her purse back. "I am grateful to the police," she explained to a friend, "but if it had not been for the security guard, I would have lost my money!"

Careers in Law and Public Safety

Keeping people safe and protecting property are some of the goals of people who have careers in law and public safety. Most people are familiar with the duties of police officers and firefighters. Police officers work to keep our communities safe. They patrol, or walk around, streets and neighborhoods. They investigate behavior that is against the law and arrest people who break laws. Firefighters also protect the public against danger. They immediately respond to fires and other emergency situations. They often give emergency medical service to people who have been injured.

There are many other careers that also serve to protect the public. Some of these careers include security guard, correctional officer, emergency dispatch operator, fire inspector, and fire investigator. People who have these careers are sometimes called public safety workers.

Many stores and workplaces have security guards, or security officers. **Security guards** are responsible for making sure that property and people on the property are safe from fire and illegal activity, such as robbery. Some security guards patrol property. Others check on property using special cameras.

Correctional officers work in prisons and jails. They keep order and make sure that the prisoners obey the rules. Correctional officers are responsible for the safety and well-being of prisoners. They must also prevent prisoners from escaping.

Emergency dispatch operators help other public safety workers do their jobs. During an emergency, people usually call 911. Calls are answered and handled by an emergency dispatch operator. Callers might need police, firefighters, or an ambulance. An emergency dispatch operator makes sure that help is immediately sent to the site of an emergency.

Did You Know ?

Correctional officers have no public safety responsibilities outside of the prison or jail in which they work.

A **fire inspector** examines buildings and other structures to make sure that they are safe from fires. He or she also makes sure that buildings meet the terms of fire prevention laws. A **fire investigator** gathers facts to determine the cause of a fire. After a fire is put out, he or she examines the area for clues to what could have started the fire.

Career Fact

A fire inspector may speak at schools and other public places about ways to prevent fires.

Job Trends in Careers in Law and Public Safety

Law and public safety is a popular career cluster. In the years between 2002 and 2012, the number of jobs in law and public safety is expected to increase at a higher rate than for most other careers. This rate is expected to be between 21 and 35 percent. The jobs affected by the increase include correctional officers, security guards, and police officers.

There are several reasons for this growth. One reason is crime. Crime is behavior that is against the law. People are more aware of the need for protection against crimes. They want to be safe in their homes. They also want safe streets and neighborhoods. The best way to fight crime is to hire more police officers and public safety workers.

When crime increases, more people go to prison. The prison population has grown rapidly in recent years. In the year 2003, there were more than 2 million prisoners in the United States. To handle the increasing prison population, new prisons will need to be built. Also, prison terms are getting longer. A prison term is the time a prisoner serves in prison. More correctional officers will be needed because of the increasing prison population and longer prison terms. By the year 2008, more than 530,000 correctional officers will be needed in the United States.

The threat of terrorism has also created jobs in law and public safety. The attacks of September 11, 2001, and other violent acts have increased the need for protection, especially in public places. To address these threats, more security workers and police officers have been hired in recent years in many cities. They patrol airports, public spaces, bridges, and tunnels.

The number of jobs for firefighters is expected to increase at the average rate for most occupations. This rate is between 10 and 20 percent. The main reason for this average growth is the lack of funding for firefighting occupations.

✓ **Check Your Understanding**

Write your answers in complete sentences.

1. What are the goals of people who have careers in law and public safety?
2. What does a correctional officer do?
3. Why are some career opportunities in law and public safety growing?

Strengths of People Who Have Careers in Law and Public Safety

People who have careers in law and public safety share similar personal strengths. These personal strengths include respect for authority, good judgment, and a sense of responsibility. If you have these qualities, then you may be a good candidate for a career in law and public safety.

Many people who have careers in law and public safety enjoy their work because they find their jobs rewarding. Serving and protecting the public is very important to them. In fact, some of these people put their lives in danger in order to save the lives of others.

A person who has a career in law and public safety may be required to have certain physical abilities. For example, in order to be considered for a job as a police officer or a firefighter, a person must be in good physical shape. Running, jumping, climbing, and lifting are all part of the job. In fact, to become a police officer in Phoenix, Arizona, a person has to run 1.5 miles and climb a 6-foot wall. He or she must also be able to do a certain number of sit-ups and lift a certain amount of weight.

The ability to work as part of a team is a very important strength that police officers and firefighters must have. Many police officers work with a partner. Police partners patrol areas. Some partners work together to solve crimes. Firefighters work together to fight fires. They connect hose lines, operate pumps, and set up other equipment. Police officers and firefighters depend on their partners or teams to help each other, especially during dangerous situations.

People who are interested in careers in law and public safety also need to be open-minded, alert, and quick-thinking. They need to be able to deal with all types of people fairly and equally. In addition, they should respond to emergency situations quickly and in the right manner. The training that people in these careers receive prepares them to handle many emergency situations.

Public safety workers also need skills to get information to solve crimes. Very often, public safety workers solve crimes by talking with people. For example, police officers talk to people who have witnessed a crime. Witnesses may not want to talk about what they have seen. Sometimes, they are not sure about what they have seen. As a result, police officers need good speaking skills and good people skills to get witnesses to talk to them. Good writing skills are also necessary because writing reports is usually part of the job.

Write About It
Make a list of the risks that you think people who work in law and public safety careers face. Then, write a paragraph describing why a career in this field may or may not be right for you.

Lifestyles of People Who Have Careers in Law and Public Safety

Career Trend

In the United States, paid firefighters held about 294,000 jobs in the year 2004. Women made up about 2 percent of the nation's firefighters. Ten years earlier, there were no female firefighters.

Careers in law and public safety can be found in just about any location. Police officers, firefighters, security officers, and correctional officers work in cities and suburbs. They also work in rural areas. Cities with large populations need the most public safety workers.

Most public safety workers are employed by federal, state, and local governments. Workplaces, however, vary with the jobs. Police officers begin and end their workday at the police station. During the time in between, however, they might be patrolling the streets on foot, in patrol cars, or on bicycles or horseback. When they are not fighting fires, firefighters can be found in the firehouse. Private security officers work in stores, offices, factories, and even private homes.

People who have careers in law and public safety can work irregular hours. Some public safety workers have to be on duty for many hours at a time. For example, many firefighters work 50 hours or more a week. Some firefighters might be on duty for 24 hours and then off duty for 48 hours. Many public safety workers work evening hours, weekends, and holidays. They may also work overtime.

The requirements for careers in law and public safety vary by job. A high school diploma is usually the first requirement. People who want to become police officers or firefighters must pass both a physical fitness test and a written test. Not having a criminal record is important, too. Employers usually look closely into each person's background.

After passing tests, law and public safety workers get specialized training. For example, police trainees attend a police academy. New firefighters attend a fire training center. Training classes might last three months or longer. A person who completes the training will be assigned a full-time job.

Graduation from a police academy occurs after about 12 to 14 weeks of training.

Workers in law and public safety usually have steady work and good benefits. Salaries vary widely from city to city and from state to state. A starting police officer may earn $35,000 a year, while a starting firefighter may earn about $32,000. Newly hired correctional officers and private security guards usually earn less.

Public safety employees who work for the government have a good retirement system. Many retire at age 50 or 55, or after 20 years of service. These people receive a pension, or monthly payment for retired workers.

Remember
In Chapter 1, you learned that a pension is usually paid to a person who has worked a certain number of years, after he or she leaves a job.

Workers in public safety often face dangerous situations. Stopping criminals, putting out fires, and rescuing people from accidents are just some of the situations that public safety workers deal with. It is easy to understand why the injury rates and stress levels in public safety careers are higher than in most other jobs. Fortunately, there are agencies that offer counseling to public safety workers. These agencies can help public safety workers to deal with their emotions and their high levels of stress.

How to Learn More About Careers in Law and Public Safety

You have read that the outlook for jobs in law and public safety is good. If you are interested in a career in this career cluster, you can do one or more of the following:

- Look through the *Occupational Outlook Handbook*, the *Guide for Occupational Exploration*, or other career resources. Many of these resources provide information about the working conditions and job trends for most careers in law and public safety.

- Search the Internet. All cities and states have Web sites. Some Web sites tell about job openings in law and public safety. Others tell what jobs are available in your city or state. These Web sites might also indicate when tests are given for people interested in applying for those jobs.

- Visit a firehouse in your community. Talk to the firefighters. Ask them to tell how they got their jobs. They might give you some good advice about what courses to study to increase your chances of becoming a firefighter.

- The next time you go shopping at a mall, look for a security guard. Ask the security guard about his or her job and the working conditions.

- Write letters to law and public safety associations. A list of these associations is given on page 136. In your letters, be sure to ask for specific career information.

- Visit a police station. Observe the activities of the police officers. Ask an officer on duty if it is possible to interview any of the officers. You may be able to schedule a personal interview with an officer. Be sure to prepare a list of questions before the interview.

Using Technology

To learn more about firefighting occupations, visit the Bureau of Labor Statistics online at www.bls.oco/ ocos158.htm. This Web site provides information about the working conditions, salary, and job outlook for firefighters.

✓ **Check Your Understanding**

Write your answers in complete sentences.

1. What are two problems that public safety workers often face on the job?

2. Why do public safety workers need good speaking skills?

3. What retirement benefits do public safety workers who work for the government often receive?

Career Path

POLICE OFFICER

When Keith graduated from high school, he joined the U.S. Army. In the Army, Keith became a military policeman, or M.P. An M.P. is a soldier in the Army who guards people and places.

After four years in the Army, Keith returned to civilian, or nonmilitary life. His first job was with a private security firm. He worked as a security guard in a large department store. Keith watched the customers in the store through a security camera. When he saw someone shoplift, or steal, he alerted another security guard working nearby.

While working as a security guard, Keith explored other careers in law and public safety that would help him to earn a higher salary. He decided to take courses at a community college. His goal was to become a police officer.

At a city Web site, Keith learned when the test for police officers was given. His experience and course work helped him pass the test. He also passed the background check. Soon, he was training at a police academy.

Now, Keith has been a police officer for three years. Every day is different and interesting. One thing stays the same, though. His main goal is to keep people safe!

CRITICAL THINKING Why do you think Keith wanted to become a police officer?

Associations for Careers in Law and Public Safety

American Correctional Association
4380 Forbes Boulevard
Lanham, MD 20706

American Society for Industrial Security
1625 Prince Street
Alexandria, VA 22314

International Association of Chiefs of Police
515 North Washington Street
Alexandria, VA 22314-2357

National League of Cities
1301 Pennsylvania Avenue, NW
Washington, DC 20004

National Sheriffs' Association
1450 Duke Street
Alexandria, VA 22314

Office of Fire Prevention and Arson Control
National Emergency Training Center
16825 South Seton Avenue
Emmitsburg, MD 21727

More Careers in Law and Public Safety

Animal control officer
Armored car guard
Computer forensics specialist
Detective
Emergency planning manager
Federal marshal
File and document manager
Fire investigator
Forest firefighter
Hazardous materials responder
Immigration and customs inspector

Jail administrator
Law clerk
Loss prevention officer
Private investigator
Probation/parole officer
Rescue worker
Security manager
Security systems installer
Warden
Youth services worker

JOB DESCRIPTION
Firefighter

Job Summary

A firefighter helps people in emergency situations. He or she puts out fires and rescues people trapped in fires. A firefighter also helps people injured in accidents. Firefighters are trained to treat injuries. They are often the first people to arrive at the scene of an accident or other medical emergency.

A firefighter must respond quickly when called to the site of an emergency. Firefighting is a very dangerous job. The number of hours that a firefighter works can be very long. Many firefighters work more than 50 hours a week. Night and weekend work is usually required.

Work Activities

A firefighter may do any or all of the following activities:

- Use heavy equipment to put out fires.

- Rescue victims and give medical treatment.

- Practice firefighting activities.

- Clean and maintain firefighting equipment.

- Take part in physical fitness activities.

Education/Training Requirements

People who want to become firefighters must be at least 18 years of age. They also must have a high school education. These people must pass a written test, a physical test, and a medical examination. Then, they go through several weeks of training. Once the training is completed, they are assigned to a fire station. Additional job requirements include training in cardiopulmonary resuscitation (CPR) and first aid training.

Think About It

Why does the job of a firefighter require physical strength?

Chapter

10 ▷ Review

Summary

- People who have careers in law and public safety protect people and property. Careers in this cluster include police officers, firefighters, correctional officers, private security officers, and emergency dispatch operators.

- Law and public safety is a popular career cluster. The number of jobs for occupations in law and public safety are expected to increase at the average rate or faster.

- People interested in careers in law and public safety need to be physically fit, quick-thinking, and fair-minded. A high school diploma is a requirement.

- People who have careers in law and public safety usually receive good pay and benefits. Stress, injuries, and danger are part of the job. Working night and weekend shifts is common. Many people in this career cluster retire with a pension.

correctional officer
emergency dispatch operator
fire inspector
fire investigator
security guard

Vocabulary Review

Complete each sentence with a term from the list.

1. A person who works in a prison as a guard is called a _____.

2. A person who examines buildings to make sure that they are safe against fires is called a_____.

3. A person who determines the cause of a fire is called a _____.

4. A person who handles emergency telephone calls is called an _____.

5. A person who protects stores or businesses from illegal activities is called a _____.

Chapter Quiz

Write your answers in complete sentences.

1. What types of decisions might an emergency dispatch operator make?

2. What is one job responsibility of a correctional officer?

3. How does a fire inspector protect the public?

4. What are two reasons why more law and public safety workers are needed?

5. Why do firefighters need to be able to work as a part of a team?

6. Why would visiting a police station help a person explore a career in law and public safety?

CRITICAL THINKING

7. Why do firefighters need to go to a fire training center before beginning work?

8. Tell why you think many people want to become firefighters and police officers.

Career Portfolio Project

For each of the careers in law and public safety described in this chapter, list two benefits and two drawbacks. Then, decide whether you are interested in one of the careers. Explain your responses in a brief paragraph.

A person who sells custom made picture frames works closely with customers. Working with customers is an important skill for a career in sales.

Lesson Objectives

- Identify some careers in sales.
- Discuss trends in careers in sales.
- Describe strengths and lifestyles of people who have careers in sales.
- List ways to find out more about careers in sales.

Chapter 11 ▸ Careers in Sales

Words to Know

retail sales	the selling of goods or services directly to customers
telemarketer	a person who sells products or services over the telephone
sales representative	a person who works to sell the products that a company makes
customer service representative	a person who handles customers' questions, requests, or complaints in person, by telephone, or through the Internet
commission	a fee paid to a salesperson for selling goods or services, usually a percentage of the selling price
bonus	an amount of money awarded to a person who sells a certain amount or does an outstanding job
entrepreneur	a person who organizes and runs a business

Mr. Jackson's tenth-grade class decided to have a dance to raise $5,000 for a homeless shelter. Read about the plans for the dance:

Alfredo and Christina worked on the dance committee. They convinced the manager of a hotel to allow them to hold the dance in one of the hotel's ballrooms. Alfredo managed to get a band to play at the dance for free.

Lisa and her friends made posters and put them up all around the city. They also wrote an article about the event in the school paper.

The dance was a big success. Mr. Jackson's class raised more than $7,500! Later, Mr. Jackson praised his students. "You are the best group of salespeople I have ever seen."

Careers in Sales

Mr. Jackson's students had not thought of themselves as salespeople. They were, however, doing what many salespeople do. They were convincing others to buy or donate goods or services.

Career Fact

Some service careers include doctors, lawyers, and teachers.

Businesses produce goods and services. Goods are things that can be seen and touched and are bought or sold. Goods include clothing, furniture, food, and books. Services are activities that are performed in exchange for money. People who teach, make things, sell things, or fix things perform a service.

Consumers are the customers who buy goods and services. People in sales are the link between businesses and consumers. Salespeople show us products, give us information, accept money, and arrange for deliveries. Without salespeople, it would be harder to buy a new car or order a cable television service.

There are as many jobs in sales as there are types of goods and services. The largest number of sales jobs is in retail sales. **Retail sales** is the selling of goods or services directly to customers. Retail salespeople sell goods including food, clothing, televisions, CDs, plants, computers, pet food, and more.

Retail salespeople work in stores. They help customers find what they need. Retail salespeople might show people how to use a product. They might also ring up the sales at cash registers, make and return change, and give receipts to customers. In the year 2002, there were more than 4 million jobs for retail salespeople. Job titles for retail salespeople include demonstrator, insurance sales agent, and cashier.

Service salespeople sell services rather than goods. For example, banks have service salespeople who help customers sign up for checking accounts and other banking services. Telephone companies employ service salespeople to sell long distance service to customers. Some job titles for these occupations include advertising sales associate, telesales representative, and financial services sales agent.

There are some salespeople who sell goods or services over the telephone. These salespeople are called **telemarketers**. Telemarketers call consumers at their homes. They describe their product or service without the customer actually seeing or using it.

There are also salespeople who are employed by manufacturers. Manufacturers are companies that make products or goods. Salespeople employed by manufacturers are called **sales representatives**.

The job of a sales representative is to sell the product or products that the manufacturer makes to stores and other businesses. For example, Jerry is a sales representative for the Colorful Paint Company. He contacts the owners of paint stores to convince them to carry Colorful Paint in their stores. When Jerry gets an order, he makes sure that the paint is delivered to the store on time. He also sends a bill for the paint to the store owner. Because he is a good sales representative, Jerry calls the store owner to make sure that he or she is happy.

There are also some people who have careers in sales but do not sell goods or services. Instead, these people, called **customer service representatives**, help customers. When customers have questions or complaints about a company's product or service, they can usually contact the company by telephone, by e-mail, or through the mail. Customer service representatives are the workers who respond to the calls, e-mail messages, or letters. By providing good customer service, these people help build strong sales for their employers.

Career Fact

When consumers order goods using the telephone, customer service representatives are the people who handle the orders.

Some salespeople sell a product and also perform a service. For example, a real estate agent helps people and businesses to buy, sell, or rent properties. These properties can be houses, other buildings, or land.

Job Trends in Careers in Sales

Career Trend

The need for temporary salespeople increases during the end-of-year holiday season.

There are many trends that can affect the sales industry. In general, the condition of the economy usually has a great effect on jobs in sales. When the economy is doing well, consumers buy many products and services. The need for salespeople is greater during these periods. This need leads to an increase in the number of jobs for salespeople.

However, when the economy is doing poorly, consumers usually do not purchase as many goods or services. As a result, the need for salespeople declines. The number of jobs in sales also decreases.

Technology can also affect the number of jobs in sales. For example, modern cash registers are able to read price tags and credit cards at a faster rate than ever before. They can also add up prices and keep track of sales information. This technology can decrease the need for salespeople.

Did You Know

Ordering goods using a computer is called "shopping online." The ability to shop online began in 1994.

In addition, computers and telephones allow people to shop for goods without leaving their homes or offices. Instead, customers can place their orders through the telephone or computer. These ways of shopping also reduce the need for salespeople.

Technology can also affect the types of jobs in sales. For example, companies who produce new technology products usually need people who know about technology to sell them. These new products may also need repairs or other kinds of services. These additional needs can create new jobs for service salespeople.

✓ Check Your Understanding

Write your answers in complete sentences.

1. What are some types of goods sold to consumers?

2. Which type of salesperson sells goods directly to customers?

3. What factors can affect the number of jobs in sales?

Strengths of People Who Have Careers in Sales

Do you like talking with people? Do you have good speaking skills? Are you the kind of person who can convince other people to do something? If you have answered yes to any of these questions, then a career in sales may interest you.

Good salespeople know how to convince people to do something. They are able to convince customers that their products or services are the best ones available. Salespeople may compare their products to other products, give demonstrations of their products, and list facts about their products in order to sell them. Most consumers want to trust the salespeople they buy from. Friendliness, honesty, charm, and determination are all personal strengths of successful salespeople.

Salespeople should also have good math and writing skills. They add up prices and, in some cases, give discounts. Discounts are lowered prices. Good writing skills are also important. Many salespeople have to write reports. Salespeople should also be able to keep good, clear records. Certain types of salespeople have to keep files on customers and what these customers have bought. These salespeople use the information in their files to stay in touch with customers and make future sales.

> **Write About It**
> Make a list of qualities or strengths that you think a good salesperson has. Compare your list with a classmate's.

Salespeople should also believe in the product or service that they are selling. Many customers can tell when a salesperson is just trying to sell them a product to make a sale. Good salespeople do not try to sell goods or services that will not satisfy a customer's needs.

Lifestyles of People Who Have Careers in Sales

The lifestyles of people with careers in sales can vary. Retail salespeople usually live near the stores that employ them. Customer service representatives and sales representatives usually live near the companies that they work for. However, some sales representatives might travel many miles to customers' business locations. Some telemarketers work at home. They can live and work wherever there are telephone lines and equipment. Many real estate agents live close to the areas where they help people buy or sell properties.

Many retail stores require that their salespeople have high school diplomas. Salespeople are often paid by the hour. They might start at the minimum wage and get small raises, or increases in salary, over time.

Remember
In Chapter 9, you learned that a license is a legal document that gives a person permission to do something.

Some companies provide training programs to teach salespeople how to sell their products. Some employers require people to pass state exams and get licenses. Real estate agents, for example, must be licensed. Higher education can also be quite helpful to people who want high-level sales careers. Both two- and four-year colleges offer business courses and degree programs for people seeking careers in sales.

A customer service representative working at a 24-hour call center might work any hour of the day or night.

The amount of time a person spends doing sales work can vary. Salespeople can work part-time or full-time. Often, businesses have 24-hour customer service call centers. Calls made to these call centers are answered by customer service representatives. These employees might work 8-hour shifts any time of day, including during evenings and weekends. Many retail salespeople work long hours during sales, when stores sell their goods at discounted prices.

The salaries that some salespeople receive are based on commissions. A **commission** is a certain percentage of a selling price. For example, Mr. Smith, a real estate agent, sells a house for $100,000. His commission is 6 percent of the sale, or $6,000.

Some salespeople may also receive a bonus. A **bonus** is an amount of money awarded to a person who sells a certain amount or does an outstanding job.

Remember
In Chapter 7, you learned that a part-time worker usually works less than 35 hours per week.

How to Learn More About Careers in Sales

Using Technology

Being a fashion model is considered a career in sales. For information about careers in modeling, visit www.opeiu.org/models/index.asp.

There are many ways to learn more about careers in sales. Look through career sources such as the *Occupational Outlook Handbook* to find out about the many different types of sales jobs there are. Here are some other suggestions that can help you to learn more about careers in sales:

- Get a job working in a store after school or during your summer vacations. You will learn basic customer service skills. You can also try working for a short time. Quite often, large department stores need extra help during holidays.

- Join a debate team. Debaters choose a subject and then present facts about that subject. They use facts to convince people to believe in what they are saying. In many ways, debaters use the same skills as salespeople. They try to convince others to believe in something.

- Become a volunteer for an organization that you believe in. For example, you can work for a group that helps children get basic needs. Asking people for donations is one of the toughest sales jobs there is. It is a great way to practice and learn sales skills.

- Take classes in business math, sales, or other business courses at your high school or community college. Not all jobs in sales require a college degree. However, taking such classes will help you to develop good sales skills.

- Write to one or more of the sales associations listed on page 150 for information about sales careers. Be sure to ask about the working conditions and employment opportunities in the careers that you are interested in.

✓ **Check Your Understanding**

Write your answers in complete sentences.

1. What are two personal strengths of people with careers in sales?

2. Which sales career requires a license?

3. What is one way to learn more about a career in sales?

Learn More About It

BEING AN ENTREPRENEUR

Stella runs her own business. She sells children's products, such as clothes, books, and videos. Stella does not own a store. Instead, she sells her items over the Internet. She has a Web site that shows many of the children's products that she sells. Stella employs customer service representatives to process the orders she receives through her Web site.

Stella is an **entrepreneur**, a person who organizes and runs a business. An entrepreneur tries to make profits from his or her business. A profit is the money left over after all the costs of running a business have been paid.

Many entrepreneurs start out with an idea for a product or service that they believe people are willing to buy. Then, they bring that product or service to people. They may use their own money to start their business, or they may borrow from other sources. Banks and certain government agencies sometimes loan money to people who want to start their own business.

Entrepreneurs usually have a lot of self-confidence. They believe in themselves and their goods or services. They are not afraid to make decisions and are willing to take risks. However, not all entrepreneurs are successful. Many businesses owned by entrepreneurs fail. Almost half of all new businesses close within four years. Those businesses that are successful require long hours and a lot of hard work.

CRITICAL THINKING What are the benefits and drawbacks to owning your own business?

Associations for Careers in Sales

American Marketing Association
311 South Wacker Drive, Suite 5800
Chicago, IL 60606

Direct Selling Association
1275 Pennsylvania Avenue, NW
Suite 800
Washington, DC 20004

National Association of Sales Professionals
11000 North 130th Place
Scottsdale, AZ 85259

National Field Selling Association
1900 Arch Street
Philadelphia, PA 19103

National Retail Federation
325 7th Street, NW
Suite 1100
Washington, DC 20004

Professional Salespersons of America
3801 Monaco, NE
Albuquerque, NM 87111

More Careers in Sales

Advertising associate
Business development manager
Circulation manager
Client relationship manager
Financial adviser
Food service manager
Fulfillment manager
Hotel manager
Manufacturer's agent
Marketing assistant

Public relations associate
Purchasing manager
Real estate broker
Retail marketing assistant
Sales engineer
Sales manager
Sales supervisor
Stockbroker
Store manager

JOB DESCRIPTION
Customer Service Representative

Job Summary
A customer service representative has many different job responsibilities. Some customer service representatives provide information about products and services to customers. Some respond to customers' problems. Other customer service representatives receive orders for products over the telephone or through the Internet.

A customer service representative spends most of his or her time sitting at a desk and talking to customers on the telephone. Most customer service representatives use fax machines and computers. Full-time and part-time positions are available.

Work Activities
A customer service representative may do any or all of the following activities:

- Help customers open accounts for home utilities, such as gas, oil, electricity, cable television, Internet, or telephone services.

- Take orders for products or services from customers over the telephone or through the Internet.

- Give information about products or services to customers.

- Work to resolve customers' complaints.

Education/Training Requirements
A high school diploma is usually the first requirement. Most employers also require good computer skills and good people skills. Training for customer service representatives takes place on the job or during company training programs.

Think About It

What strengths should a customer service representative have?

Summary

- People with careers in sales are the link between businesses and consumers. Salespeople show products, give information, accept money, and arrange for deliveries. Retail salespeople work in stores. They sell goods to consumers. Service salespeople sell services.

- The condition of the economy usually has a great effect on the sales industry. When the economy is doing well, consumers buy more products and services. When the economy is doing poorly, consumers usually do not buy as many goods and services.

- Friendliness, honesty, charm, and determination are some personal strengths that many salespeople have. Good math skills and record-keeping skills are also important strengths.

- Some sales jobs require travel, while others are done at home or in stores. There are part-time and full-time opportunities. Sales training can be found in companies and in two-year and four-year colleges.

- To learn more about sales, you can get a temporary sales job, join a debate team, or take certain business classes. You can also write to sales associations for information about sales careers.

bonus

customer service representative

entrepreneur

telemarketer

Vocabulary Review

Complete each sentence with a term from the list.

1. A person who organizes and runs a business is called an _____.

2. A person who handles customers' questions, requests, or complaints in person, by telephone, or through the Internet is called a _____.

3. An amount of money awarded to a person who sells a certain amount or does an outstanding job is called a _____.

4. A salesperson that sells products or services over the telephone is called a _____.

Chapter Quiz

Write your answers in complete sentences.

1. What are goods?

2. What are services?

3. What are salespeople employed by manufacturers called?

4. How can technology decrease the need for salespeople?

5. Why are good writing skills important to a salesperson?

6. What kind of hours might a customer service representative work?

CRITICAL THINKING

7. If you sell a microwave oven, are you a retail salesperson or a service salesperson? Explain your answer.

8. Many real estate agents are only paid a commission on the sale of a property. They receive no other salary. Explain a benefit and a drawback to this type of career.

Career Portfolio Project

Mike is a salesperson in an electronics store. He is told that he will get a bonus if he can sell a certain number of CD players. Mike could use the bonus money to pay for his next vacation. If you had Mike's job, explain how you would sell the CD players.

Unit 2 **Review**

Choose the letter of the best answer to each question.

1. Which of the following occupations are clerical workers?
   A. receptionists
   B. shipping and receiving clerks
   C. bookkeepers
   D. all of the above

2. What do most people in education and training do?
   A. research information
   B. organize the work of others
   C. help others to learn
   D. work in museums

3. What types of jobs are found at a Federal Job Information Center (FJIC)?
   A. jobs for career counselors
   B. jobs for organizations
   C. jobs for social workers
   D. federal government jobs

4. What does having a license mean?
   A. It allows a person to drive a car.
   B. It provides a person with a form of identification.
   C. It gives a person permission to do a certain job.
   D. It allows a person to retire from a career.

5. What kinds of skills do people who have careers in law and public safety need?
   A. skills to explore careers
   B. skills to prepare them for emergency situations
   C. skills to work overtime
   D. skills to determine the cause of a fire

6. Which of the following would a customer service representative do?
   A. deliver mail
   B. help people choose healthy food
   C. keep neighborhoods safe
   D. answer customers' questions and complaints

Critical Thinking
There are some factors that can cause the number of jobs to increase. Give an example of a factor that can cause an increase in the number of jobs in a certain area. Be sure to name the type of jobs that are affected.

Unit 3

Careers in Trade and Industry

Before You Read

In this unit, you will learn about careers in trade and industry. You will read about the special training that many people in these careers need in order to perform their jobs.

Before you start reading, ask yourself these questions:

1. What is a trade?
2. What skills are needed for these types of careers?
3. What are the job trends for these careers?

155

This environmental worker is gathering information about rainwater. Most environmental workers work to keep Earth's air, water, and land clean.

Learning Objectives

- Identify some careers in agriculture and the environment.

- Discuss trends in careers in agriculture and the environment.

- Describe strengths and lifestyles of people who have careers in agriculture and the environment.

- List ways to find out more about careers in agriculture and the environment.

Chapter 12 ▷ Careers in Agriculture and the Environment

Words to Know

livestock	animals raised on farms
agricultural inspector	a person who inspects farms and the crops and animals raised on farms to make sure that farmers follow laws on health and safety
forester	a person who works to keep a healthy balance between wildlife, plant life, and water quality in forests
wastewater treatment operator	a person who operates equipment that cleans and treats wastewater from sewers and certain types of businesses
environmental activist	a person who works to change laws and attitudes about the environment

Tanya is going to a tree-planting ceremony. Read how she is trying to convince her friend Gerald to join her:

"Planting trees is very important. Without trees and other plants, the quality of air will get worse," Tanya told Gerald. "Air pollution is bad enough with the many harmful chemicals that come from cars, trucks, and factories."

"Wow! I never thought about trees affecting the air we breathe," replied Gerald. "You know so much about the environment. Maybe you should become an environmental worker!"

Careers in Agriculture and the Environment

Career Fact

Other jobs in agriculture can be found in nurseries where flowers and plants are grown.

Careers in agriculture deal with farming or raising livestock. **Livestock** are animals that are raised on farms. Careers in agriculture include farmers, farm managers, and agricultural inspectors.

Farmers may own or rent the land on which they raise their crops. Many farmers raise food crops, including fruits, vegetables, and grains. Some farmers raise animals such as pigs, chickens, and cattle. Certain types of fish and shellfish can also be raised by farmers. These marine animals are raised, fed, and harvested in ponds.

Farm managers help farmers organize and run their farms to make the largest profit possible. Farm managers might decide which types of crops to grow, the best time to plant the crops, and how much money to spend on farm equipment.

Agricultural inspectors work for the United States federal and state governments. They inspect crops, livestock, farm equipment, and soil to make sure that farmers are following health and safety laws.

Careers in the environment deal with keeping Earth's air, water, and soil clean. People who have these types of careers are often called environmental workers. Environmental workers include foresters, wastewater treatment operators, and environmental activists.

Did You Know

Pollution is the release of harmful materials into the environment. Environmental workers usually work to prevent pollution in the air, water, and soil.

A **forester** works to keep a healthy balance between wildlife, plant life, and water quality in forests. He or she may supervise the planting of trees or the clearing, or cutting down, of trees with diseases.

A **wastewater treatment operator** runs the equipment at a water treatment plant. At these plants, wastewater from sewers and certain types of businesses is cleaned and treated with chemicals.

An **environmental activist** works to change laws and attitudes about the environment. Some activists try to raise money to support programs that keep the environment clean and healthy. Some activists help clean areas that have been polluted. Other activists write laws and work to get them passed.

Job Trends in Careers in Agriculture and the Environment

In general, the number of jobs in agriculture and the environment, between the years 2002 and 2012, is expected to slowly grow between 3 and 9 percent. Some of the expected slow growth in agricultural careers is due to small farms joining large farms. Also, farmers are using better and faster farming equipment. Both of these factors lead to a loss of farm jobs. Less government money for land management is one reason for expected slow growth in jobs in the environment.

Career Trend

Although slow growth in many environmental jobs is expected, there may be good job opportunities for foresters in the southeastern states. These states have privately owned forests that may be in need of forest management.

Some farmers use technology to help them manage their farms.

Write your answers in complete sentences.

1. Name three careers in agriculture.

2. Describe one job activity that a forester performs.

3. What is the trend for most jobs in agriculture?

Strengths of People Who Have Careers in Agriculture and the Environment

Agricultural workers should enjoy working outdoors and be willing to work hard. Farmers and farm managers need to understand how the economy and the marketplace affect the amount of profit their farms will make. Also, knowing the latest and most advanced ways of farming can help improve their profits. Good mechanical skills are also useful in fixing farm equipment.

Environmental workers want people to be aware of the need to keep soil, water, and air clean. They should understand the conditions that can harm the relationship between living things and nonliving things. Environmental activists usually need good writing skills and speaking skills. They may write speeches and other material to convince people to spend their time, money, and voting power on the environment. They may also talk to people to help them understand the need to keep the environment clean.

Some environmental workers need good mechanical skills. For example, wastewater treatment operators may install and run equipment in water treatment plants. These people may also make repairs or replace parts on equipment.

Write About It

Natural resources are materials found in nature that people use. Write a list of five natural resources. For each resource, write one way that environmental activists can prevent it from being overused.

Lifestyles of People Who Have Careers in Agriculture and the Environment

People who have careers in agriculture usually work outdoors. Working on a farm might include long hours, hard physical work, and working in bad weather conditions, such as rain and frost. In addition, farm work may only be seasonal. There might not be work during winter months.

Much of the work on a farm can be learned through on-the-job training. A high school diploma is not usually required. However, courses in business and farm management are helpful to farmers and farm managers. Agricultural inspectors usually need a college degree in biology or agricultural science.

The income that farmers make usually depends on the prices that they can get for their crops. Because prices change from year to year, incomes can also change.

Many people who have careers in the environment also work outdoors. For example, foresters spend much time examining tree growth in forested areas. However, many other people with careers in the environment work indoors. Wastewater treatment operators work inside a water treatment plant. Some environmental activists work in offices making plans to raise money.

The working hours of environmental workers can vary. Many activists work weekends talking to people about the environment. Wastewater treatment plants operate 24 hours a day. Operators at these plants work shifts, including during weekends and holidays.

Many environmental jobs require education beyond high school. For example, a forester needs a college degree in forestry. An activist who writes material to increase environmental awareness usually needs a college degree in science or writing.

Remember

In Chapter 2, you read that getting an education can increase your chances of finding a job.

Wastewater treatment operators usually need a high school diploma. However, the completion of a 1-year certificate program or a degree in water quality or liquid waste treatment increases a person's chance of getting a job in this area. In 2002, wastewater treatment plant operators earned an average salary of $33,390. In 2002, the average salary of a forester was $46,730.

How to Learn More About Careers in Agriculture and the Environment

To learn more about careers in agriculture and the environment, you can write to any of the associations listed on page 164 for more information. You might also consider following any of the suggestions listed below:

- Search through resources such as the *Occupational Outlook Handbook*. You can find out more about the trends and working conditions for these types of careers.

- Visit a farm. You might be able to observe how it operates. You might also think about a summer job working on a farm.

- Visit a wastewater treatment plant. Some plants offer tours. Take a tour and find out how important these plants are to the environment.

- Volunteer to work for an environmental organization. These organizations often need help raising money and running various programs. You might find the work interesting and personally rewarding.

Using Technology

The Society of American Foresters publishes a list of schools that offer courses in forestry. You can get a copy of this list from the organization's Web site at www.safnet.org.

✓ Check Your Understanding

Write your answers in complete sentences.

1. Why would it be useful for a farmer to have good mechanical skills?

2. Why do some environmental activists need good speaking skills?

3. Why would the *Occupational Outlook Handbook* be helpful in exploring careers in agriculture and the environment?

Career Path

AN ENVIRONMENTAL ENTREPRENEUR

When Sheri was 12 years old, her state passed a recycling law. To recycle means to turn waste materials into materials that can be used again. Newspapers, glass, and metal can all be recycled. Stores in Sheri's state were required to give ten-cent refunds for certain cans and bottles that were returned to the store for recycling.

Sheri decided to start her own recycling program. She collected bottles and cans that were left on sidewalks or on lawns every day. At the end of each week, Sheri would bring the bottles and cans to a nearby store. In return, Sheri received ten cents for each bottle or can. Week after week, the money that she collected increased.

When Sheri turned 17, she used the money that she had saved to buy a used truck. She began to pick up anything that could be recycled. She found clothing, furniture, books, and more. Certain stores paid her cash for many of the things she found.

Sheri saved enough money to open her own store. Her store sells recycled goods. According to Sheri, "I like the idea of running my own business while helping the environment. For me, it is the best of both worlds."

CRITICAL THINKING How has Sheri's concern for the environment helped her to make a career choice?

Associations for Careers in Agriculture and the Environment

Association of National Park Rangers
P.O. Box 104
Larned, KS 67550

National Environmental, Safety, and Health Training Association
5320 North 16th Street, Suite 114
Phoenix, AZ 85016

The New England Small Farm Institute
275 Jackson Street
Belchertown, MA 01007

North American Association for Environmental Education
Bruknew Nature Center
2000 P Street, NW, Suite 540
Washington, DC 20036

The Society of American Foresters
5400 Grosvenor Lane
Bethesda, MD 20814

Student Environmental Action Coalition
P.O. Box 51
Chapel Hill, NC 27599

U.S. Department of Agriculture Forest Service
1400 Independence Avenue, SW
Washington, DC 20250

The Wildlife Society
5410 Grosvenor Lane
Bethesda, MD 20814

More Careers in Agriculture and the Environment

Agricultural worker
Animal breeder
Environmental technician
Fish and wildlife technician
Fisher
Geology technician
Incinerator operator
Land survey technician
Logger

Logging equipment operator
Natural resource management technician
Nursery worker
Parks and recreation technician
Range manager
Recycling plant operator
Tree trimmer and pruner

JOB DESCRIPTION
Forester

Job Summary

A forester helps take care of and protect the plant life, animal life, and water quality in forests. A forester also helps care for the public areas in a forest, such as campsites and roads.

A forester usually works outside in all kinds of weather. A forester has to be in good physical shape. He or she must be able to lift heavy equipment. Full-time and part-time positions are usually available.

Work Activities

A forester may do any or all of the following activities:

- Use digging and planting tools to plant seeds and young trees.

- Remove dead trees.

- Measure harmful pollutants around trees.

- Clear away trees and dead bushes from hiking trails and camping areas.

- Examine and keep track of tree growth.

Education/Training Requirements

Most foresters need a college degree in forestry. However, some government jobs for foresters might only require a high school diploma and related work experience. Some foresters learn how to operate equipment on the job.

Think About It

Why do you think that the number of jobs for foresters is expected to decrease in future years?

Summary

- Careers in agriculture include farmers, farm managers, and agricultural inspectors. Careers in the environment deal with keeping Earth's air, water, and soil clean. Some careers in the environment include forester, wastewater treatment operator, and environmental activist.

- In general, the number of jobs in agriculture and the environment, between the years 2002 and 2012, is expected to grow more slowly than the average rate. This slower growth is expected to be between 3 and 9 percent.

- Strengths that people in agricultural careers have include enjoying working outdoors, being willing to work hard, understanding the economy and the marketplace, and having good mechanical skills. Strengths that people in environmental careers have include good speaking skills, good writing skills, and good mechanical skills.

- Careers in agriculture and the environment vary in training and education requirements. Farmers may not need a high school diploma. Foresters and environmental activists need a college degree or higher.

agricultural inspector

environmental activist

forester

livestock

wastewater treatment operator

Vocabulary Review

Complete each sentence with a term from the list.

1. A person who works to change laws and attitudes about the environment is called an _____.

2. A person who operates equipment that cleans and treats wastewater from sewers and certain types of businesses is called a _____.

3. Animals raised on farms are called _____.

4. A person who inspects farms and the crops and animals raised on farms to make sure that farmers follow the laws on health and safety is called an _____.

5. A person who works to keep a healthy balance between wildlife, plant life, and water quality in forests is called a _____.

Chapter Quiz

Write your answers in complete sentences.

1. What are livestock?

2. For whom do agricultural inspectors work?

3. What type of occupation might involve writing materials to increase environmental awareness?

4. What is a reason that the number of jobs for foresters will grow more slowly than the average rate?

5. Why do some wastewater treatment operators need good mechanical skills?

6. What is one way to learn more about careers in agriculture?

CRITICAL THINKING

7. Why would knowing about the economy and the marketplace help a farmer?

8. Why does wastewater need to be treated?

Career Portfolio Project

Suppose that you find a summer job as an assistant to a forester. You are asked to help count the number of different types of trees in a certain area. You must help identify each type of tree and the types of animals that live in or around the trees. Your observations need to be written in a report. Which high school classes helped you to prepare for this job? Explain your answer.

When a large structure is being built, ironworkers connect sections of steel together to provide support for the structure.

Learning Objectives

- Identify some careers in construction trades.

- Discuss trends in careers in construction trades.

- Describe strengths and lifestyles of people who have careers in construction trades.

- List ways to learn more about careers in construction trades.

Chapter 13 — Careers in Construction Trades

Words to Know

trade	an occupation that requires certain skills
carpenter	a skilled worker who builds structures by cutting and putting together wood and other materials
ironworker	a skilled worker who works with the steel that will become the framework for large structures
bricklayer	a skilled worker who builds walls, fireplaces, patios, or walkways with brick; also called a brickmason or blockmason
manufacturing	the name of the industry that makes things, especially by using machines
assembler	a factory worker who puts together the pieces that make up a product
machinist	a factory worker who uses tools or machines to make metal parts
tool and die maker	a skilled worker who makes parts for machines that are used to make metal products
apprenticeship program	a special type of program in which a student learns skills on the job and also in a classroom
journeyman	a person who has mastered his or her trade
trade union	an organization of trade workers whose main goal is to protect the working conditions and wages of members of the organization

Read about Jenny's first day at work at a construction site:

Jenny went to work wearing jeans, a long-sleeved shirt, and a tool belt. Her supervisor handed her a hard hat. "Put this on," he said. "I don't want anyone getting hurt on my work site."

Jenny knew that she would have to prove her skills. All day long, she worked hard to help build the frame of a new house. She measured the wood carefully before cutting it. She nailed pieces together quickly. By the end of the day, the frame of the house was almost finished.

As Jenny packed up her tools, the supervisor spoke to her. "You did a good job. Keep it up."

"Thanks," said Jenny. She began to walk away. It had been a good day.

Careers in Construction Trades

Remember
In Chapter 5, you learned that a specialist is a person who does work in one certain field.

Jenny has a career in the construction trades. The term *trades* refers to groups of skilled occupations. People who have careers in construction trades include carpenters, electricians, plumbers, ironworkers, roofers, and bricklayers. These workers are trained specialists. They perform work that most other people cannot do.

Construction trade workers are the builders of our country. They build office buildings, bridges, tunnels, and machines. They lay water pipes. They wire buildings for electricity. They also repair and remodel structures.

A **carpenter** is a skilled worker who performs many different kinds of construction activities. He or she builds structures by cutting and putting together wood and other materials. Some carpenters build houses and other large structures. Other carpenters build smaller items, such as cabinets or chairs. Carpentry is the largest construction trade.

A construction laborer usually performs tasks that involve heavy, physical labor. These tasks include operating equipment, preparing a work site, cleaning a work site, and removing dangerous materials.

An electrician sets up electrical systems in houses, offices, factories, and other structures. He or she may also connect wires to fire alarm systems, telephone systems, or security systems.

A plumber is a skilled worker who lays the pipes and other parts that allow water or gas to run through a structure. A plumber might also repair pipes, faucets, or other plumbing fixtures.

Did You Know
Plumbers install sinks, faucets, toilets, showers, bathtubs, dishwashers, washing machines, dryers, and hot-water heaters.

A steelworker is a person who works in a factory making steel by using iron, carbon, and other materials. At construction sites, an **ironworker** works with steel to create the framework for many large structures. Some ironworkers operate equipment that lifts the steel. Other ironworkers connect the steel pieces together.

A roofer builds or repairs the roofs on buildings. Roofs protect buildings, including houses, from water damage. A roofer nails down layers of waterproof materials on top of a structure to prevent water from leaking into the structure.

A **bricklayer**, also called a brickmason or blockmason, builds walls, fireplaces, patios, or walkways with brick. He or she may be hired by businesses or private home owners.

There are many other types of construction trade workers. Some specialize in floor or tile work. Others operate or repair equipment.

In some career clusters, manufacturing is considered to be an industry related to construction trades. **Manufacturing** is the making of things, especially by the use of machines. Some careers in manufacturing include assembler, machinist, and tool and die maker.

An **assembler** usually works in a factory, or plant, that makes finished goods. These goods include computer, engine, dishwasher, televison, and bicycle parts. An assembler helps put together the pieces that make up the finished goods.

A **machinist** uses tools or machines to make metal parts. The metal parts might be used in other tools or machines, such as automobiles, engines, or airplanes.

Machines that make metal products have parts called tools and dies. Tools hold metal in place. Dies shape and form the metal. A **tool and die maker** uses machines to make these parts.

Career Fact

There are people with occupations in manufacturing who make plastic parts and plastic products. These occupations include plastics-working machine setter, operator, and tender.

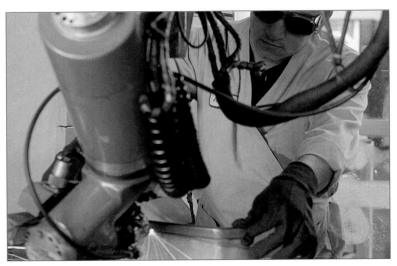

In a factory, a machinist uses machines to make metal parts.

Job Trends in Construction Trades

Construction workers make up the largest group of workers in the United States. In 2002, more than 6 million construction trade workers were employed.

In general, the outlook for jobs in construction trades between the years 2002 and 2012 is good. More jobs in construction trades will be created because of the need for new housing and house repairs. Also, workers are always needed to repair aging highways, dams, bridges, and office buildings.

The outlook for many skilled workers in manufacturing between the years 2002 and 2012 is also expected to be good. Although there are factors that can cause the number of jobs to decrease, there are also factors that can cause the number of jobs to increase. For example, some companies have moved their factories to other countries where workers are paid less. Sometimes U.S. workers lose their jobs when companies move their factories. Also, technology, such as robots and high-speed machines, can do the work of many workers, causing these workers to lose their jobs.

However, the overall demand for goods is expected to grow because the U.S. economy is expected to be strong. This growth in demand for goods is expected to increase the number of manufacturing jobs.

> **Career Trend**
>
> In the year 2000, one-fourth of all carpenters were self-employed. In the year 2002, one-third of all carpenters were self-employed.

✓ Check Your Understanding

Write your answers in complete sentences.

1. What are five careers in construction trades?
2. Name two occupations in manufacturing.
3. Give one reason why the outlook for jobs in construction will be good in coming years.

Strengths of People Who Have Careers in Construction Trades

Workers in construction trades usually enjoy working with their hands. Many trade workers like to produce visible changes in the world. At the end of the day, they can see the results of their labor. They may take pride in helping to build a new house, a bridge, a table, or a patio.

When you see a construction laborer hammering nails into a wall, you might not think of that worker as an artist. Many trade workers, however, do have artistic interests and skills. A carpenter, for example, might carve designs into wood. A bricklayer might lay bricks into a beautiful garden walkway.

Almost all trade workers need good mechanical skills. To do their jobs well, these workers need to operate both large and small tools. They might also need the skills to read blueprints, plans for buildings, or instruction manuals for machines.

As a rule, trade workers must be strong and in good health. People who work mainly with machines may have to stand long hours on the job.

Lifestyles of People Who Have Careers in Construction Trades

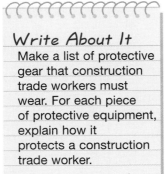

Write About It

Make a list of protective gear that construction trade workers must wear. For each piece of protective equipment, explain how it protects a construction trade worker.

Construction trade work can be dangerous. Working high off the ground, working with heavy machinery, running electricity through wires, and working with certain materials can lead to accidents and injuries. Construction trade workers dress for safety and comfort—not fashion. They wear safety glasses, gloves, steel toe boots, harnesses or belts, and hard hats. The noise level on many job sites can also be dangerous. Many workers wear earmuffs to protect their hearing.

An electrician must wear gloves and other protective gear when working with "live" electrical wires.

Some construction trade workers work full-time for construction companies. Other construction trade workers might be hired only part of the year when weather conditions are good for working outdoors. During the other part of the year, these workers may find other types of employment or not work at all. Some construction workers start their own businesses.

There are a number of ways to learn a trade. High schools, community colleges, and vocational schools offer classes in construction trades. Some workers receive on-the-job training. These workers may not need a high school diploma.

Many people seeking careers in the trades go through **apprenticeship programs**. During this special type of program, a student learns skills on the job and also in a classroom. He or she earns a salary at a lower rate of pay than a skilled worker. Apprenticeship programs can last from two to six years. As skills are mastered, the apprentice works toward becoming a journeyman. A **journeyman** is someone who has mastered his or her trade. A journeyman gets higher wages and better choices of jobs.

Career Fact

In 2002, there were 897,000 female construction workers. On most job sites, however, there were many more men than women. In that year, there were 8.8 million male construction workers.

Skilled workers in construction trades often belong to a trade union. A **trade union** is an organization of workers whose main goal is to protect the working conditions and wages of its members. For certain jobs, large businesses often hire only union members.

In the year 2002, the average hourly wage of a bricklayer was $20.11. The average salary of a carpenter in the year 2002 was $36,840. The average salary of a machinist was $33,410.

How to Learn More About Careers in Construction Trades

Using Technology

For more information about the work of electricians, visit the Independent Electrical Contractors Web site at www.ieci.org.

To learn more about careers in construction trades, you can write to one of the associations listed on page 178 for more information. You can also follow any of the suggestions listed below:

- Take wood shop or machine shop classes. Some high schools offer such classes. In these classes, you will learn to use tools for building and repair.

- Read "how to" books on home projects. These books are usually written for home owners, not for professionals. However, they can give you a good idea of what skills are needed to do carpentry, electrical work, and plumbing.

- Get a part-time job in a hardware store. Hardware stores are great places to learn about different types of tools. You will learn about hammers, saws, nuts, bolts, paint, and more.

- Find a summer job on a construction crew. You will learn what it is like to work on a construction site. Your school counseling center or a city employment office can help you apply for a job.

✓ Check Your Understanding

Write your answers in complete sentences.

1. What are two strengths of people with careers in construction trades?

2. What is one reason why construction work can be dangerous?

3. What is one way to learn more about careers in construction trades?

Learn More About It

TRADE UNIONS

In the 1800s, a workday in the United States could last 14 hours. Factories hired young children to work for very low wages. Safety conditions were poor. Finally, workers joined together to form trade unions. Trade unions worked with factory and business owners to get better wages and working conditions for their members. In 1866 the National Labor Union (NLU) was formed. That organization fought for an eight-hour workday for its members.

The NLU only lasted until 1872. Workers, however, created other unions and found ways to have employers meet their working needs.

Today, the working conditions and wages that many workers receive are due to the unions that were formed long ago. The eight-hour workday, the 40-hour workweek, paid vacations, and sick leave are working conditions and benefits that those labor unions fought hard to get from employers.

Today, many workers, especially construction trade workers, are trade union members. Being a union member has many benefits including financial assistance during long illnesses, unemployment, and old age. Members must pay dues to the union. Dues are payments that go toward running the union.

CRITICAL THINKING Why would a construction trade worker join a trade union?

Associations for Careers in Construction Trades

American Council for Construction Education
1300 Hudson Lane, Suite 3
Monroe, LA 71201

Associated General Contractors of America
333 John Carlyle Street
Suite 200
Alexandria, VA 22314

International Union of Bricklayers and Allied Craftsmen
1776 Eye Street, NW
Washington, DC 20006

The Joint Apprenticeship Training Fund
1750 New York Avenue, NW
Washington, DC 20006

Technology Student Association
1914 Association Drive
Reston, VA 22091

United Brotherhood of Carpenters and Joiners of America
101 Constitution Avenue
Washington, DC 20001

More Careers in Construction Trades

Boilermaker
Building inspector
Carpet installer
Cement mason
Concrete finisher
Construction equipment operator
Drywall installer
Elevator inspector
Elevator repairer
Fabricator
Floor installer
Glazier

Insulation worker
Marble setter
Painter
Pipe layer
Plasterer
Plumbing inspector
Sheet metal worker
Steamfitter
Stonemason
Stucco mason
Tile installer
Welder

JOB DESCRIPTION
Electrician

Job Summary

An electrician is responsible for installing and repairing electrical equipment. Electrical equipment can include electrical outlets, security systems, electrical switches, computer equipment, telephone systems, and streetlights.

An electrician may stand for long periods of time and work in dusty, wet, or hot spaces. He or she must wear gloves and other protective gear. Part-time and full-time positions are available. Many electricians work during evenings and weekends.

Work Activities

An electrician may do any or all of the following activities:

- Install and repair electrical systems in factories, office buildings, and houses.

- Follow the National Electric Code and state and local building codes when setting up electrical systems.

- Inspect electrical equipment to locate and correct problems.

- Use power tools and hand tools to install and repair electrical systems.

- Test electrical systems to make sure they are safe.

Education/Training Requirements

Most electricians complete a four- or five-year training program. Students in this training program must be at least 18 years old and have a high school diploma. People wanting to become electricians must also pass an exam that shows they have the required skills.

Think About It

What kind of person would make a good electrician?

Summary

- The term *trades* refers to groups of skilled occupations. People who have careers in construction trades include carpenters, electricians, plumbers, ironworkers, roofers, and bricklayers.

- Manufacturing is a related industry to the construction trades. Manufacturing is the making of things, especially by using machines. Some careers in manufacturing include assembler, machinist, and tool and die maker.

- The outlook for jobs in construction trades between the years 2002 and 2012 is good. More jobs in construction trades will be created because of the need for new housing and house repairs. The outlook for many skilled workers in manufacturing is also expected to be good.

- Construction trade workers should have good mechanical skills and enjoy working with their hands.

assembler
bricklayer
carpenter
manufacturing
trade
trade union

Vocabulary Review

Complete each sentence with a term from the list.

1. An occupation that requires certain skills is called a _____ .

2. The name of the industry that makes things, especially by using machines, is _____ .

3. A skilled worker who builds structures by cutting and putting together wood and other materials is called a _____ .

4. A factory worker who puts together the pieces that make up a product is called an _____ .

5. An organization of trade workers whose main goal is to protect the working conditions and wages of its members is called a _____ .

6. A skilled worker who builds walls, fireplaces, patios, or walkways with bricks is called a _____ .

Chapter Quiz

Write your answers in complete sentences.

1. What small items might a carpenter specialize in making?

2. What does an ironworker do?

3. What does a machinist do?

4. When the owners of manufacturing plants in the United States move their factories to other countries, how are manufacturing workers in the United States affected?

5. How do construction trade workers usually dress?

6. What classes can a high school student take to learn more about construction trades?

CRITICAL THINKING

7. Joe does not have good mechanical skills. Why would Joe not like working in a construction trade?

8. Ironworkers do not usually work during windy conditions. Explain why windy weather conditions would be dangerous to ironworkers.

Career Portfolio Project

Make a list of the things that you would like if you had a career in a construction trade. Make a list of the things that you would not like if you had a career in a construction trade. Review both of your lists. Then, write a brief paragraph explaining whether you would consider a career in a construction trade.

There are many different careers in sports. Some careers involve playing the sport. Others involve organizing the players.

Learning Objectives

- Identify careers in sports and the arts.
- Discuss trends in careers in sports and the arts.
- Describe strengths and lifestyles of people who have careers in sports and the arts.
- List ways to find out more about careers in sports and the arts.

Chapter 14 ▷ Careers in Sports and the Arts

Words to Know

athlete	a person who is trained to play a certain sport
umpire	a person who watches the plays during baseball and other games to make sure that players follow the rules
referee	a person who watches the plays during sporting events, such as football or basketball, to make sure that players follow the rules
scout	a person who identifies the most talented athletes in a sport
set designer	a person who builds and paints sets, or furniture and scenery, for plays, movies, or television shows
floral designer	a person who creates flower arrangements using live, dried, or plastic flowers

Vince and Eddie are members of their high school football team. Read about their plans for the future.

"We could both use more practice," Vince said to Eddie. "Let's forget about going to class."

"No way," Eddie answered. "I need to go to class. I want to be a professional player, but if I don't make it, I'll need a college education. If my grades are not high enough, no college is going to accept me," Eddie told Vince.

"You're right. I need good grades, too." Vince walked away. "I'm going to class. We can practice later."

Careers in Sports and the Arts

Many **athletes**, or people who are trained to play a certain sport, have hopes of becoming professional athletes. A professional athlete is paid to play a certain sport. Some professional athletes include football, basketball, and tennis players, golfers, and ice skaters. Some professional athletes earn high salaries and are well known.

Playing any sport well takes hours of practice. There are also many other players to compete against. Professional athletes have to be among the best players in their sports. The chances of becoming a successful professional athlete are very small.

Fortunately, not everyone who has a career in sports has to be a professional athlete. Coaches, for example, help players to improve their skills. They also organize and manage teams during practice sessions and games. Sports instructors teach people of all ages how to play different kinds of sports. **Umpires** and **referees** watch games to make sure that the athletes play by the rules. They may also decide what penalties are given to teams or individuals for breaking the rules of a game. **Scouts** identify the most talented amateur, or nonprofessional, athletes in a sport. They visit high schools and colleges to search for athletes to join professional sport or college teams.

Careers in the arts can be as competitive as careers in sports. The arts, or the art industry, are made up of people who express themselves in creative ways. Many of these people are artists. Artists include actors, singers, dancers, painters, and writers. Like athletes, artists face a lot of competition among other artists. Many artists spend much of their time improving their abilities. Like many professional athletes, some artists make high salaries and are well known. However, the chances of an artist becoming rich and famous are also very small.

Write About It
Writers express themselves using words. Make a list of the different ways in which other kinds of artists express themselves. Make a check mark next to the ways in which you express yourself.

Not everyone who has a career in the arts works as an actor, a dancer, or a painter. Some of the other careers in the art industry include fashion designer, set designer, camera operator, illustrator, and floral designer.

A fashion designer usually designs clothes for men, women, or children. He or she may also design shoes, belts, scarves, or handbags. A **set designer** builds and paints sets, or furniture and scenery, for plays, movies, or television shows. A camera operator uses cameras and other equipment to film television shows or motion pictures. An illustrator creates pictures for books, magazines, and other products, such as greeting cards and posters. A **floral designer** creates flower arrangements using live, dried, or plastic flowers.

Did You Know ?

High-fashion designers usually design clothes for fashion shows and for famous people. Most clothing designers, however, work for companies that produce clothes sold in department stores.

Job Trends in Careers in Sports and the Arts

There are many people who train to become professional athletes, actors, singers, or musicians. There are usually many more people seeking jobs in these areas than there are jobs. As a result, many of these people work in other occupations while trying to find jobs as professional athletes or artists.

Some careers in sports, however, have a fairly good job outlook. For example, the number of jobs for coaches and sports instructors between the years 2002 and 2012 will increase about as fast as the average rate. The average rate is between 10 and 20 percent. One reason for this increase is due to the growing population. As the population grows, more schools are built. Schools, especially at the high school level, offer sports programs. Coaches and instructors usually play important roles in these programs.

The number of jobs for umpires and referees between the years 2002 and 2012 is also expected to increase between 10 and 20 percent. These jobs will be found in high school, college, or professional sports.

In general, the trends for many jobs in the arts are positive. Between the years 2002 and 2012, the number of jobs for illustrators, set designers, and camera operators will increase at the average rate or even faster. Most of these increases are due to the expected growth in motion picture and cable television production.

The number of jobs for fashion designers is also expected to increase at a rate between 21 and 35 percent. One reason for this strong growth is that people demand new styles and fashions in clothes, shoes, belts, and handbags. The trend for jobs for floral designers is also expected to be strong.

Career Trend

The growth in the cable and satellite television industries will also result in an increase in the number of jobs in sports.

✓ Check Your Understanding

Write your answers in complete sentences.

1. What is a professional athlete?
2. Name three careers in sports other than professional athlete.
3. What is the general trend for careers in the arts?

Strengths of People Who Have Careers in Sports and the Arts

Professional athletes care a great deal about their physical ability and sports skills. They also deal with high levels of stress. For professional athletes, competing against other athletes and winning gives them satisfaction.

Other people who have careers in sports, such as coaches, instructors, and scouts, have to know a great deal about the sport. For example, a football coach needs to know which plays will help his team win. An umpire needs to know the rules of baseball in order to know whether a pitch is a strike or a ball. Some people who have careers in sports also need good teaching, communications, and people skills. A scout needs good people skills in order to get talented players to sign up with his or her team. A tennis instructor must have all of these skills in order to teach people how to play tennis.

Actors, singers, musicians, and many other artists enjoy performing in front of an audience. These people use their abilities to act, sing, play a musical instrument, or perform in some other way to entertain people. Like professional athletes, these artists are hardworking, spend many hours improving their performance, and deal with high levels of stress.

Many other people who have careers in the arts are highly talented as well. For example, a set designer may build and paint objects to make a stage for a movie or play look like a dark forest. A fashion designer may sew material together to make a wedding gown. These people must also have good communications and people skills. They must be able to communicate their ideas to people who would hire them for jobs or would buy their work.

Camera operators need good technical skills. They need to know how to operate camera equipment in order to make motion pictures. They also need to be creative in knowing what subjects will look good and interesting on film.

Career Fact

Motivation, team spirit, and fair play are qualities that coaches and instructors try to encourage among their players.

A camera operator should have knowledge of camera operation and a steady hand in order to film motion pictures, including sporting events.

Lifestyles of People Who Have Careers in Sports and the Arts

You have read that professional athletes and artists work hard. They spend hours improving their skills. They may compete or perform during the day, in the evening, on weekends, or on holidays. They must deal with large amounts of stress. In addition, professional athletes worry about injuries. However, for many of these people, being successful has great rewards. These rewards include traveling around the world, meeting different kinds of people, and making high salaries.

Coaches, instructors, and scouts in professional sports may also travel a great deal. Like professional athletes, they work in the evenings, on weekends, and on holidays. However, they usually do not earn the high salaries of many professional athletes.

Knowledge of certain sports is the most important requirement for coaches and instructors. Many coaches and instructors start out teaching or working in schools. They usually coach or instruct after the school day has ended. However, some schools hire people who have related experience in sports. In the year 2002, coaches earned an average salary of $34,170.

Fashion designers, floral designers, and illustrators usually work indoors. Good lighting is important while these people do their work. Many of these artists are self-employed. They do not work for a company or a manager. Instead, self-employed artists sell their creations directly to companies or people. They may work during the day, in the evening, during weekends, or on holidays.

Training requirements for careers in the arts can vary. A college degree in design is usually required for fashion designers. Many illustrators and set designers complete training in art programs. However, some illustrators are hired based upon their work experience and work samples.

Classes in floral design are offered at some vocational schools, however, most floral designers receive on-the-job training. Camera operators can also be trained on-the-job. However, many camera operators have taken courses in camera operation at vocational schools or community colleges. College degrees in communications often require courses on camera operation.

In the year 2002, fashion designers earned an average salary of $60,160. Floral designers earned $20,600. Illustrators earned an average salary of $43,750, and camera operators earned an average salary of $36,880.

Using Technology

Technology has helped many people with careers in the arts. For example, computer programs can be used to draw illustrations. Special cameras, guided by computer technology, can be used to film action-packed motion pictures.

How to Learn More About Careers in Sports and the Arts

There are many resources that can provide you with information about careers in sports and the arts. The *Occupational Outlook Handbook* and the *Guide for Occupational Exploration* are two helpful books. You can also follow the suggestions below to learn more about careers in these areas:

- If you feel that you are a talented athlete, talk to a coach at your school. The coach may be able to help you contact a scout. He or she may also have information about colleges or universities that offer athletic scholarships.

- Volunteer to coach children at a community recreation center. You will find out if you have the patience and desire to teach or coach others.

- If you are interested in becoming a fashion designer, contact schools that offer programs in fashion and design. Find out what the requirements are and what courses are offered.

- The next time you watch a television program or view a movie, focus on the objects and scenery on the screen. Think about how a camera operator films an action scene.

- If you are interested in acting, try out for school plays. Take acting classes. You will find out if performing in front of an audience is right for you.

- Read biographies, or stories about the lives of famous people, in the field you are exploring. Learn what made these people successful.

- Write to one of the associations listed on page 192 for more information about careers in sports and the arts.

✔ Check Your Understanding

Write your answers in complete sentences.

1. What are some strengths of people who have careers in sports?

2. What are the training requirements for a set designer?

3. What is one way to learn more about a career as an athletic coach?

Career Path

BECOMING A SINGER

Since she was a child, Lila has always enjoyed singing. She sang while taking a bath, doing chores around the house, and along with her favorite songs on the radio. When she was ten years old, Lila joined a choir. Soon she was giving solo performances and being praised for her ability to sing.

While attending high school, Lila continued to sing. She sang in school musicals. She performed at friends' parties. She and two of her friends formed a singing group. They sang during school talent shows. They even won a contest for young nonprofessional singers.

When she graduated from high school, Lila was determined to have a career in music. She took a job selling instruments in a music store. On weekends, she sang with a band at weddings, as well as in a choir.

After three years of working, Lila is now taking private lessons from a voice coach. Her coach is helping Lila to improve her voice. Lila is planning on trying out for singing parts in professional musicals. According to Lila, "I don't need to become a star. I just want to be able to do what I love doing, which is singing."

CRITICAL THINKING How has Lila gained experience in singing in front of an audience?

Associations for Careers in Sports and the Arts

American Alliance for Health, Physical Education, Recreation, and Dance
1900 Association Drive
Reston, VA 20191

American Dance Guild
P.O. Box 2006
Lenox Hill Station
New York, NY 10021

American Guild of Musical Artists
1430 Broadway, 14th Floor
New York, NY 10018

The Athletic Institute
200 Castlewood Drive
North Palm Beach, FL 33408

National Art Education Association
1916 Association Drive
Reston, VA 20191

National Association of Schools of Dance
11250 Roger Bacon Drive, Suite 21
Reston, VA 20190

National Endowment for the Arts
1100 Pennsylvania Avenue, NW
Washington, DC 29506

Screen Actors Guild
5757 Wilshire Boulevard
Los Angeles, CA 90036

Society for Technical Communications
901 North Stuart Street
Suite 904
Arlington, VA 22203

More Careers in Sports and the Arts

Assistant coach
Cartoonist
Composer
Costume attendant
Dancer
Director
Disc jockey
Editor
Graphic artist
Jeweler
Makeup artist

Music arranger
Potter
Radio operator
Sculptor
Singer
Sketch artist
Songwriter
Sound engineering technician
Sports announcer
Talent director
Writer

JOB DESCRIPTION
Karate Instructor

Job Summary

A karate instructor teaches children and adults a Japanese method of self-defense called karate. Karate training involves learning to use parts of the body to kick and strike.

A karate instructor usually works in a karate school. He or she may work with individuals or with a class of students. Some karate instructors have other full-time jobs and teach karate classes in the evenings or on the weekends. Some travel to competitions with their students.

Job Responsibilities

A karate instructor may do any or all of the following activities:

- Show individuals or small groups of students the correct way to perform karate moves.

- Test students' knowledge of karate.

- Give students colored belts to promote them to higher levels of karate training.

- Teach qualified students to become karate instructors.

- Supervise and judge karate competitions.

Education/Training Requirements

All karate instructors are trained in karate. They are experts in most of the skills and movements in karate. Many employers require that instructors have a high school diploma and be at least 18 years old. Karate instructors must also have good communications skills. Additional requirements include training in cardiopulmonary resuscitation (CPR) and first aid.

Think About It

Why do you think many karate instructors have other full-time jobs?

Chapter

14 ▷ Review

Summary

- Some careers in sports include professional athletes, coaches, umpires, referees, and scouts. The arts, or the art industry, includes people who express themselves in creative ways. Careers in the arts include fashion designers, set designers, camera operators, illustrators, and floral designers. Careers in the arts can be as competitive as careers in sports.

- The job outlook between the years 2002 and 2012 is generally good for many careers in sports and the arts. The number of jobs for coaches, umpires, referees, fashion designers, set designers, and illustrators is expected to increase at the average rate or faster.

- People who have careers in sports have to know a great deal of information about certain sports. Set designers, fashion designers, floral designers, and illustrators create art. Camera operators must have good technical skills.

- Looking through the *Occupational Outlook Handbook* and the *Guide for Occupational Exploration* are good ways to learn more about careers in sports and the arts.

| athlete |
| floral designer |
| scout |
| set designer |
| umpire |

Vocabulary Review

Complete each sentence with a term from the list.

1. A person who creates flower arrangements using live, dried, or plastic flowers is called a _____.

2. A person who is trained to play a certain sport is called an _____.

3. A person who watches the plays during baseball games to make sure that players follow the rules is called an _____.

4. A person who identifies the most talented athletes in a sport is called a _____.

5. A person who builds and paints sets for plays, movies, or television shows is called a _____.

Chapter Quiz

Write your answers in complete sentences.

1. What does a referee do?

2. What is the job of a fashion designer?

3. What are the chances of a person becoming a professional athlete or a famous artist?

4. What is the job trend for illustrators in the years between 2002 and 2012?

5. For whom do coaches and instructors usually work?

6. Why will reading biographies about professional athletes help a person to learn more about a career in sports?

CRITICAL THINKING

7. How is a professional athlete different from a person who plays sports on the weekends only?

8. Why do many artists work at other jobs?

Career Portfolio Project

There are many benefits to becoming an athlete or artist. There are also drawbacks to these careers. Write a list of the benefits and drawbacks for these careers. Then, decide if you would consider a career in sports or the arts. Explain your decision.

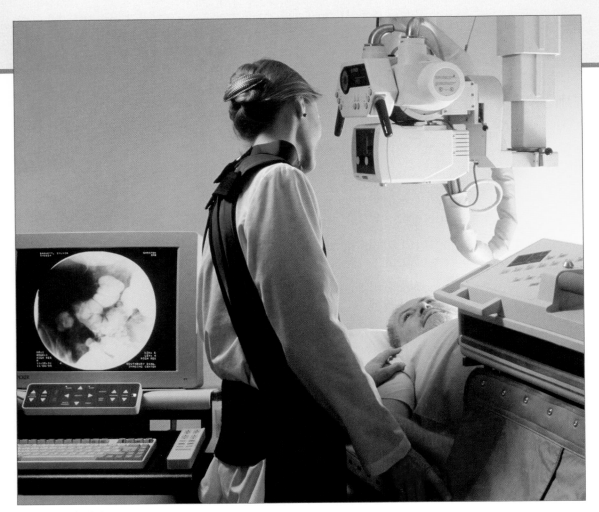

X-ray technicians use machines to take x-rays, or pictures, of people's inner organs and tissues.

Learning Objectives

- Identify some careers in healthcare.
- Discuss trends in careers in healthcare.
- Describe strengths and lifestyles of people who have careers in healthcare.
- List ways to find out more about careers in healthcare.

Chapter **15** Careers in Healthcare

Words to Know

nursing aide	a hospital worker who helps care for patients
x-ray technician	a person who takes x-rays of a patient's body; also called a radiologic technician
emergency medical technician (EMT)	a person who treats people who need immediate medical care before they get to a hospital
licensed practical nurse (LPN)	a person who has completed a training program in caring for patients
dental hygienist	a person who cleans and takes x-rays of teeth
dental assistant	a person who helps dentists care for patients
mental health assistant	a person who helps people suffering from mental illness
veterinarian	an animal doctor, also called a vet
veterinary assistant	a person who helps veterinarians in caring for animals
home health aide	a person who cares for sick, injured, or older people in their homes
pharmacy technician	a person who helps fill prescriptions for medical drugs
registered nurse (RN)	a nurse who has completed a two- or four-year program in patient care

Read how a baseball player learned about careers in healthcare in the story below.

Bill held the bat high and waited for the pitch. *Thunk!* Bill fell to the ground. The baseball had hit him on his head.

Bill was taken to the hospital. After being examined completely, Bill was told that he could go home.

On the way home, Bill told his mother, "I never realized all the different jobs there are in a hospital. There was a **nursing aide** who helps care for patients. An **x-ray technician** took an x-ray of my head." Bill continued, "I always thought that people who worked in healthcare were just doctors and nurses. But there are other interesting jobs in a hospital."

"Sounds like that ball knocked some sense into you!" said Bill's mother.

Career Fact

An x-ray technician is also called a radiologic technician. Radiology is the science of dealing with x-rays.

Careers in Healthcare

Like Bill, many people think of only doctors and nurses when they think about healthcare careers. However, there are many different kinds of healthcare workers. The goal of most healthcare workers is to help improve the health of others.

Although many careers in healthcare are in a hospital setting, there are also many healthcare careers that are in different settings. For example, **emergency medical technicians**, or EMTs, may treat people who need immediate medical attention in ambulances. EMTs usually treat patients before the patients get to a hospital. **Licensed practical nurses**, or LPNs, have completed a training program in basic patient care. Some LPNs work in doctors' offices.

Did You Know ?

Basic care includes recording a patient's body temperature, blood pressure, and pulse rate.

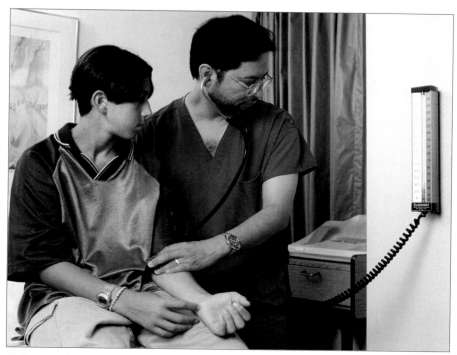

A licensed practical nurse (LPN) is trained to take a patient's blood pressure.

There are some healthcare careers that focus only on teeth. A dentist works to correct problems with teeth and gums. A **dental hygienist** cleans a patient's teeth and may take x-rays. A **dental assistant** helps a dentist examine and care for patients.

Healthcare also includes treating people with mental illness. **Mental health assistants** work with patients who suffer from a variety of mental illnesses. These patients may feel sad or unhappy with their lives. Mental health assistants closely watch their patients and report their behavior to mental health doctors.

There are also careers in animal health. Animal doctors are called **veterinarians**, or vets. Vets treat pets, farm animals, zoo animals, and animals in other settings and environments. Vets often have veterinary assistants. **Veterinary assistants** may give medicine to animals, clean cages, and exercise animals.

Job Trends in Careers in Healthcare

Career Trend

Healthcare is one of the largest industries in the United States today. It is estimated that healthcare will also be the fastest-growing industry through the year 2012.

The job trend for careers in healthcare between the years 2002 and 2012 is good. Since the 1980s, the number of jobs in healthcare has been increasing. By the year 2008, the number of healthcare jobs is expected to be well over 13 million. One reason for this increase is the growing population of older people. As people age, they need more healthcare services. Another reason is that health technology is changing quickly. New equipment is used to help people. Skilled workers will be needed to operate these new machines.

The cost of medical treatment has also affected many types of healthcare jobs. For example, it has become very expensive to care for people in hospitals. It is less costly to care for people in their homes. As a result, the number of jobs for home health aides is also increasing. A **home health aide** cares for sick, injured, or older people in their homes.

✓ Check Your Understanding

Write your answers in complete sentences.

1. What is the difference between a dental hygienist and a dentist?

2. What are two careers in animal health?

3. What is one reason why the number of jobs in home healthcare services is increasing?

Strengths of People Who Have Careers in Healthcare

How can you decide if a career in healthcare is right for you? Think of your strengths and interests. Do you have an interest in science? Would you like to help people or animals to improve their health? If so, a career in healthcare might interest you.

Many healthcare careers need people who care about other people. Do you fit that description? To succeed in these careers, you must also be a good listener. People should feel comfortable around you. Also, depending on the job, you must be willing and able to do some unpleasant tasks. These tasks may include cleaning open wounds or giving vaccinations.

Other healthcare careers need people who are healthy and strong. Often, these workers have to move patients from one place to another. Many healthcare workers must be able to deal with sickness and death. They must be able to handle their own feelings in order to do their jobs.

Healthcare workers must also be careful about details. For example, a **pharmacy technician** helps fill prescriptions for medical drugs. He or she must be able to mix and measure medicines in the right amounts. A small mistake could cause serious problems for a patient.

Career Fact

Some healthcare workers never come into personal contact with patients. For example, a dental technician works with tools in a lab to make false teeth.

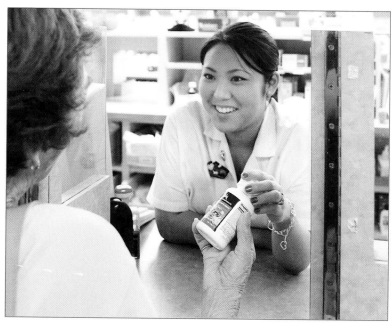

A pharmacy technician must be very careful when helping to prepare prescriptions for medicines.

Lifestyles of People Who Have Careers in Healthcare

Careers in healthcare offer a wide range of lifestyles. Healthcare jobs can be found just about anywhere. Large cities usually have large hospitals. Less populated areas may have smaller hospitals. Doctor's offices, schools, pharmacies, and other businesses employ healthcare workers. Some healthcare workers live and work in the homes of their patients.

Hospitals are the largest employer of healthcare workers. Hospitals are clean, well-lighted spaces. Many hospital workers wear a special type of uniform to protect workers and patients against germs. Because hospitals operate day and night, they need workers for every shift. A shift is an eight- to twelve-hour period. There are morning, afternoon, evening, and night shifts. Weekend workers are also needed.

Healthcare workers work closely with each other and patients in a doctor's office. Most doctors' offices are open only during the day, and they might be closed on weekends. Some doctors may practice only one type of medicine. Healthcare workers in such offices may practice only that type of medicine.

As you read earlier, healthcare is also given in a patient's home. Home healthcare workers may develop a close working relationship with their patients. These men and women may work night shifts if a patient needs around-the-clock care.

Education, training, and salary vary widely in the healthcare field. Usually, the more education and training a person has, the greater the salary. Colleges, community colleges, and vocational schools offer training for many healthcare careers. These training programs can last several months to several years. Some hospitals also train people for beginning-level jobs as well.

Career Fact

Many healthcare workers in hospitals work on holidays. When working on a holiday, these workers are usually paid more than their normal daily salary.

Remember
A vocational school offers programs that help prepare students for certain careers.

Write your answers in complete sentences.

1. What skills do most healthcare workers need?

2. If you were a nurse and wanted to work a night shift, where might you apply?

3. What is an LPN?

Career Path

FROM NURSING AIDE TO REGISTERED NURSE

Lyle has had a career in healthcare for 15 years. He first started out in his career by learning on the job. Then, as he received more formal training, Lyle advanced in his career.

After Lyle graduated from high school, he took a job as a nursing aide in a home for elderly people. He received on-the-job training from a trained nurse. Lyle helped dress and feed people. He earned the minimum wage. (In the year 2002, the average salary for a nursing aide working in a nursing home was about $19,282.)

After 3 years, Lyle enrolled in a training program to become a licensed practical nurse (LPN). He took classes at a local community college. After he completed his classes, Lyle took a test required by the state to become licensed. At the nursing home, Lyle's salary and job duties both increased. (In the year 2002, the average salary of an LPN was about $31,440.)

Lyle continued to take nursing courses. Finally, he completed a four-year program and became a **registered nurse** (RN). As an RN, Lyle could supervise the work of other nurses. He left the nursing home and took a job at a hospital. (In the year 2002, the average salary of a registered nurse was about $48,090.)

CRITICAL THINKING Why do you think Lyle chose to become a registered nurse?

How to Learn More About Careers in Healthcare

Does a career in healthcare sound right for you? If so, you might want to do more research on careers or occupations in healthcare. Here are some ideas:

Using Technology

For information on healthcare careers, visit the American Medical Association's Web site at www.ama-assn.org.

- Read job descriptions for different healthcare positions. The *Occupational Outlook Handbook (OOH)* is a good place to start. Healthcare careers may be divided into different career clusters, so look carefully. For example, doctors and nurses are listed under *Professional and Related Occupations*. Dental assistants are listed under *Service Occupations*.

- Do research on the Internet. There are many Web sites that can provide you with specific career information, such as working conditions and average salaries.

- Visit the career center in your school or at a library. These centers may also have counselors that can help you find the healthcare careers that interest you most.

- Speak with someone you know who has experience in or knowledge of healthcare careers.

- Hold informational interviews with people who have careers in healthcare. Remember to prepare a list of questions before the interviews.

- Volunteer in a nursing home or hospital. You will find out what it is like to work in these settings. Also, you may find a healthcare professional to interview.

- Write letters to different healthcare associations for information on healthcare careers. A list of healthcare associations appears on page 206.

Writing for Information

When you write a letter to request information, be clear about what you want to know. For example, John is a high school student who wants to learn about careers in animal health. He decides to write a letter to an animal health association.

In his letter, John includes a description of his own interests, and where he wants to live. John's personal information could help the person receiving the letter to send John the right kind of information. Here is the letter that John wrote.

Write About It
Write a letter to an association for more information about becoming an x-ray technician. Be clear about the information that you are looking for.

21 Forest Road
Columbus, OH 43206

U.S. Animal Health Association
6924 Lakeside Avenue, Suite 205
Richmond, VA 23228

May 1, 2004

Dear USAHA,

I am a high school student who loves animals. I think I would enjoy a career working with animals. I am writing to you for career information.

I am an average science student and a hard worker. I am not interested in going to college for four years. However, I would be willing to take some classes if they would help me to prepare for a career working with animals.

Can you suggest any jobs in animal care that might be good for me to look into? Also, any information on training programs in my area would be helpful. I would like to work in Ohio, if possible.

Thank you for your help.

Sincerely,

John Sherman

John Sherman

Associations for Careers in Healthcare

American Medical Association
515 North State Street
Chicago, IL 60610

American Dental Association
211 East Chicago Avenue
Chicago, IL 60611

U.S. Animal Health Association
P.O. Box K227
Richmond, VA 23228

American Nurses Association
600 Maryland Ave, SW
Suite 100 West
Washington, DC 20024

American Health Care Association
1201 L Street NW
Washington, DC 20005

National Mental Health Association
2001 North Beauregard Street
12th Floor
Alexandria, VA 22311

More Careers in Healthcare

Cardiovascular technician
Cardiovascular technologist
Clinical laboratory technician
Clinical laboratory technologist
Dental technician
Licensed vocational nurse
Medical assistant
Nuclear medicine technologist
Occupational therapist
Occupational therapist aide
Occupational therapist assistant
Optician
Optometrist

Orthodontist
Paramedic
Pediatric nurse
Pharmacist
Physical therapist
Physical therapist aide
Physical therapist assistant
Physician
Physician assistant
Psychologist
Respiratory therapist
Surgical technologist
Veterinary technologist

JOB DESCRIPTION
Physical Therapist Assistant

Job Summary
A physical therapist helps people who have an injury or disease to gain movement in their body. A physical therapist assistant helps physical therapists to provide services to these patients. Such services include improving movement in different parts of the body, preventing further injury, and reducing pain.

A physical therapist assistant may work in a hospital or in an office of physical therapists. Work schedules depend on full-time or part-time work.

Work Activities
A physical therapist assistant may do any or all of the following activities:

- Help a physical therapist plan and carry out treatment for patients.

- Help patients perform exercises using special equipment or on mats.

- Give patients special treatments such as hydrotherapy, or water therapy; massages; bandaging; and paraffin, or wax, baths.

- Observe and record patients' reactions to treatment.

- Order equipment, fill out forms, file paperwork.

Education/Training Requirements
Many states require completion of a physical therapist assistant program. Some states require physical therapist assistants to be licensed. Licensing is given after taking special courses and passing a state exam. An additional requirement may include certification in cardiopulmonary resuscitation (CPR).

Think About It
What kinds of qualities might a physical therapist assistant need to do his or her job well?

Chapter

15 ▷ Review

Summary

- There are many healthcare careers. The goal of most healthcare workers is to help improve the health of others. Some healthcare workers work with animals.

- The number of jobs in healthcare is increasing. This increase is due to an aging population, changing technology, and the high cost of medical treatment.

- It is helpful for a healthcare worker to be interested in science. He or she should also like working with people. Healthcare workers must be careful about details.

- Careers in healthcare offer a variety of lifestyles. Work shifts are available days, nights, overnight, and on weekends. Usually, a healthcare worker's salary increases with training and education.

- Healthcare career training programs can be found in colleges, community colleges, and vocational schools. Hospitals sometimes offer on-the-job training for beginning-level positions.

- There are many ways to find out more about healthcare careers. The Internet, libraries, and career centers provide information about careers.

dental hygienist
home health aide
pharmacy technician
registered nurse
veterinary assistant

Vocabulary Review

Complete each sentence with a term from the list.

1. A person who helps fill prescriptions is called a _____.

2. A person who cleans and takes x-rays of the teeth is called a _____.

3. A nurse who has completed a two- or four-year program in patient care is called a _____.

4. A person who helps veterinarians in caring for animals is called a _____.

5. A person who cares for a sick or injured person in the home is called a _____.

Chapter Quiz

Write your answers in complete sentences.

1. What are two careers in the field of dental health?

2. What are two careers in a hospital setting?

3. What kinds of treatment can a licensed practical nurse give to a patient?

4. How many healthcare jobs are there expected to be in 2008?

5. Why must a pharmacy technician pay attention to details?

6. Name four places where a person might be able to train for the healthcare field.

CRITICAL THINKING

7. Who will probably have a higher income, an LPN or an RN? Explain your answer.

8. Optometric technician is another career in healthcare. This healthcare worker gives vision tests and helps fit patients with eyeglasses. What strengths and interests do you think an optometric technician should have?

Career Portfolio Project

Make a two-column chart on a separate sheet of paper. Label the left column *Strengths*. Label the right column *Yes*. In the left column, list ten strengths a healthcare worker should have. In the right column, write a check mark next to each strength that you have. Look over your chart. Decide whether you would be interested in a career in healthcare. Write your explanation in a short paragraph.

An automotive service technician uses technology to help repair cars and light trucks.

Learning Objectives

- Identify some careers in technology.
- Discuss trends in careers in technology.
- Describe strengths and lifestyles of people who have careers in technology.
- List ways to find out more about careers in technology.

Chapter 16 ▷ Careers in Technology

Words to Know

computer software engineer	a person who designs, develops, and tests computer programs that enable computers to perform their functions
software program	a set of instructions that tells a computer what to do
computer programmer	a person who writes software programs that computers follow in order to perform their functions
computer support specialist	a person who helps people solve problems with their computers
Web developer	a person who designs or creates Web sites for the Internet, also called a Web designer
data entry keyer	a person who types information into a computer or updates information already stored in a computer
automotive service technician	a person who uses technology to inspect, repair, and maintain cars or light trucks
line installer	a person who sets up electrical wires and cables to provide customers with electricity, telephone, or cable network services

Read how Darryl helps people solve problems with their computers in the story below.

"My computer doesn't seem to be working. I can't print anything," a customer told Darryl.

"Well, your printer connection seems fine, but your software is out-of-date," Darryl explained. "Let me install the newest version. Then, you won't have any problems!"

"Thanks! I would not have known what to do," the customer said gratefully.

Careers in Technology

Look around you. You are very likely to see equipment, tools, or machinery that make doing chores much easier. For example, telephones, dishwashers, and microwave ovens can be found in almost every home in the United States.

Outside of our homes, we also depend on other types of machines, such as automobiles, cash registers, and automated bank machines. People need these tools and machinery in order to live comfortably, to be safe, and to be able to communicate with others.

Offices and other places of business depend on machines, too. Without fax machines, photocopiers, and computers, most companies would find it difficult to run their business.

Remember
In Chapter 1, you learned that technology is the use of science to create new or better products or ways to produce goods.

Today's machines, tools, and equipment are produced using technology. Technology applies scientific ideas to make useful products. Engineers, scientists, and other professionals are the people who plan and direct the production of machines. Technicians are the people who help carry out the plans of scientists, engineers, and other professionals. Most technicians set up, run, program, and repair equipment and machines.

Quite often, when people think of technical careers, they think of computers. There are many careers in the computer industry. For example, a **computer software engineer** designs, develops, and tests software programs. A **software program** is a set of instructions that tells a computer what to do. A **computer programmer** writes the software programs. A **computer support specialist** helps people solve problems with their computers. A computer repairer replaces broken parts in computers, printers, and other computer equipment.

People whose jobs involve using a computer include computer operators, Web developers, and data entry keyers. A computer operator monitors computer parts to make sure that a computer's programs are running properly. A **Web developer**, also called a Web designer, designs or creates Web sites for the Internet. A **data entry keyer** types information into a computer or may update information already stored there.

There are many other technology-related jobs that are not in the computer industry. For example, an **automotive service technician** uses technology to inspect, repair, and maintain cars and light trucks. An office machine repairer works to repair fax machines, photocopiers, and mail processing equipment. A heating and air conditioning technician sets up, repairs, and maintains these kinds of systems in homes and business locations. A **line installer** sets up electrical wires and cables to provide customers with electricity, telephone, or cable network services. Many of the people in these jobs use electronic tools or other forms of technology to identify problems in the machinery that they install, maintain, and repair.

Using Technology

Automotive service technicians use computers to locate problems during automobile inspections.

A line installer sets up, maintains, and repairs electrical and cable wires.

Job Trends in Careers in Technology

Career Trend

Many U.S. companies employ workers in other countries to perform computer-related work. These companies save money because workers in these countries are paid a lower salary than American workers.

The outlook for many jobs in the computer industry between the years 2002 and 2012 is very good. Some computer careers are expected to be among the fastest-growing occupations. For example, the number of jobs for computer software engineers, computer programmers, and some other computer-related occupations is expected to grow 36 percent or more. This growth is much faster than the average rate. However, the number of jobs for computer operators and data entry keyers is expected to decrease. One of the reasons for the decrease is that improvements in technology replace the need for many of these types of workers.

The number of jobs for office machine repairers is expected to increase at about the average rate. This rate is between 10 and 20 percent. One reason for this increase is that businesses depend heavily on computers, fax machines, photocopiers, and mail-sorting machines. These tools and equipment often need to be repaired or replaced. Another reason for the increase in jobs for office machine repairers is that certain businesses are also expected to grow. When businesses grow, they hire more workers. These workers need equipment that works properly to help them to perform their jobs.

The outlook for the number of jobs for other technology-related careers also looks good. The number of jobs for automotive service technicians and line installers is expected to increase between 10 and 20 percent. Between 2002 and 2012, the number of jobs for heating and air conditioning technicians is expected to increase 21 to 35 percent. One reason for this large increase is due to growth in the population and the economy. More home owners and businesses will demand heating and cooling systems.

✓ Check Your Understanding

Write your answers in complete sentences.

1. List three careers in the computer industry.

2. How does an automotive service technician use technology?

3. What is the job trend for office machine repairers?

Strengths of People Who Have Careers in Technology

People who have careers in the computer industry usually enjoy working with computers. Most of these people understand how computers and computer-related equipment work. People who have service-related careers that use technology usually have good mechanical skills. They often use hand tools, such as drills and screwdrivers, to do their work.

People who create software programs must know what computer users want and need. They design computer programs that make it easier and faster for people to do their work. For example, a computer software engineer may design a program to help people file their tax forms on a computer. This person has to understand how the tax system works in order to design a computer program easy enough for people to use.

People who use technology to install, repair, or maintain equipment need to understand how machines work and how electrical systems run. For example, an automotive service technician should know when a car's engine is not running properly. He or she should also know how a car battery runs the electrical systems in a car.

Did You Know ?

Computer software engineers help design computer games. Computer programmers work with computer software engineers to write the instructions that tell the computer how to make a game run, including the images and the sounds.

Knowing how to follow detailed instructions and reading handbooks is also important. In order to become a heating and air conditioning technician or an office machine repairer, a person has to learn how these systems or machines operate. Instructions and handbooks give these people the information that they need.

People in these careers should also have good communications skills. An automotive service technician needs to speak with customers to find out what problems they are having with their cars. A line installer may be a part of a team of workers that sets up lines and cables. He or she needs to communicate with other members of the team.

Career Fact

Because wires and cables may be color-coded, line installers must be able to identify certain colors.

Lifestyles of People Who Have Careers in Technology

Computer technology is a fast-growing industry. A few large companies produce most of the computer equipment or software that is used by businesses and individuals. These large companies employ computer software engineers and many other people in computer-related positions. Although computer companies are found throughout the United States, many of these companies are located near San Jose, California. This area is often called Silicon Valley because so many companies located there produce computer parts made of silicon.

People with careers in computer technology usually work in offices. Many of these people work the usual 40 business hours a week. However, because many computers run 24 hours a day, some computer operators may work evenings, weekends, or holidays.

Some computer support specialists may be required to work during nonbusiness hours if problems occur at those times. They may travel to customers' offices to solve computer-related problems. Other computer support specialists or computer repairers work to repair computer parts in a shop.

Most employers require computer software engineers and computer programmers to have college degrees. Completion of a certification program in computer technology helps many computer support specialists find jobs. However, many computer support specialists and computer repairers are hired based on their knowledge of electrical systems and related work experience. Many employers hire data entry keyers for their speed in typing. However, computer-related training gives a person a better chance of being considered for a job in these careers.

Line installers usually work 40 hours a week. However, they may work during bad weather to make emergency repairs to storm-damaged lines and cables. Line installers also work high above the ground, and they lift heavy equipment. Line installers must wear protective clothing and equipment to prevent themselves from falling or from being injured by an electric shock.

Many automotive service technicians complete a formal training program in high school or at a vocational school. However, some people in this career learn automotive repair on the job by working with experienced workers. Line installers also learn on the job, but most employers require a high school diploma.

In the year 2002, computer software engineers earned an average salary of $70,900. Computer operators earned an average salary of $29,650. A computer repairer earned an average hourly wage of $15.98. An automobile service technician earned an average hourly wage of $14.71 in 2002. A line installer earned an average hourly wage of $23.33. A heating and air conditioning technician earned an hourly wage of $16.78.

Write About It
Choose a technology career that interests you. Make a list of the skills needed for that career. You may need to do research to help you create the list. Make a check next to each skill you do not have and explain how you can learn that skill.

How to Learn More About Careers in Technology

There are many ways to learn more about careers in technology. A list of suggestions appears below. You can also write to any of the associations listed on page 220 for more information.

- Look through the *Occupational Outlook Handbook* or other books on careers in technology. These books can be found in the career section of a library. First, look at the table of contents. Find the chapters listed for occupations in technology. Then, read the descriptions of the occupations that interest you.

- Study images on different Web sites if you are interested in becoming a Web designer. Look at how the words are arranged. Think of how you could improve the way these pages look.

- Take a course in computer programming or computer repair if you are interested in a computer-related career. Understanding how a computer operates is an important part of any computer-related career.

- Take classes in physics, algebra, and trigonometry. These classes will help you develop the skills that you will need for a career in technology.

- Take a class in automotive repair. You will find out what skills an automotive service technician needs. Even if you do not become an automotive service technician, you can still learn how a car operates.

- Look at the available jobs listed in a local paper. Find the technology-related jobs. Read what the requirements for these jobs are.

- Find a summer job working for a company whose workers use technology to install, maintain, or repair equipment or machinery. You will find out if you have a talent for this type of work and if you would enjoy a career in this area.

✓ Check Your Understanding

Write your answers in complete sentences.

1. What strength do most people in the computer industry share?

2. How do line installers protect themselves from falling and being injured by an electric shock?

3. Describe one way to learn more about careers in technology.

Career Path

AIRCRAFT MECHANIC

Rob has always had good mechanical skills. When he was a young boy, he took apart many of his toys. With his father's help, he put them back together again. When he was a teenager, Rob took apart his bicycle and rebuilt it alone.

Rob chose to go to a technical vocational high school. In addition to courses in English and mathematics, Rob took courses in mechanics, physics, electrical systems, computers, and aviation, or airplane, technology. After graduating from high school, Rob completed a 30-month training program approved by the Federal Aviation Administration (FAA). Rob then passed written and oral exams that showed he had learned the required skills to become an aircraft mechanic.

Rob now works for an aircraft repair shop at a large airport. His main task is to make sure that aircraft are safe to fly. His job responsibilities include inspecting engines, checking landing gear, brakes, and valves, and replacing or repairing worn parts.

Rob usually works a 10-hour day. However, he does not mind the long hours. In fact, to Rob, the hours go by quickly because he enjoys what he does.

CRITICAL THINKING Why is being an aircraft mechanic a good occupation for Rob?

Associations for Careers in Technology

Association of Computer Operations Management
722 East Chapman Avenue
Orange, CA 92860

Association of Computer Support Specialists
218 Huntington Road
Bridgeport, CT 06608

Automotive Youth Educational Systems
50 West Big Beaver, Suite 145
Troy, MI 48084

Computing Technology Industry Association
1815 South Meyers Road, Suite 300
Oakbrook Terrace, IL 60181-5228

International Brotherhood of Electrical Workers Telecommunications Department
1125 15th Street, NW
Washington, DC 20005

National Automotive Technicians Education Foundation
101 Blue Seal Drive, SE, Suite 101
Leesburg, VA 20175

National Workforce Center for Emerging Technologies
3000 Landerholm Circle, SE
Bellevue, WA 98007

Society of Broadcast Engineers Information Office
7002 Graham Road, Suite 118
Indianapolis, IN 46220

More Careers in Technology

Aircraft mechanic
Automotive air conditioning repair specialist
Avionics technician
Broadcasting and sound engineering technician
Central office installer
Computer scientist
Computer systems analyst
Database administrator
Diesel service technician
Electrical and electronics installer and repair specialist

Electrician
Heating equipment technician
Home appliance repair specialist
Industrial machinery mechanic
Motorboat mechanic
Motorcycle mechanic
Radio and telecommunications equipment installer
Radio mechanic
Radio operator
Refrigeration mechanic
Small engine mechanic
Vending machine servicer

JOB DESCRIPTION
Computer Support Specialist

Job Summary

A computer support specialist is responsible for installing and updating computer systems. A computer support specialist helps people when they have a problem with their computer or computer-related equipment. He or she may also train people to use computers and computer software programs.

Most computer support specialists work about 40 hours a week. Overtime may be required if problems occur within a computer or in a computer system. Some computer support specialists are required to work evenings and weekends. Part-time and full-time positions are usually available.

Job Responsibilities

A computer support specialist may do any or all of the following activities:

- Travel to customers' offices to help fix computer problems.

- Answer telephone calls from computer users who have problems or questions.

- Install and update computer software programs.

- Clean and repair computer monitors, keyboards, printers, disk drives, and mice.

Education/Training Requirements

Education requirements range from a high school diploma to a college degree. A person wishing to become a computer support specialist might consider going through a certification training program. Many companies offer training programs.

Think About It

What type of person would make a good computer support specialist?

Summary

- Careers in technology include computer software engineers, computer programmers, computer support specialists, computer repairers, Web developers, data entry keyers, automotive service technicians, office machine repairers, heating and air conditioning technicians, and line installers.

- The outlook for jobs in technology between the years 2002 and 2012 is good. Some computer-related occupations are expected to grow 36 percent or more.

- People who have computer-related jobs usually enjoy working with computers. People who use technology to install, repair, or maintain equipment need to understand how machines work and how electrical systems work. They must also have good mechanical skills.

- Looking through the *Occupational Outlook Handbook*, taking courses in computer repair or automotive repair, and studying the design of Web pages are some ways to learn more about careers in technology.

---

automotive service technician

computer software engineer

line installer

Web developer

Vocabulary Review

Complete each sentence with a term from the list.

1. A person who designs, develops, and tests the computer programs that allow computers to perform their functions is called a _____.

2. A person who designs or creates Web sites on the Internet is called a _____.

3. A person who uses technology to inspect, repair, and maintain cars or light trucks is called an

_____.

4. A person who sets up electrical wires and cables to provide customers with electricity, telephone, or cable network services is called a _____.

Chapter Quiz

Write your answers in complete sentences.

1. What does a computer programmer do?

2. What does a computer support specialist do?

3. What does a data entry keyer do?

4. What is the job trend for office machine repairers between the years 2002 and 2012?

5. What is the expected increase in the number of jobs for heating and air conditioning technicians?

6. How can a person become an automotive service technician?

CRITICAL THINKING

7. What does technology have to do with things such as CD players, computers, cable television, and heating systems?

8. What is the difference between an engineer and a technician?

Career Portfolio Project

Choose two occupations mentioned in this chapter. Use career resources to write job descriptions for those occupations. Read over both of your job descriptions. Then, write an essay that compares and contrasts both occupations. Decide if you are interested in either occupation. Explain your decision in your essay.

Men and women who have careers in transportation hold a variety of jobs, such as directing airplanes on runways.

Learning Objectives

- Identify some careers in transportation.
- Discuss trends in careers in transportation.
- Describe strengths and lifestyles of people who have careers in transportation.
- List ways to find out more about careers in transportation.

Words to Know

transportation	the movement of people or goods from one place to another
pilot	a person who controls, or flies, an airplane
navigate	to steer, or control the direction of, something
air traffic controller	a person who manages the movement of airplanes in and around an airport
tractor-trailer truck driver	a person who is licensed to drive a large truck used for transporting goods
hand packer	a person who prepares items for shipment by hand
crane operator	a person who is licensed to operate a vehicle that lifts large objects
stevedore	a person who loads and unloads ships
ship engineer	a person who maintains the engines, boilers, and other machinery on a ship

Emma is holding an informational interview with Frank, an aircraft pilot. After telling Emma the requirements to becoming an aircraft pilot, Frank describes how to fly an airplane. Read his description below.

"One of the most difficult parts about flying an airplane is the takeoff. During takeoff, the pilot watches the runway while the copilot monitors the instrument panel. When the airplane reaches takeoff speed, the copilot tells the pilot. The pilot then raises the nose of the airplane to lift it off the ground."

"Wow! That sounds exciting," said Emma. "It's a good thing that pilots are so well trained."

Careers in Transportation

Transportation is the business, or industry, of moving people or goods from one place to another. Careers in transportation can be divided into three groups. Air transportation careers are related to airplanes and helicopters. Ground transportation careers are related to vehicles that move on the ground. Water transportation careers are related to vessels that move on water.

Careers in Air Transportation

Many people are needed to prepare an airplane for flight, direct the airplane on the runway, and fly the airplane. **Pilots** fly airplanes. Before takeoff, the pilot checks the engine, controls, weight of the cargo, amount of fuel, and anything else that will affect the flight. During the flight, the pilot must **navigate**, or control the direction of, the airplane.

Pilots depend on **air traffic controllers** to tell them if other airplanes are near them in the sky or on the ground. The two main responsibilities of air traffic controllers are to make sure airplanes are safe and to help airplane pilots take off and land on time.

Careers in Ground Transportation

Careers in ground transportation include truck, bus, and taxicab drivers, train conductors, and subway attendants. Some people in these careers are responsible for delivering goods. **Tractor-trailer truck drivers** pick up and deliver goods in large trucks called tractor-trailers. Many of the routes they drive are thousands of miles long. Truck drivers can spend many hours driving each day.

Other people with careers in ground transportation are responsible for the safety of their passengers. These people include bus drivers, railroad conductors, and taxicab drivers.

Using Technology

Air traffic controllers often work in airport towers. They check the position of airplanes on computers. Then, they use radios to give information and directions to pilots.

Career Fact

Sometimes, two truck drivers will help to drive one route. This way, one drives while the other sleeps.

A bus driver is responsible for transporting people from one place to another.

Another industry listed in the transportation career cluster is called material moving. This industry involves packing and loading cargo, or material, onto different forms of transportation. Some material movers, called **hand packers**, usually pack boxes by hand. They record the items packed and prepare the boxes for shipping. Another type of material mover is a crane operator. **Crane operators** use large machines called cranes to lift and move very heavy objects.

Careers in Water Transportation

A type of material mover who works on ships is called a stevedore. **Stevedores** load and unload a ship's cargo. Because ships roll and sway a lot, stevedores must secure the cargo carefully in the ship.

Ship engineers are responsible for maintaining the engines, boilers, and other equipment on board a ship. Ship engineers start the engines when a ship is ready to move and make sure that the engines continue to work properly during a trip.

Did You Know

The types of ships used to transport people and cargo across water include tugboats, oil tankers, cruise ships, ferries, and barges.

Job Trends in Careers in Transportation

Career Trend

A growing population can affect the number of jobs in transportation. For example, the number of jobs available for school bus drivers increases when the population grows.

The job trends for careers in transportation for the years between 2002 and 2012 are expected to vary. One factor that will affect the number of jobs for people in this career cluster is the condition of the economy. When the economy is doing well, the number of jobs for aircraft pilots and truck drivers will increase. More people travel and more goods are produced and transported in a good economy.

A factor that can cause a decrease in the number of jobs is technology. The increasing use of computers will cause the number of jobs for certain occupations in transportation, such as air traffic controllers, to decrease.

✓ **Check Your Understanding**

Write your answers in complete sentences.

1. What are the three different groups of transportation careers?

2. Name at least three careers in ground transportation.

3. What is the general trend for careers in transportation?

Strengths of People Who Have Careers in Transportation

People who have careers in transportation share some common personal strengths. The ability to handle stress is one of them. For example, air traffic controllers are responsible for the safety of the passengers and crews on airplanes. Bus drivers often drive in heavy traffic and must keep to strict schedules. Ship engineers must be able to quickly repair mechanical problems on their ships.

Good physical health is another strength that some people with careers in transportation have. Many material movers, such as stevedores, must be able to lift and move heavy objects. The jobs of pilots and truck drivers are also physically demanding. Pilots and truck drivers have to sit for long periods of time, which can be very uncomfortable.

Some people who have careers in transportation must have the ability to navigate, plan routes, and read a map. Truck drivers must plan which roads to take and how many hours to drive each day in order to reach their destinations on time. A pilot must know the number of miles to a destination so that he or she can calculate the amount of fuel the airplane needs.

Lifestyles of People Who Have Careers in Transportation

There is probably a job in transportation to fit the lifestyle of almost every person. Someone who likes to travel and work alone may succeed as a truck driver. A person who enjoys working 8 hours per day with a set schedule may prefer driving a bus route. Those people who do well using physical strength may become stevedores. People who like to work with machines may become crane operators.

Many jobs in transportation provide on-the-job training. New employees receive training from more experienced workers. Beginners who work hard and learn from others can often advance to better jobs. Some jobs also require special training or licensing.

Salaries among transportation workers can vary according to experience, job responsibilities, and technical skill. A beginning-level hand packer will probably earn close to minimum wage.

Write About It
Compare the lifestyles of two careers in transportation. Describe the benefits and drawbacks of each career. Then, explain whether you would be interested in either career.

The average annual salary of air traffic controllers in the year 2002 was $91,600. Bus drivers earned an average hourly wage of $14.22. Hand packers made an average hourly wage of $8.03. The average hourly wage of tractor-trailer truck drivers in the year 2002 was $15.97. Some ship engineers earned an average hourly wage as high as $37.37. Overtime pay can increase earnings for all those workers paid by the hour.

How to Learn More About Careers in Transportation

There are many resources that can provide you with information about careers in transportation. You can write to one of the associations listed on page 232 for more information. You can also follow the suggestions below to learn more about careers in this area:

- Speak with a U.S. military recruiter if you are interested in a career in ground, water, or air transportation. The U.S. military provides training in the latest technology in these careers. Sometimes, people with military training are preferred over other job applicants.

- If you are interested in becoming a bus or truck driver, find out what your state's requirements are for these types of jobs.

- If you are interested in a career in water transportation, contact your local Coast Guard office or check the Coast Guard's Web site at www.uscg.mil for more information. The U.S. Coast Guard trains, issues certificates of training, and hires people to work in many water transportation careers.

✔ **Check Your Understanding**

Write your answers in complete sentences.

1. What are some strengths of people who have careers in transportation?

2. What affects salaries of transportation careers?

3. What is one way to learn more about a career in water transportation?

Career Path

BECOMING THE BEST TAXICAB DRIVER

Peter is the best taxicab driver in Chicago. At least, that is what he tells his customers.

After he graduated from high school, Peter began working for his uncle's taxicab company in Chicago. At first, he worked as a dispatcher. A dispatcher answers customers' calls and then contacts drivers by radio to pick up the customers.

Only people with driver's licenses and chauffeur's licenses can drive taxicabs in Chicago. So, Peter enrolled in a chauffeur training course offered by a city college. For two weeks, Peter studied city maps, driving rules, and practiced his people skills, such as being courteous and having good manners. At the end of the course, Peter passed a written exam and was given his chauffeur's license.

Peter began driving customers to and from Chicago's airports. The more he worked, the more familiar he became with all of Chicago's streets. Peter was polite and friendly and always seemed to know how to get to his customers' destinations quickly.

However, Peter wanted to be known as the best taxicab driver in Chicago. He began studying Chicago's history. He started taking people on tours of famous locations in Chicago and telling them stories. Soon, people were calling his uncle's company requesting Peter. He was proud of the career he made for himself.

CRITICAL THINKING What were some of the skills Peter needed to become a successful taxicab driver?

Associations for Careers in Transportation

Airline Pilots Association
1625 Massachusetts Avenue, NW
Washington, DC 20036

American Bus Association
1100 New York Avenue, NW
Suite 1050
Washington, DC 20005

American Public Transportation Association
1666 K Street, NW
Suite 1100
Washington, DC 20006

American Trucking Association, Inc.
2200 Mill Road
Alexandria, VA 22314

Association of American Railroads
50 F Street, NW
Washington, DC 20001

International Organization of Masters, Mates, and Pilots
700 Maritime Boulevard
Linthicum Heights, MD 21090

Specialized Carriers and Rigging Association
2750 Prosperity Avenue
Suite 620
Fairfax, VA 22301

More Careers in Transportation

Chauffeur
Conductor
Copilot
Deck officer
Excavating operator
Flight engineer
Locomotive engineer
Machine feeder
Marine oiler
Offbearer
Operating engineer
Paratransit driver
Pile-driver operator

Rail yard engineer
Railroad brake, signal, and switch
  operator
Sailor
Ship captain
Ship mate
Streetcar operator
Subway operator
Taxicab driver
Tractor operator
Yardmaster

JOB DESCRIPTION
Railroad Conductor

Job Summary

A railroad conductor is responsible for all of the activities that take place on a train. On a passenger train, the railroad conductor is responsible for the safety of all the traveling people. On a freight train, the railroad conductor is responsible for the cargo.

Most railroad conductors are required to work nights, weekends, and holidays. Some work more than 40 hours per week. Railroad conductors may have to spend time away from home if they work on a train that travels long distances.

Job Activities

A railroad conductor may do any or all of the following activities:

- Make sure that all passengers on a train are safe and comfortable.

- Collect tickets from passengers riding on a train.

- Meet with other staff on a train to discuss the train's route and the time it is scheduled to depart and arrive.

- Receive information about any equipment problems on another train or on the train rails.

- Arrange for any repairs to be done on the train at the nearest station.

Education/Training Requirements

Railroad conductors are required to have a high school diploma. In addition, they must have good mechanical skills. All job applicants must pass a physical exam and a test that shows they have all the skills necessary for the position.

Think About It

Why do you think railroad conductors should have good mechanical skills?

Chapter

17 ▷ Review

Summary

- Careers in transportation involve moving people and cargo across land and water and through the air. The three main groups of transportation careers are ground, air, and water.

- Most air transportation careers are related to airplanes, and water transportation careers are related to ships. Ground transportation careers are related to moving people or goods across the ground, with or without a vehicle.

- The job trend for careers in transportation between the years 2002 and 2012 is expected to vary. Factors that can affect the number of jobs in transportation include the economy and technology.

- Strengths that people working in transportation have are varied. They include an ability to handle stress and good physical health. Careers in transportation vary in training and education requirements.

air traffic controller

hand packer

pilot

ship engineer

stevedore

tractor-trailor truck driver

Vocabulary Review

Complete each sentence with a term from the list.

1. A person who prepares items for shipment by hand is called a _____.

2. A person who loads and unloads ships is called a _____.

3. A person who flies airplanes is called a _____.

4. A person who manages the movement of airplanes from the ground is called an _____.

5. A _____ is a person who maintains the engines, boilers, and other machinery on a ship.

6. A _____ is a person who drives a large vehicle used to transport goods.

Chapter Quiz

Write your answers in complete sentences.

1. What are three main groups of careers in transportation?

2. To which transportation career group do air traffic controllers belong?

3. A person in which type of occupation might unload new cars from a cargo ship?

4. What is one factor that can affect the number of jobs in transportation?

5. Why do tractor-trailer truck drivers need to know how to read a map?

6. What is one way to learn more about careers in transportation?

CRITICAL THINKING

7. Why would knowing about the weather help an air traffic controller?

8. Why do some material-moving jobs require experience?

Career Portfolio Project

Suppose that you find a summer job packing boxes at a local shipping company. You notice that many small items are being packed in larger, more expensive boxes. You think that the company could save money if it used the correct size box for each item. Write a memo to your supervisor explaining what you have observed. Be sure to tell the supervisor how and why you think the company can save money.

Unit 3 Review

Choose the letter of the best answer to each question.

1. What do people who have careers in agriculture usually work with?
   A. goods and services
   B. children and elderly people
   C. food
   D. crops and livestock

2. What is one factor that will cause the number of jobs in construction trades to increase between the years 2002 and 2012?
   A. They are fun jobs that a lot of people want.
   B. There will be a need for new housing and house repairs.
   C. Companies are moving their factories to other countries.
   D. The use of robots at construction sites.

3. Why is it difficult to become a professional athlete?
   A. There are too many injuries involved.
   B. There is too much competition.
   C. Professional athletes do not have enough talent.
   D. The professional athlete only plays sports on weekends.

4. In what kinds of settings can you find healthcare careers?
   A. in ambulances
   B. in doctors' offices
   C. in hospitals
   D. all of the above

5. Why do people with careers in technology need to know how to follow instructions and read manuals?
   A. Instructions and manuals give them the information they need.
   B. They want new jobs.
   C. Their managers told them to.
   D. They will not get paid otherwise.

6. Why is it important for pilots to be well-trained?
   A. They have no one to help them.
   B. Pilots have a lot of responsibility.
   C. They may want to become air traffic controllers.
   D. none of the above

Critical Thinking

What are some ways to learn more about a career?

Unit 4

Career Preparation

Before You Read

In this unit, you will learn how to plan your career and get started finding the right job.

Before you start reading, ask yourself these questions:

1. What are some important steps in career planning?
2. Why should I stay in school?
3. How do I find jobs that are right for me?

A job in a restaurant is a possible first step toward a career in the food industry.

Learning Objectives

- Describe four steps that can be used to help choose a career.
- Set short-term career objectives and a long-term career goal.
- Describe how to stay focused on a career plan.
- List four ways to get work experience.

Chapter 18 | Making a Career Plan

Words to Know

career plan	an outline of what a person wants to achieve with a career, including details of ways to reach a career goal and a timeline
career objective	one step toward meeting a long-term career goal
recommendation	a positive statement that tells that a person is qualified for a job
reference	the name of a person who will provide a statement that describes another person's character or job responsibilities
internship	an on-the-job learning and training experience
mentor	an experienced person who helps and advises a person with less experience
protégé	a person who is guided or helped by a more experienced person
job shadowing	going to a workplace to learn about the daily activities of a person who does the job every day by following that person on the job

Making a career plan is an important step. A **career plan** is an outline of what you want to achieve with a career. It may include details of how and when you hope to achieve your career goal.

An important part of career planning is figuring out how to get experience. Employers like to hire workers who have worked elsewhere.

Experience of any type can be useful, especially for students. On page 240, you will read a conversation between Ethan and a friend about getting work experience. Ethan was looking for summer work. He had just filled out a job application at an auto body shop.

"I really don't know why I'm bothering," Ethan said to his friend Keisha. "Even if I do get the job, it has nothing to do with my career plans."

"What career are you planning?" asked Keisha.

"I want a career in food service," said Ethan. "I like cooking and working with people. I applied for a job at a few restaurants, but I don't have experience."

"Well," Keisha said, "If you were to work at a restaurant, you would have to talk to lots of people, get to work on time, and work well with others, right?"

"Yes, but so what?" Ethan answered.

"Well, you would probably be doing those things at an auto body shop."

Ethan agreed, "I suppose working at almost any job is a way to get experience."

Making a Career Choice

Remember
Lifestyle is the way in which a person lives. Different things affect a person's lifestyle, including where a person lives and works, salary, and family commitments.

You read in earlier chapters why career planning should be important to you. You identified your strengths, made lifestyle choices, and did research. You will learn more about getting work experience later in this chapter. Now, it is time to make a career choice. Here are the first four steps toward doing that:

STEP 1 **Match possible careers to your strengths and lifestyle choices.**

Narrow your choices to two or three careers that you think might suit you. Trust yourself to be able to make a good career choice. Remember that nobody knows you as well as you do.

STEP 2   **Make a chart.**

Make a chart like the one Ethan made below. At the top of the page, write your two career choices. Then, list what you want from a career. Be specific. Include such things as where you want to live. Complete the chart by writing an *X* beside what you will get with each career choice. Write an *O* beside what you will not get.

What I Want From a Career	Chef	Banquet Manager
Learn skills on the job.	X	X
Work with food.	X	X
Cook food.	X	O
Meet new people.	O	X
Work in San Francisco, California.	X	X
Eventually work in a large hotel or restaurant.	X	X
Make at least $18,000 my first year.	X	X

STEP 3   **Weigh choices based on your values.**

Weighing choices means comparing what makes something appealing and what makes something unappealing. Ethan saw that if he was a chef, his contact with new people would be limited. He would probably see the same kitchen staff every day. For Ethan, the drawback to being a banquet manager was that he would not be cooking.

STEP 4   **Make the choice.**

Ethan decided that it was more important to him to meet and work with new people. He decided to become a banquet manager. Ethan knew that later, he might want to change his plan. Still, he was glad to have set a direction for himself.

Write About It

Write a story about a typical day on the job in the career you have chosen. Include how your day begins, how busy you are, what the people you work with are like, and what assignments you might be handling. Have at least one "crisis" occur on that day. Tell how you handle that crisis.

✓ Check Your Understanding

Write your answers in complete sentences.

1. What is a career plan?
2. What is the first step in making a career plan?
3. What does it mean to weigh career choices based on your values?

Setting a Long-Term Goal

After you have made a career choice, it is time to make a career plan. A career plan is an outline of what you want and how and when you will get it.

Begin your career plan by setting a long-term career goal. A career goal is a statement of what you want to achieve and when you want to achieve it. Make your goal realistic. Set yourself up to succeed, not to fail. Here are three examples of long-term career goals:

Career Trend

The food-service industry is expected to be one of the fastest-growing industries between the years 2002 and 2012. The number of jobs is expected to increase by 15.9 percent during this time period.

- "I will be a banquet manager at a large hotel in San Francisco, California, in the next 5 years."

- "I will be a radio sportscaster in Miami, Florida, in 6 years."

- "I will be a self-employed plumber working in my hometown in 10 years. My income will be $40,000 per year."

Notice that these goals are stated as "I will be," not as "I want to be." Writing the goal in this way will help you keep a positive attitude. Each goal also includes the time by which the goal is to be achieved. Long-term goals may also include where a person wants to work or the salary he or she expects to earn. The more details you include, the easier it will be to know when you have reached your goal. Remember, too, that you can always change your mind!

Short-Term Career Objectives

When you know where you want to go in your career, you must plan how to get there. You do this by setting short-term career objectives. **Career objectives** are steps that will help you meet your long-term career goal. They are ways to gain the skills, knowledge, and experiences your chosen career requires. Like your career goal, career objectives should be detailed and include target dates.

Here are some examples of short-term career objectives:

- Get an *A* in my health class.

- Volunteer at a nursing home this summer.

- Get a part-time job as a sales clerk to learn customer service skills.

Review Ethan's career plan below. His long-term career goal is to be a banquet manager at a large hotel in 5 years. As he completes each career objective, he will be one step closer to his long-term career goal.

Career Objective	Date to be Completed
Take home economics and business math courses in high school and get *B*s or better.	December 2006
Apply to a food-service management training program at a community college.	January 2008
Graduate from high school with good grades.	June 2008
Get a part-time food-service job in a large hotel in San Francisco, California.	July 2008
Begin a food-service management training program.	September 2008
Complete the food-service management training program.	May 2010
Get a job as an assistant banquet manager.	July 2010
Apply for banquet manager jobs.	October 2011

Staying Focused

Following your career plan can be hard work. Here are four things you can do to stay focused:

1. **Write your career plan and keep it where you can see it.**

   Hang it up in your room or inside your locker at school. Look at your plan often as a reminder. When you meet an objective, cross it off.

2. **Put off what you want now in return for future rewards.**

   This action is called "delayed gratification." For example, instead of playing ball after school, you decide to work at a part-time job.

3. **Be flexible.**

   As you grow and experience new things, your values and goals will probably change. As they do, change your career plan.

4. **See problems as challenges.**

   It is easy to make excuses when things do not go right. However, excuses will not get you where you want to go. Think about these examples. Ludwig von Beethoven, who was deaf, wrote music. The African American athlete Wilma Rudolph overcame crippling polio as a child. In 1960, she became the first American woman to win three gold medals in track in the Olympic games. These people met their challenges with courage and drive. When problems arise in your life, try to do the same.

✓ Check Your Understanding

Write your answers in complete sentences.

1. What is an example of a career goal?

2. What is an example of a career objective?

3. What does it mean to "delay gratification?"

Getting Experience

If you have ever applied for a job, you have been asked, "What experience do you have?" Employers ask this question because they like to hire people with experience.

Quite often, employers ask for recommendations. A **recommendation** is a positive written or spoken statement that tells that someone is qualified for a job. It lets an employer know that a worker has done well in the past. The worker can therefore be expected to do well in the future. A recommendation is similar to a reference. A **reference** is the name of a person who will provide a written or spoken statement that tells what qualifications a person has for a job or describes his or her character. When you give someone's name as a reference, an employer will call or e-mail the person and ask questions about you.

How can you get experience if you are just starting in a career? Sometimes, you can get jobs that do not require any experience. "First jobs" include babysitting, dogwalking, and working in restaurants.

Even first jobs can be hard to get, though. However, there are three other ways for a young person to get experience. A brief discussion of each of these follows.

Internships

Heather is doing an internship at a local radio station. An **internship** is an on-the-job learning and training experience. Heather spends 2 hours a day after school there. She has many job duties. These duties include taking calls and answering mail from listeners. In exchange, Heather learns how the radio station operates.

Career Fact

First jobs are good jobs to have while you are still in school. They help you develop skills, gain experience, and earn some money. Your employers can give you recommendations for later jobs, too.

Using Technology

The Web site of the Congressional Youth Leadership Council, www.cycl.org, lists internship opportunities for the Washington, D.C., area. Most of these internships are for college students or adults.

Heather also meets people who have careers in radio. She hopes that these contacts will someday help her find a job.

Most interns, or people like Heather who do internships, are high school or college students. The work can be part time or full time, and is sometimes unpaid. Many internships are offered during the summer months.

To receive an internship, you will have to apply for it, much as you apply for a job. Usually, you must apply at least four to six months before the work is to begin. The application will probably ask why you want the internship. One reason might be that being an intern is one objective in your career plan.

Mentoring Programs

Mentoring programs are different from internships. In a mentoring program, an experienced person, the **mentor**, is paired with a less experienced person, the **protégé**. The mentor becomes an adviser to his or her protégé. The mentor may provide advice, job contacts, or tutoring. The mentor and protégé decide together which activities suit their strengths and needs.

Did You Know

The Black Achievers Program is a mentoring program. One of its goals is to help inner-city youth from grades 7 to 12 finish school. Mentors in this program also help their protégés get job experience.

One of the best-known mentoring programs is Big Brothers Big Sisters of America. In this program, an adult works with a young person to provide support. The Big Brother or Big Sister also acts as a role model for the younger person.

You may want to join a mentoring program either as a mentor or as a protégé. If you join as a protégé, decide what you want from your mentor before you join. If you become a mentor, make sure you join a program that provides training. Mentors must know how to listen well, give support and advice, and help their protégés achieve. In most cases, mentors are not paid.

Some mentors provide help with schoolwork.

Volunteering

Volunteers are unpaid workers. They are hired by many organizations. Hospitals, clinics, schools, places of worship, animal shelters, and homeless shelters are just a few of the places where volunteers work.

Review your career plan. If you are thinking of a health career, perhaps nursing homes in your area could use your help. If you like to work with animals, there are many animal shelters that hire volunteers. Projects that build community housing offer volunteer opportunities to those interested in the construction trades.

How do you find a place to volunteer? In the front of many telephone books is a section called "Community Services Numbers." The services listed there often need volunteers. You can also check the Internet or your school's guidance office or career resource center.

Call any organizations that interest you. Be clear about the kind of work you want to do and the days and hours you can work. Also, ask about volunteer training. First-time volunteers should get training in how to perform their jobs.

Career Fact

The Volunteers of America has more than 41,000 volunteers plus 12,000 paid employees. It provides about 100 different kinds of services and helps more than 1.7 million people each year.

For more information about where and how to volunteer, go to the Volunteers of America Web site at www.voa.org. At this Web site, you can find information about volunteering opportunities in many different career fields.

✓ Check Your Understanding

Write your answers in complete sentences.

1. What are recommendations used for?

2. What is a mentor?

3. Why would you ask a volunteer organization if it offers training?

Learn More About It

SCHOOL TO WORK

School to work (STW) is a phrase that has been around since the early 1990s. In 1994, President Bill Clinton signed the School-to-Work Opportunities Act into law. The goal of this law is to help students better connect what they learn in school with what they will earn on the job. Since that time, many different STW programs have been created.

One important activity that grew out of STW programs is **job shadowing**. Job shadowing is going to a workplace and following someone around who actually does the job every day. The purpose of job shadowing is to learn more about a job. STW also includes learning about different careers while you are still in school and how to interview for a job. Speakers may come to schools to tell what they do, students may go on company tours, and some students may even try out different jobs while still in school.

For more information on school-to-work programs in your area, go to the Jobs for the Future Web site at www.jff.org.

CRITICAL THINKING What can you learn by shadowing someone at a job?

JOB DESCRIPTION
Chef

Job Summary
A chef works in a kitchen preparing meals for people. The kitchen may be in a restaurant, school, university, hospital, or nursing home. A chef usually manages food preparation workers who help peel and cut vegetables, make sauces, and do other duties in the kitchen.

Most of a chef's time is spent working in a kitchen. Working conditions can vary, depending upon the type of kitchen a chef is working in. Chefs usually stand for most of the day. They may also lift heavy pots and work near hot stoves. A chef often has to work early mornings, late nights, and weekends. Full-time and part-time positions are available.

Work Activities
A chef may do any or all of the following activities:

- Measure, mix, and cook ingredients according to recipes.

- Manage and direct other staff in the kitchen.

- Plan meals and menus.

- Shop for or order food supplies.

- Create new recipes.

Education/Training Requirements
Some employers require a high school diploma or previous work experience. Many chefs train at cooking schools. Some chefs start out as short-order cooks. Short-order cooks prepare foods in restaurants that serve food quickly. After short-order cooks have learned some skills, they can move up to higher positions. It usually takes many years of training and experience to become a chef at a well-known restaurant.

Think About It
Why do you think many chefs have to work early mornings?

Summary

- A career plan outlines what a person wants to achieve with a career. It also includes details of how and when he or she will achieve the career goal.

- A long-term career goal is a positive statement of the job a person wants to have and when he or she wants to have it. Most long-term career goals look 5 to 10 years into the future.

- A short-term career objective is a single step toward meeting a person's long-term career goal.

- Employers like to hire workers who have experience. To get experience, young people can apply for "first jobs," such as dogwalking, that require little or no experience.

- Internships, mentoring programs, and volunteer programs are other ways to get experience.

career objective

career plan

internship

mentor

recommendation

Vocabulary Review

Complete each sentence with a term from the list.

1. Each _____ is a step toward meeting a long-term career goal.

2. A positive written or spoken _____ is a statement that someone is qualified for a job.

3. When you make a _____, you are outlining what you want to achieve in your work life and how long it will take you to achieve your career goal.

4. One type of on-the-job learning and training experience is called an _____.

5. A _____ is someone who helps and advises someone who is less experienced than himself or herself.

Chapter Quiz

Write your answers in complete sentences.

1. Where should you keep your career plan?

2. List three "first jobs" that do not usually require a person to have experience.

3. Why do employers ask if you have experience?

4. How do employers check to see if a job applicant was a good worker in past jobs?

5. What is an internship?

6. What are three good places to volunteer?

CRITICAL THINKING

7. Why should values play a role in a career choice?

8. Which do you feel would help you most with your long-term career goal—an internship, mentoring, or a volunteer program? Explain why.

Career Portfolio Project

By now you should have a career plan in place. In a three-ring binder, divide the pages so that each of your short-term career objectives gets its own section. Put in your binder information you collect from Web sites, magazines, newspapers, interviews—anything that could help you learn how to achieve your objectives. This information may be names of contacts, data, and names of organizations or companies you are interested in. Include a section toward the back of your binder called "General Research." Place your career plans or goals at the beginning of the binder.

The skills you learn in your classes, such as working as a group, can be useful in many different jobs.

Learning Objectives

- Identify two ways in which high school can help a person prepare for a career.
- Tell how to develop a positive self-image and attitude.
- Describe what time management is.
- List high school classes that can help build career skills.

Chapter 19 ▶ Skill-Building in School

Words to Know

self-image	how you feel about yourself
attitude	a way of acting, thinking, or feeling that shows a person's true nature
pre-employment tests	exams given by possible employers that may test your skills, your personality, or your attitudes
positive self-talk	replacing negative thoughts with positive ones
feedback	a reaction from someone about what you have done or how you have performed at something
time management	learning to use time well
procrastinate	to put off doing things without a good reason
communications skill	a skill that involves sharing information
language arts skill	a communications skill using writing, reading, or speaking
proficiency	being able to do something well

Emilio sat in history class trying to listen to Mr. Hays talk about the Civil War. Soon, however, Emilio's eyes began to close. Then, his head fell on the desk with a bang.

Startled, Emilio awoke to find the whole class laughing. Mr. Hays said, "Emilio, please stay after class. I want to talk to you." When class ended, Emilio stayed behind. Read the conversation between Emilio and Mr. Hays, which follows on page 254.

"This is the third time this month that you've fallen asleep in class," Mr. Hays said. "Are you having any trouble?"

"No," Emilio said. "I took a job after school. I'm helping a friend of my father's build a room in his house. I get home late, which is why I am tired in school. I think I want to work as a builder after high school. What use is history class to me, anyway?"

"A general comes up with battle plans," Mr. Hays said. "A builder plans houses. In some ways, those plans are alike. In some ways, they are different. Think about that."

That night, Emilio read about Civil War battle plans. History began to look a little more meaningful to him.

High School and Your Career

In Chapter 2, you read that high school graduates usually earn more money than people who drop out of school. This fact is one of many good reasons to stay in school. As Emilio learned, high school can also help you prepare for a career. In school, you can explore your interests and aptitudes. Music, art, writing, debate, and sports can all help you learn about yourself and help you to choose a career. Most importantly, high school is a time to gain knowledge and build skills.

Remember
Hard skills are skills related to a specific job or task. Knowing how to operate a cash register is a hard skill. Soft skills are more general skills that can apply to many different jobs.

Applicants who have good skills will have a better chance of getting a job than those who do not have good skills. Good skills include technical, or hard, skills as well as the soft skills you learned about in Chapter 3. In high school, you should begin to prepare yourself for a career. Your first task is to look at how you feel about yourself.

The Importance of Self-Image

Your **self-image** is your view of yourself. Self-image is made up of two things: self-esteem and self-confidence. Self-esteem is thinking of yourself as having value. Self-confidence is trusting in yourself.

Training yourself to have a positive self-image is very important for your career. People with a positive self-image usually show a positive attitude. An **attitude** is a way of acting, thinking, or feeling that shows a person's true nature. People with a positive attitude look for the good in what happens. They think things will work out right.

Many companies today give pre-employment tests. **Pre-employment tests** may judge your skills, your personality, or even your attitudes. Some tests try to see how you would react to different situations. Other tests examine your outlook on life.

You have the power to change your attitude. Here is how you can develop a positive attitude:

1. Before you go to sleep at night, focus on one positive event in the day. It could be something you learned or a fun time you had with a friend.

2. When you wake up in the morning, think of the good things that will happen to you that day. Throughout the day, keep these positive thoughts in mind.

3. Another way to improve your self-image is through **positive self-talk**, or replacing negative thoughts with positive ones. Your thinking has a strong effect on your behavior. You may not be able to stop thinking negative thoughts altogether. However, trying to replace negative thoughts with positive ones will make a difference.

4. Ask people for positive feedback. **Feedback** is a reaction from someone about how you have performed at something.

Did You Know ?

Most of the messages people give themselves are negative messages. When presented with a problem, they may think, "I am not smart enough to solve this."

Career Trend

Employers today look for workers with a positive attitude. Positive people enjoy their work. Their co-workers find them easy to be around. They usually see problems as opportunities rather than as barriers.

Another way to change your attitude is to look for the positive side of not-so-positive events. A poor grade on a test or a defeat in a basketball game at school are all opportunities to learn something.

Use situations like these to develop a positive attitude. For example, tell yourself that you will do better on the next test or that during the next basketball game you will score more points.

Managing Time Well

Write About It

Make a list of all the usual activities you do in a week. Then, place each activity in a daily slot on a calendar. Now, you have a schedule for an average week. Label each activity as *Must Do* (MD), *Routine Task* (RT), or *If There Is Time* (IFT).

To achieve the career goals you have set for yourself, you will need to learn time management. **Time management** means learning to use your time well. Using time well is a critical workplace skill. Employers want workers who show up regularly, who are on time, and who get their work done on time.

How do you develop the skill of time management? Begin by recording how you use your time right now. Keep a diary of what you do on an average day. You could find that you spend 4 hours each day in front of the television. Or, you might be spending 2 hours on the telephone. Having some time to relax—"downtime"—is a good thing. However, you may have to cut down on this amount of time to meet your career goals.

Next, set your goals and objectives for school. One goal could be to try to get good grades in all your classes this year. Another goal might be to join a club. An objective could be to be complete homework each day before playing video games or watching television.

When people **procrastinate**, they put off doing things without a good reason. People procrastinate for many reasons. Perhaps a goal is not realistic or seems too far off. A part of managing your time well is to not procrastinate.

Time Management Tips

- Set aside time for homework. Schedule at least 1 to 2 hours for homework at the same time each day. Ask for help with big projects or difficult schoolwork.

- Make to-do lists. Check off tasks as they get done.

- Reward yourself after you have completed a difficult project or homework assignment. Give yourself small rewards, such as 15 minutes of extra downtime or a new CD.

- Do not expect perfection from yourself. Set reasonable goals, so you do not set yourself up for failure.

- Learn to say no, especially to people who ask you to do too many tasks. Also, do not change plans that you have made just because you do not want to turn someone down.

- Learn to prioritize. Plan to complete each of your tasks or chores in order of importance.

- Combine several activities to be done at the same time. For example, while heading to school, listen to taped notes. This practice allows up to an hour or two a day of good study review. While you are showering, make a mental list of the things that need to be done. As you listen to music, make up your next day's to-do list.

✓ Check Your Understanding

Write your answers in complete sentences.

1. What are some ways high school can help you prepare for a career?

2. What is a positive attitude?

3. Why is setting unreasonable goals for yourself damaging?

Building Communications Skills

There are many possible careers in the field of communications. Advertising and public relations, broadcast media, speech therapy, news directing, and technical writing are just a few. Many colleges and vocational schools offer programs in communications.

Almost every employer wants workers who have good communications skills. **Communications skills** involve sharing information with others. A stock clerk communicates when writing down the number of items in a warehouse. A salesperson communicates with customers when telling them about a product.

High school language arts classes are good places to build communications skills. **Language arts skills** are communications skills that use reading, writing, or speaking. Writing classes teach you how to organize written information. Reading novels, poems, and essays teaches you how to understand and apply written ideas and information. Speech classes teach you how to present information aloud in a clear, entertaining way.

Many schools offer fun ways to build different communications skills. Students on debate teams learn how to argue a point. Students on school newspapers write stories about school events. In school plays, student actors learn to entertain an audience.

Performing in a school play is a way to improve your communications skills, such as speaking in front of a group.

Building Math Skills

Basic math skills are also needed for just about every job. A nurse's aide counts a pulse for 10 seconds. She then multiplies the number by 6 to find a patient's heartbeats per minute. A drywall installer measures the square footage of a room to decide how much building material to buy. Workers also need math skills to make sure that their paychecks are correct.

Most high schools require students to pass a basic math proficiency test. **Proficiency** means "being able to do something well." Basic math proficiency tests check that students know how to add, subtract, multiply, and divide. They may also test the ability to use calculators and computers to do math.

For a career in technology, advanced math classes are helpful. Some high schools offer classes in business math. In a business math course, you can learn about investments and taxes, how to read charts and graphs, and how money is managed by banks. Business math is especially helpful for those people who want sales careers or careers working in the finance departments of companies. Owners of small businesses also find business math helpful.

Classes and Activities for Chosen Careers

Megan wants to be a nurse. She takes health and biology classes. Ian wants to run for political office someday. He takes history and government classes. He also runs for student office. Tanya wants to be a graphic designer. She takes art classes.

Career research includes learning how to prepare for a career. Your school counselor can direct you to those classes that match your career goals.

Using Technology

There are many classes available for people who want to study either business math or business writing. The American Management Association (AMA) is one group that offers these courses. To find out what is available from the AMA, go to www.amanet.org.

✓ **Check Your Understanding**

Write your answers in complete sentences.

1. What is self-image?

2. Why is learning how to manage your time well an important skill to learn?

3. Why should everyone who earns a paycheck have basic math skills?

Learn More About It

SCANS

In the early 1990s, the U.S. government created the Secretary's Commission on Achieving Necessary Skills, or SCANS. The purpose of SCANS was to identify the skills young people need to succeed in the workplace. Other tasks were to suggest ways to prepare students to become highly skilled workers and to share the group's findings with schools, businesses, and the public.

During the SCANS research, information was gathered from different sources. Workers and managers in shops, plants, and stores in many industries were interviewed. The SCANS published its work in a report called "What Work Requires of Schools: A SCANS Report for America 2000."

The report contains a detailed list of important workplace skills. SCANS skills include reading, writing, and math. They also include thinking skills, such as decision making, problem solving, and reasoning. Leadership skills and teamwork are also part of SCANS. Many of the skills we have talked about in this chapter are SCANS skills. To find a complete listing of the skills and how they are broken down, you can visit the U.S. Department of Labor at wdr.doleta.gov/SCANS.

CRITICAL THINKING Why would decision making be a SCANS skill?

JOB DESCRIPTION
Bookkeeper

Job Summary
A bookkeeper is responsible for the financial records of a company. He or she keeps track of money that comes into and goes out of a business. Most bookkeepers record this information using a computer. A bookkeeper is also responsible for keeping the financial records of a company up-to-date.

Most bookkeepers work in an office. They spend a lot of time on a computer. Bookkeepers usually work normal business hours. Overtime work may be required during busy times of the year, such as when tax forms are sent out to employees. Part-time and full-time jobs are available.

Work Activities
A bookkeeper may do any or all of the following activities:

- Record expenses and income.

- Keep track of company accounts, especially accounts where money is due.

- Prepare financial statements.

- Prepare reports for managers.

- Use computers or special books called ledgers to calculate and record data.

- Calculate pay for employees.

Education/Training Requirements
Most employers require bookkeepers to have at least a high school diploma. Some employers require courses in accounting, business, or finance. Some employers will provide on-the-job training. Most employers require good math, communications, and computer skills.

Think About It

What do you think are the most important tasks a bookkeeper does?

Summary

- To prepare for careers, students should use high school to discover their interests and aptitudes. High school is also an important time for gaining knowledge and developing important career skills.

- Getting and keeping a positive attitude is an important skill. Work on a positive attitude by focusing on successes and seeing the good side of things. Use positive self-talk to improve your self-image.

- Learning how to manage time can help you in school and at work. Keep track of how you use time now. Set objectives for what you want to achieve in school. Avoid letting procrastination become a bad habit. Change the way you use your time to meet your objectives.

- Communications skills are needed on almost every job. Language arts classes help build reading, writing, and speaking skills. School activities such as acting, debating, and writing for the school paper can also be helpful.

- All workers need at least basic math skills. Students who want technical careers should also take advanced math classes as well as learn computer skills. Business math is helpful for many careers.

communications skill
positive self-talk
procrastinate
proficiency
self-image

Vocabulary Review

Complete each sentence with a term from the list.

1. To _____ means to put off doing things without a good reason.

2. Having _____ means being able to do something well.

3. A skill that involves sharing information is a _____.

4. Your _____ is how you feel about yourself.

5. A technique called _____ involves replacing negative thoughts with positive ones.

Chapter Quiz

Write your answers in complete sentences.

1. What is one way that high school can help a person prepare for a career?

2. What two things make up a positive self-image?

3. What is one way to develop a positive attitude?

4. Why do employers like to hire people with good time management skills?

5. What is the first step in managing time?

6. What communications skills are learned in language arts classes?

CRITICAL THINKING

7. What are some skills that can be developed by working on the school yearbook?

8. Why would a business math class be helpful for the owner of a business?

Career Portfolio Project

List two bad habits you have that could prevent you from becoming successful in your work life. Do you have a poor self-image? Are you always late for school? Do you daydream away your free time? Are you lacking good communications skills?

Make a plan for doing something about one of your bad habits now. Write your plan in your Career Portfolio. Include when you will achieve your goal. Continue making up a weekly calendar, like the one you did for the Write About It assignment on page 256. Be sure to stick to your written plan. Review your plan after 3 weeks. Write a paragraph that describes how well you did.

Looking for a job should be considered a job itself. Plan to spend a certain number of hours each day on your job search.

Learning Objectives

- List five ways to make a job search successful.
- Explain how to find job possibilities using personal contacts.
- Describe how to find job possibilities using published resources.
- Discuss how to find job possibilities using employment offices.
- Explain how to find job possibilities using the Internet.

Chapter 20 ► Searching for Jobs

Words to Know

job prospect	a future possibility of employment
networking	being in touch with a wide variety of people, called contacts, who can pass along information on job opportunities to you
directory	a published resource that lists information for a certain area or subject
trade magazine	a magazine that contains articles about a particular industry
blind ad	an ad in which the name of the hiring company is not given
alumni	students who have graduated from a school; former students

Two high school friends talked about searching for jobs after graduation. Here is their conversation.

"To find a job, I guess I should look in the local newspapers," Chloe said. "They have job ads for people to do all kinds of work."

"Not all the job openings are in the newspapers," Zach replied. "There must be other ways of finding jobs."

"Well, I know that there are employment agencies. You can also look on the Internet," Chloe told Zach.

"Do you know anyone who found a job through the Internet?" Zach asked.

"Not really," Chloe said. "We should ask the guidance counselors at school. They might know of some other ways to find jobs."

The Job Search

There are very few, if any, sure ways of finding a job. However, there are many ways to find jobs other than the ways Chloe and Zach talked about.

As you begin your job search, you should have a good idea of your interests, aptitudes, and goals. Clear goals and objectives are important for a successful job search. You should also know your priorities. Finally, you should have a few career choices.

Soon, perhaps, you will be looking for a job. How prepared are you for planning and carrying out a successful job search? How do you find opportunities that meet your needs and fit your talents? Here are five things to think about as you begin your job search:

1. **Finding job possibilities is hard work.**

   A **job prospect** is a future possibility of employment. Looking for job prospects takes time and energy. Job seekers must have good job-hunting skills.

   A rewarding career is one that suits you. Keep your goals in mind at all times!

2. **Take time to learn as much as you can about your chosen career.**

   Review your career research and career plan before searching for a job. Decide which jobs will best match your strengths and desires. Review your lifestyle choices as well. Think about the working conditions that appeal to you. Aim for a realistic starting salary.

   You learned about trade unions earlier. If the trade you are interested in has a union, find out how to become a member. Ask a union official about any training programs the union offers. In some industries, all employees are, or must become, union members.

Career Fact

Some experts recommend that you begin an active job search 6 to 9 months before the date you hope to be employed. Begin your job search by talking to career or school counselors.

3. **Be realistic about how long it takes to find a job.**

Surveys show that the average time it takes to find a job is between 12 and 24 weeks. In 2003, the average time to find a new job was about 18 weeks. If you start out knowing this, you are less likely to become discouraged. There is one possible way to shorten the overall search length, however. Most job seekers spend only about 5 to 7 hours a week searching for jobs. The more hours you spend looking for a job, the sooner you will find one.

4. **Prepare a personal data sheet with all your employment-related information.**

This sheet will make filling out any employment applications easier and can be used to prepare a special form that you will send to possible employers.

5. **The more resources you use to find a job, the more likely you are to be successful.**

If, for example, you look in the newspaper job ads and ask friends about job openings, you are more likely to find a job than someone who only looks in the newspaper. Keep this in mind when searching for jobs. Make use of every opportunity.

Did You Know ?

Many job hunters give up looking for a job because it can take a long time. Those people who give up are not counted in the unemployment rate reported by the federal government.

Where to Learn About Job Openings

What are some different ways to find jobs? The following chart shows the most useful ways:

Different Ways to Find Jobs	
• Personal contacts	• Labor unions
• School career offices	• Private employment agencies
• Employers	• Community agencies
• Newspaper job ads, professional journals, and trade magazines and newsletters	• Local bulletin boards in shopping centers, churches, and community centers
• The Internet	• Teachers and school administrators
• State and federal government offices	• Former students

Did You Know ?

Nearly 80 percent of job openings are not advertised. Most employers find enough applicants without advertising. Also, most employers prefer to hire people whose names were given to them by someone they know.

The most popular way to find a job is by responding to job ads—also called the help wanted or classified ads. These ads are found in newspapers and other printed sources. However, looking at job ads is not the most effective way to find a job. The way most people actually find a job is by contacting people who can help them. You should spend the most time putting together a list of these people.

Networking to Find Jobs

A network is a group of connected individuals or items. Individuals in a network cooperate and share information. **Networking**, in the world of work, is being in touch with a wide group of individuals, called personal contacts. These personal contacts can share job information with you.

Personal contacts can help you find a job by providing names of people who may be aware of job openings, giving advice, or writing recommendations. They may also help people learn on the job. People need to work together for a business to run smoothly. Success in the business world often depends on the networks you build with others.

How do you go about networking? The first step is to make a list of all the people you know. Include friends and family members, teachers, neighbors, local store owners, and old friends.

Remember

An informational interview is an interview you set up to gather information from someone who has a job or career that you are interested in.

Review the career research you have already done. Did the people you held informational interviews with tell you about any companies that might have open job positions? Did they give you the names of any other people you might be able to contact? If not, try calling these people again. Tell them you are ready to look for work. Ask if they have any job leads for you.

When you are ready to actively seek work, begin by making telephone calls. When you call, explain who you are and why you are calling. Tell what kind of work you are looking for. You can also write letters or send e-mails, but these methods are not as effective as telephoning. Keep a log or record of your efforts.

While making telephone calls, do not ask for a job. If there is one available, the person you are calling will probably tell you about it. Ask the person if he or she can provide you with information. For example, what is currently important in that industry? What companies in the area does he or she know of? Can the person give you the names of anyone who can help you with your job search?

Keep notes on all the responses that you receive. Also, ask your contacts to stay in touch with you if a job that might be right for you becomes available. Be sure to give the person either your telephone number or your e-mail address. Politely thank the person for his or her time and help.

Do not give up on networking after a few weeks have passed. Try to contact everyone you know or whose name you have been given. Wait a few weeks and then call your original contacts again. Remember, networking is very important in the world of work. Everyone networks at some time in his or her career.

> **Write About It**
> Make a list of at least 10 people who could be part of your network. Write a short paragraph about what you would say when you telephone them.

✓ Check Your Understanding

Write your answers in complete sentences.

1. What is a personal data sheet?

2. What do most people think is the best way to find work?

3. In a job search, what does it mean to network?

Using Published Resources

Before you begin your job search, you should make a list of possible employers. As your job search progresses, you will continually add to this list.

A public library is an excellent place to find the names of companies that may have job openings. Libraries contain a wide variety of published resources that can be used to find jobs. Specific resources include the telephone book, Chamber of Commerce listings, employer profiles, industry guides, and newspapers. Jordan, for example, wants to be a television scriptwriter. He went to his local library and found a book called *Jobs for Writers*. It described writing careers and places to apply. Jordan applied for jobs at some of the companies listed in the book.

Libraries also have directories that can be very useful in job hunting. **Directories** list professional groups, schools, and employment resources. Some of these directories may also provide names of people who can be contacts for your networking list.

The most popular printed resources used by job seekers are help wanted ads. Help wanted ads appear in newspapers and trade magazines. A **trade magazine** is a magazine that contains articles about a particular industry or business. Professional journals and trade newsletters may also contain help wanted ads for jobs.

Most ads for jobs give job titles and brief job descriptions. They may include the skills and experience the employer wants. Sometimes, the ads give information about income and hours as well. The ads also tell you how and where to apply for the jobs.

Some ads are blind ads. **Blind ads** are ads in which an address, a telephone number, or an e-mail address is given but the name of the employer is not.

Career Trend

In recent years, the Internet has become a major resource for job seekers. However, the career information available through the Internet is almost the same as what is available through most libraries and career centers.

Help wanted ads are usually listed in alphabetical order by job title or job area. For example, jobs for teachers can be found under *education*.

When applying for jobs in help wanted ads, be aware that other job seekers, hundreds—even thousands—of people, may answer the same ad that you do. You should still answer the ads. Just be sure to use other methods of job-searching as well.

Career Fact

When you are job hunting, read the help wanted ads in newspapers every day. Be sure to read them on Sundays. The Sunday edition of a newspaper contains the most help wanted ads.

Contact possible employers listed in newspaper help wanted ads immediately. Most of these jobs are filled quickly.

Another way to find work is through job ads on town bulletin boards. Bulletin boards can be found in libraries, schools, and supermarkets. With this method, you are more likely to find temporary, part-time work, rather than permanent, full-time work. A typical bulletin board could carry ads for babysitters, dog walkers, and gardeners.

A person seeking a job can advertise his or her availability on bulletin boards, too. If you post this type of ad, include the type of work you do, the hours you are available, and a way that you can be contacted. Include the date that you post the ad.

Learn More About It

READING HELP WANTED ADS

To save space, newspaper help wanted ads use many abbreviations, or shortened forms of words. The list below will help you understand what common abbreviations mean.

Abbreviation	Meaning
adm. asst.	administrative assistant (secretarial position)
appt.	appointment
B.A./B.S.	Bachelor of Arts/Bachelor of Science (four-year college degree)
co.	company
emp. agy.	employment agency
EOE	Equal Opportunity Employer
exc. opty.	excellent opportunity
exp'd	experienced
exp. nec.	experience necessary
exp. pref.	experience preferred
exp. req.	experience required
P/T or F/T	part-time or full-time
mgr.	manager
perm.	permanent
Refs req.	references required
sal. reqs.	salary requirements
temp.	temporary
W/P	word processing
$20K–$22K	$20,000 to $22,000 per year salary

CRITICAL THINKING What is the difference between "experience necessary" and "experience preferred"?

Using Employment Offices

Many job seekers use employment offices when searching for jobs. Employment offices have lists of job openings. They usually have employment specialists who help match workers with jobs.

Colleges, vocational schools, and some high schools have employment, or placement, offices. These offices operate free of charge. Usually, only people who have attended the school can use the employment services. School placement offices work hard at placing graduating students and former students, or **alumni**, in jobs. Whenever a student is placed, it helps the school show that it can successfully prepare students for careers.

The state employment service is sometimes called the Job Service. The Job Service operates under the U.S. Department of Labor's Employment and Training Administration (ETA). Local offices are found nationwide and do not charge employers or job seekers a fee. These offices help match job seekers to employers.

There are also private employment agencies. These agencies charge fees to help people find jobs. The fee is paid either by the employer, the employee, or both. Some agencies specialize in listing certain types of jobs. For example, an agency may only list positions for word processors and administrative assistants.

Before using a private agency, review the agency's policies. Ask who pays the fees. Ask about the agency's success rate in finding jobs for people. If possible, talk with someone who has used the agency's services.

Temporary agencies are another source of employment. Many people have found full-time positions in a company by first working there as a temporary employee. Temporary jobs are also an excellent way to build skills and gain experience.

Using Technology

To find the Job Service office nearest you, look in the state government section of a telephone directory under *job service* or *employment*. You can also search the ETA Web site, www.doleta.gov, for specific state Web sites and contacts.

Using the Internet

Most companies and government agencies have Internet sites. These sites provide information about the organizations and their activities. The sites also often include listings of job openings and job application information. To find these sites, use a search engine and the search terms *vocations* or *careers*. You can also use the Internet to identify possible employers, evaluate them, and contact them.

Develop a list of possible employers in your career field by researching on the Internet. Look on these employers' Web sites for lists of job openings. Even if there are no current openings, contact the employer or the company's human resources department to try to set up an informational interview. Directly contacting employers is one of the most successful ways of job hunting.

There are many government Web sites that give job information. For example, America's Job Bank (AJB) is run by the U.S. Department of Labor. AJB lists more than 1 million job openings within the United States on any given day. The AJB Web site is www.ajb.org. For a job with the federal government, you can visit www.usajobs.opm.gov.

Using Technology

Careers.org is a nonprofit group with a Web site containing many links to useful job Web sites. Their address is www.careers.org. You can also try www.job-hunt.org for links to job databases. Many different employers maintain this Web site.

✓ Check Your Understanding

Write your answers in complete sentences.

1. What are two kinds of published resources that you might use to look for help wanted ads?

2. What do state employment agencies charge for their services?

3. What does America's Job Bank do?

JOB DESCRIPTION
Floral Designer

Job Summary
A floral designer is one type of artist. He or she cuts and places live, dried, or artificial flowers into special arrangements using vases, baskets, or other containers. Some of these floral arrangements are sold to customers who visit flower shops or florists. Other arrangements are specially ordered by customers to use at special events, such as weddings. A floral designer also designs wreaths and baskets of flowers and plants.

Some floral designers own their own business. However, most floral designers work in flower shops. Some may work out of their home. Work hours can vary. Floral designers usually work regular hours. Overtime may be required for holidays or special events. Full-time and part-time positions are available.

Work Activities
A floral designer may do any or all of the following activities:

- Arrange flowers for customers.

- Purchase flowers for a flower shop.

- Keep financial records for a flower shop.

- Grow flowers and plants.

- Manage workers in a flower shop.

- Create new designs for floral arrangements.

Education/Training Requirements
Creativity is the key requirement for a job in floral design. Some employers require a high school diploma. Employers also look for people who are willing to learn new skills. Most floral designers learn their skills on the job. Some colleges and vocational schools offer courses in floral design. There are also many adult education classes in floral design.

Think About It

Where can a person learn skills in floral design?

Summary

- Searching for a job takes time, energy, and effort. To make the job search effective, keep your career goals and objectives in mind. Be prepared to spend many weeks or longer on your job search. Use as many job-seeking methods as possible to increase your chances of finding a job.

- Networking is a good way to collect job information and find personal contacts. Tell friends, family, and acquaintances about your job search. Ask the people you did informational interviews with for job ideas.

- There are many published resources that can provide job information. These include books and directories from a library and help wanted ads in newspapers and trade magazines.

- Employment agencies try to match workers with jobs. School placement offices and state employment offices provide this service for free. Private employment agencies charge fees paid by the employer, the employee, or both.

- The Internet is another helpful resource for job hunting. You can use it to locate possible employers and find job openings.

blind ad

directory

job prospect

networking

trade magazine

Vocabulary Review

Complete each sentence with a term from the list.

1. A _____ is a published resource that lists information for a certain area or subject.

2. When you do _____, you are in touch with a wide variety of people, called contacts, who can pass job information on to you.

3. A future possibility of employment is called a _____.

4. You would look in a _____ for articles about a particular industry.

5. A _____ is an ad in which the name of the company is not given.

Chapter Quiz

Write your answers in complete sentences.

1. What is one way to learn more about your chosen career?

2. What is one way to shorten the overall time it takes to find a job?

3. What are three methods of finding a job?

4. When a job seeker is networking, what is he or she doing?

5. What are three kinds of jobs that might be found on a bulletin board?

6. How would you find the state employment office in your area?

CRITICAL THINKING

7. You read that using the Internet can be helpful when job hunting. What are some of the skills you might need to use the Internet for a job search?

8. What should you spend the most time doing in looking for a job? Explain your answer.

Career Portfolio Project

Job seekers sometimes place "Work Wanted" ads in newspapers and on bulletin boards. Write a work wanted ad for a job that you would like to have. Keep the ad under 30 words in length. Include your skills and experience. Also, include the salary you hope to receive and how long you would want to be employed (temporary or permanent, part time or full time). Use abbreviations from the chart on page 272. If you wish, design your ad on a computer, using different typefaces and adding some pictures. Put this work wanted ad in your career portfolio.

First impressions are very important when you apply in person for a job. Always try to look and act your best.

Learning Objectives

- Understand how to successfully apply for jobs.
- Describe how to fill out a job application.
- Learn how to write a résumé.
- Learn how to write a cover letter.

Chapter 21 ▶ Applying for Jobs

Words to Know

résumé	a written statement of a worker's job goals, experience, and education
candidate	a person seeking employment
human resources department	the people in a section of a business who interview job applicants and handle employee records; also called a personnel department
Social Security number	a set of numbers assigned to each citizen of the United States by the federal government for tax purposes
proofread	to carefully read written material and mark any corrections needed
cover letter	a short letter to an employer that is included with a résumé

Caitlin and Maya had just finished track practice. Both girls decided to jog home from school. They ran at an easy pace toward their neighborhood. Suddenly, Caitlin stopped.

"Look," Caitlin said to Maya. "There's a sign in that new clothing store. It says, 'Part-time work available. Apply within.' I've been looking for part-time work. Plus, I like the clothes in that store. You know I want to be a fashion designer someday. I think I should go in and apply for the job."

Maya laughed. "Are you sure? Look at yourself." She turned Caitlin around so that Caitlin could see herself in the store window.

Caitlin started to laugh, too. "I see what you mean. I guess I may need to change my clothes before I apply."

Applying for Jobs

Remember
In Chapter 20, it was suggested that you create a personal data information sheet. This sheet will help you organize information about yourself when applying for a job.

Like Caitlin, someday you may learn about a job that seems right for you. Your first thought might be to ask for the job as quickly as you can. Enthusiasm is fine. However, you must also be prepared. You should look professional and have the information you need with you when applying for a job.

Most employers ask job seekers to fill out job application forms, supply résumés, or do both. A **résumé** is a written statement of a job seeker's job goals, experience, and education. Generally, the same information appears on both a résumé and job application form. Well-prepared job applications and résumés can lead to job interviews. After interviews, the best candidate for a job is hired. A **candidate** is a person seeking employment.

How can you increase your chances of getting an interview? When possible, apply in person. Contact the person who is doing the hiring. In small companies, this person may be the manager or the owner. In large businesses, you may have to contact a person in a human resources department, or employment office. The people in a **human resources department** review job applications. They also handle employee records. Sometimes, a human resources department is called a personnel department.

Did You Know

Psychologists say that during job interviews you are judged in the following ways: 55 percent by appearance, 38 percent by behavior, and 7 percent by what is said. Of course, you still need to watch what you say!

When you apply for a job in person, look your best. A first impression can be formed in less than 10 seconds! Dress simply and neatly in clean clothing. Do not wear overly bright colors or wild prints. Smile, shake hands gently but firmly, and be polite and friendly. Make eye contact, but do not stare.

Sometimes, you will have to mail in a job application or a résumé. When you mail your application or résumé, use a business envelope and fold your papers neatly.

The Job Application

Most job applications ask for personal information, such as name, address, telephone number, and Social Security number. The federal government assigns each citizen of the United States a **Social Security number** for tax purposes.

Filling out a job application may seem like a simple task. However, it is very common to make mistakes or to forget to include important information. If you can, take the job application home to fill out. Photocopy it. If you have to fill out the application at the company, ask for two copies of it.

Fill out the photocopy of the application first. Make sure all blanks are filled in except where you see the words "For Employer Use Only." Then, proofread your application. To **proofread** means to carefully read written material and mark any corrections needed. Check that all the information and spelling are correct.

Career Fact

The federal government requires parents or guardians to apply for a Social Security number when a child is born. If you do not have a Social Security number or have lost your number, you can apply online at www.socialsecurity.gov.

APPLICATION FOR EMPLOYMENT

Name: _____
         Last   *First*   *Middle*

Address: _____
            Street and Number   *City*   *State*   *Zip Code*

Phone: (____)_____ (____)_____ Social Sec. No.: _____
         Home Number   *School or Business Number*

Are you at least 18 years of age?   ☐ Yes   ☐ No

Are you legally eligible to work in the U.S.?   ☐ Yes   ☐ No

Do you have relatives working in this company or any of its operations?   ☐ Yes   ☐ No

If so, name: _____ Company/Department: _____

Position Objective

Type of Employment: ☐ Full Time   ☐ Temporary   Total number of
                                 ☐ Part Time   ☐ Seasonal   hours per week desired: _____

Please describe the type of position you are seeking: _____

Salary required $ _____ per _____ What day would you be available to begin work? _____

A job application asks for a lot of information. Be sure to proofread your job application.

Lastly, transfer the information onto the second, blank application. If you need to make any final corrections, be sure to do so neatly.

✓ Check Your Understanding

Write your answers in complete sentences.

1. How should you prepare before you apply for a job in person?

2. What are four pieces of personal information usually asked for on job applications?

3. What is the purpose of a Social Security number?

Writing a Résumé

A résumé is a statement of who you are, what you have done in your life, and what you hope to do next. A well-written résumé will help you to get an interview.

Your résumé should be neatly printed on white paper. It should contain only true information. Résumés should be no longer than two pages. People just starting out should keep their résumés to one page.

There are many different ways to organize, or format, a résumé. Choose the format that best highlights your skills, training, and experience. Most résumés include the following sections:

Remember
Data means "information." The contact data in a résumé or job application is standard information that you are required to supply. Contact data is different from personal information, which is discussed on page 283.

- **Contact data** Résumés usually begin with how the employer can contact you. Include your full name, address, telephone number, and e-mail address, if you have one.

- **Job objective** A job objective should be short and clear. It should state your immediate goal and the type of work or the job title you are seeking, such as, "part-time salesperson."

- **Education** Your education information should be placed after your job objective, especially if it is the most important qualification you have. Include degrees or certifications awarded to you, school names and addresses, and dates you attended. Consider including any courses that might be related to a particular job.

- **Work experience** Work and volunteer experience should take up more space on your résumé than anything else. Put your most recent experience first. Be sure to include any unpaid or volunteer work. Provide employment dates, job titles, company names, and city and state. Do not include mailing addresses or telephone numbers. These items will be asked for on the job application. For each job, briefly describe your duties and accomplishments. Show your accomplishments in a measurable way. For example, instead of writing "served food," write "served food to 200 people during a 3-hour lunch shift."

- **Skills** It is important to emphasize job skills in addition to experience on a résumé. Computer skills, communications skills, foreign language skills, and any other skills should be listed.

- **References** References are the names and contact data for past employers, co-workers, or teachers. These people should be able to give positive information about your work experience or skills. Ask people for permission to use them as references. Most job applicants write, "References are available upon request" on their résumés. After an interview, be prepared to give a neatly typed list of references to the employer.

- **Personal information** List any organizations that you are a member of. You may also mention hobbies and other interests. You can also state whether you would be willing to travel or move to another city for a job.

Career Trend

Today, many employers are looking for people with SCANS skills. SCANS stands for Secretary's Commission on Achieving Necessary Skills. Choose SCANS skills that you think would have value in the jobs that you are applying for. Include these skills on your résumé.

Write About It

Write a rough draft of a résumé for a job you think you would like to have. Use your data information sheet and items in your career portfolio to help you.

Did You Know ❓

Many job seekers create their own professional Web sites, using information from their résumé.

There are companies that you can hire to write your résumé for you. However, this service can sometimes cost several hundred dollars. Plus, writing your own résumé helps you find out what strengths and abilities you have to offer an employer. It helps you to appreciate qualities about yourself that you may not have been aware of.

Now, look at the résumé that Caitlin used to apply for the part-time job in the clothing store. Caitlin had no prior paid work experience other than babysitting. However, her volunteer experience was important.

Caitlin Johnson
777 Mitchell Street, Apartment A
Northway, Michigan 48167
(313) 555-4227
cljohnson@comcast.com

Objective   Part-time sales position in a fashion clothing store

Education   Currently enrolled in Northway High School; due to graduate June 2006

Work Experience

6/04   Model, Northway Children's Hospital
                Modeled clothing for a community fundraising event

2/04–5/05   Costume Design Assistant, Northway High School
                Designed clothing for three school plays; sewed costumes; altered costumes

2004–present   Babysitter
                Work weekends caring for children aged 6 months to 8 years

Skills
- sewing
- clothing coordination and fit
- basic math skills
- excellent interpersonal skills

References are available upon request.

Learn More About It

USING ACTION VERBS

Whenever possible, use action verbs on your résumé or job application. Action verbs describe actions in a lively way. *Run*, *write*, *direct*, and *plan* are some examples of action verbs. Action verbs allow you to say a lot in a short space.

Below are examples of how you can improve what you have to say by using action verbs to describe your accomplishments.

Without Action Verbs	With Action Verbs
Was a babysitter	Cared for two children
Have animals	Raise show dogs from puppies
Went to high school	Graduated from high school
Had a story in the school paper	Wrote and published a story in the school paper

CRITICAL THINKING Describe one of your accomplishments using action verbs.

Your Résumé and Computers

Using a computer makes it easy to customize, or change, your résumé to fit a specific job. Few jobs are exactly alike. By customizing your résumé, you can focus attention on your experiences or skills that most closely fit the job's requirements.

The Internet contains a lot of career information. It has employer Web sites and job openings. Most Web sites that have job openings also let you apply for the job online. Some Web sites provide large national or local classified listings. These Web sites usually allow job seekers to place their résumés online. However, you may be charged for this service. In addition, you may not be able to customize your résumé for specific jobs.

Write About It
Some other helpful action verbs for job seekers include: *planned, created, coached, supervised, prepared, operated, tested, reported, improved,* and *built.* Choose five of these words and write a paragraph for a cover letter.

Using Technology

When you send your résumé to a company through e-mail, you may be required to use plain text format. Most computer programs can read plain text résumés. The main problem with plain text format is that you lose special formatting in your résumé.

The Cover Letter

Sending a **cover letter** with your résumé makes a much better impression than sending your résumé alone. A cover letter should be short and to the point. State which job you are applying for and how you meet the requirements. Here is Caitlin's cover letter:

Caitlin Johnson
777 Mitchell Street, Apartment A
Northway, Michigan 48167
(313) 555-4227

May 21, 2006

Jack Carlson, Manager
Threads
4250 Finlay Road
Northway, Michigan 48167

Dear Mr. Carlson:

I would like to be considered for the part-time sales position. I am currently a senior in high school. Next year, I plan to study fashion design at Northway College. Someday, I hope to have a career as a fashion designer. Working part-time at Threads would greatly help me in my long-term career goal.

I have excellent fashion sense and good people skills. I believe I would make a good salesperson. I hope you will give me a chance to work for you.

I look forward to hearing from you.

Sincerely,

Caitlin Johnson

Caitlin Johnson

✓ Check Your Understanding

Write your answers in complete sentences.

1. What is a résumé?

2. What information should a cover letter include?

JOB DESCRIPTION
Automotive Service Technician

Job Summary
An automotive service technician inspects and repairs cars and light trucks. He or she speaks with owners of cars or light trucks to find out about the problems. Then, he or she tries to locate the damaged parts and fixes or replaces them.

Most automotive service technicians work indoors in repair shops. They have to lift heavy parts and tools. Automotive service technicians work about 40 hours per week. Some are required to work evenings and weekends. Full-time and part-time positions are available.

Work Activities
An automotive service technician may do any or all of the following activities:

- Use power tools to repair cars and trucks.

- Inspect cars and trucks and replace worn parts.

- Repair exhaust systems, air conditioners, wheels, and transmissions on cars and light trucks.

- Replace brakes, belts, hoses, and spark plugs on cars and light trucks.

- Test drive cars and light trucks to make sure problems have been fixed.

Education/Training Requirements
Most employers require formal training in a high school or vocational school. The training includes completing classroom instruction and practicing working on cars and light trucks. Training programs for automotive service technicians can last from six months to one year. Some training programs also teach customer service skills.

Think About It
What kinds of qualities might an automotive service technician need to do his or her job?

Summary

- You can increase your chances of being hired for a job by applying in person. Dress neatly and be polite and friendly. Make sure your job application and résumé are complete, correct, and well organized.

- A job application is a form that job seekers must fill out. Applications ask for personal information, job experience, and skills.

- A résumé is a written statement about you. It usually includes your job objective, education, and work experience. Good résumés use action verbs and list accomplishments in an interesting and lively way.

- A computer can be used to customize résumés, contact employers, and send out résumés.

- A cover letter is a short letter sent with a résumé or a job application. Sending a cover letter with a résumé makes a much better impression than sending a résumé alone. It is also an opportunity for the job seeker to point out his or her qualifications for the job.

cover letter

human resources department

proofread

résumé

Social Security number

Vocabulary Review
Complete each sentence with a term from the list.

1. Your _____ is a letter that is sent along with a résumé.

2. When you carefully read written material for errors, you _____ it.

3. A written statement of your career goals, education, and experience is called a _____.

4. For tax purposes, every U.S. citizen needs to have a _____ from the federal government.

5. Interviewing job applicants and handling employee records are the main responsibilities of the _____.

Chapter Quiz

Write your answers in complete sentences.

1. Why is it important to make job applications and résumés complete, correct, and neat?

2. Why is it a good idea to ask for two copies of a job application?

3. What are three types of personal information often found on a résumé?

4. How long should most résumés be?

5. Where should the education section of a résumé be listed?

6. What is a cover letter for?

CRITICAL THINKING

7. Why should you be careful about whom you choose for references?

8. In what ways could you customize your résumé?

Career Portfolio Project

Earlier in this book, you were asked to list several different careers you might be interested in. Review the rough draft of the résumé you created in the activity on page 283. How could you customize that résumé to fit a different job or career? Rewrite the résumé to fit a second choice of occupation. Include a new job objective. Reformat, or make a new style for, your résumé to look different and highlight different things. Perhaps add a personal information section. Finally, write cover letters for both of your résumés.

Job seekers should show interest and enthusiasm during an interview.

Learning Objectives

- Explain the purpose of a job interview.
- List ways to prepare for a job interview.
- Tell what to do after a job interview.
- Describe what you might learn from a job interview.

Chapter 22 ▶ Interviewing for Jobs

Words to Know

job interview	a meeting between someone looking for a job and someone wanting to hire a person for a job
mission	purpose
public relations department	a department in a company that is responsible for giving out information about the company
annual report	a book or booklet published yearly that describes a company and its finances

Rachel has always liked to read. She thinks she wants to work in a library. Rachel met with a person needing to hire a library technician. Her friend Sandra came over that evening to ask her about it. Read their conversation below.

> **Career Fact**
>
> A library technician prepares and organizes library materials.

"So how did the meeting go?" Sandra asked. "Did you get the job?"

Rachel thought for a moment. "I went there well prepared," she said. "I answered all the questions the best I could. But the job is different from what I thought it would be. It turns out that the main part of the job is sitting in front of a computer. I thought I would be working more with people."

Sandra replied, "It sounds like the job may not be exactly what you are looking for."

"I'm not really sure," replied Rachel. "I guess I should have done more research on jobs in libraries."

Interviewing for a Job

Rachel is a job seeker, or someone looking for a job. She met with someone who wanted to hire a library technician. The person with whom she met is called an interviewer. A meeting between a job seeker and an interviewer is called a **job interview**.

The purpose of a job interview is to help both the interviewer and the job seeker come to a decision. The interviewer has to decide if the job seeker is the best person for the job. The job seeker uses the job interview to convince employers to hire him or her. A job seeker also uses the job interview to decide if the job is right for him or her.

Preparing for an Interview

As a job seeker, you need to be well prepared for a job interview. To be prepared, follow the steps below:

STEP 1   Research the company or place that has the job opening. Also, find out whether the job description fits your idea of the job you want.

STEP 2   Write questions that you might be asked during the interview.

STEP 3   Prepare your responses to those questions.

STEP 4   Write a list of questions to ask about the company and the job.

Research the Company

Before an interview, find out as much as you can about the company or place where you will be interviewed. Knowing the company's **mission**, or purpose, can help you to answer the interviewer's questions. If you can show the interviewer that you researched the company, the interviewer will know that you are serious about wanting the job.

Did You Know ?

Things that you might want to find out about a company include the products and services it has to offer, how many employees the company has, and how long the company has been in business.

To find information about a company, you might contact the public relations department of the company. The **public relations department** is the department responsible for giving out information about the company. Ask for **annual reports.** These books or booklets are published every year. They describe the company and its finances.

You can also search the Internet or go to a library to look for newsletters or articles about the company. Talking to someone who works for the company may also help. Take notes so you can better remember what you learn.

Make a List of Possible Questions

The next step in preparing for an interview is to write a list of questions that the interviewer may ask. The first thing most interviewers say is, "Tell me about yourself." However, you may be asked many different kinds of questions. You should be prepared to answer at least these questions:

- Why do you want to work here?

- Do you have the skills to get the work done?

- Why should you be hired instead of another person?

By asking these questions, an interviewer is trying to find the worker who is best for the job opening. Interviewers are looking for people who can work well at their companies. They want employees who will believe in the goals of the company and fit in well with others who work there.

Prepare Answers

Before going on an interview, make sure that you have answers to your list of questions. In addition, be prepared to talk about your strengths. The interview is a time to talk about your talents and abilities.

Using Technology

Many companies have Web sites. To locate a Web site, go to a search engine and enter the name of the company. You may find more information about a company at its Web site.

Career Fact

Keep your questions and research in a folder. This will help to refresh your memory if you go back for a second interview. Also, the information in the folder will be useful for interviews with other companies.

You will also have to convince the interviewer that you are the best person for the job. To do this, outline your goals. Explain to the interviewer exactly how you will accomplish your goals. Be specific. Avoid general statements such as "I hope to get more education." Be honest about what you want to do and what you can do. Be positive about your future.

Interviewers sometimes ask if you have any weaknesses. Again, answer honestly, but also tell how you make up for weaknesses. For example, you might say, "I type about 35 words a minute. But I am taking a typing course that will help me to improve my speed."

Prepare Your Own Questions

The job interview is also your time to ask questions. The answers to your questions will help you decide if the job is right for you. Here are some questions that you might want to ask:

- What kinds of projects or duties does the job require?

- What qualities should the person in this job have?

- When will you be deciding whom to hire?

Quite often, the employer will answer these questions during the interview before you ask them. Be prepared, however, to ask these questions if your interviewer does not talk about them.

Write About It
Write a list of 5 to 10 questions that you might ask during an interview.

✓ Check Your Understanding

Write your answers in complete sentences.

1. What is the purpose of a job interview?

2. How can a job seeker get information about a company?

3. What three questions are employers likely to ask?

Practicing for an Interview

You have researched a company to prepare for an interview. You have made up a list of questions and answers. You have also thought of questions to ask. Now, it is time to practice for the interview.

Some people feel silly practicing for job interviews. However, you should not feel silly. Practice is very important. Athletes train for games. Actors rehearse for plays. Job seekers must practice just as these people do if they want to do their best. A successful job seeker is one who has practiced.

There are several ways to practice interviewing. You can read your questions and answers into a tape recorder and then play them back. You can interview yourself in front of a mirror. You can videotape yourself. You can also ask a friend or teacher to play the part of the interviewer.

To prepare for a job interview, practice asking and answering questions.

When you practice, follow this list of dos and don'ts:

- Do pronounce your words in a strong, clear voice.

- Do keep your answers short and to the point.

- Do make eye contact. However, do not stare.

- Do smile occasionally. Do not grin or frown.

- Do nod your head up and down thoughtfully. Do not look away or down.

- Do sit up straight. Do not slouch.

- Do keep your legs together and your feet flat on the floor. Do not move your legs up and down.

If you find yourself nervous or forgetting things as you practice, do not worry. Now is the time to improve. Practice as much as you need to. Each time you do, you will get a little bit better.

Presenting Yourself at an Interview

To make a good impression at a job interview, dress neatly. You might wear a business shirt, pants, or a skirt, or perhaps a tie and jacket. Your hair should be neatly combed or brushed. Brush your teeth and wear deodorant. Stay away from strong perfumes or aftershave lotions.

Arrive ten minutes early for the interview. Employers want workers who will be on time. When the interviewer greets you, shake his or her hand politely but firmly.

As you ask and answer questions, let your positive attitude shine through. A good attitude is one of the key things interviewers look for. Keep your answers short—at the most, 2 minutes. At the end of the interview, shake the interviewer's hand again. Thank the interviewer and ask when you might hear about the job.

Did You Know ?

As you are being interviewed, smile and lean slightly forward. This body language will tell the interviewer that you are very interested in what he or she is saying.

Writing a Thank-You Letter

As a job seeker, you want to continue to make a good impression even after the interview. One way to do so is to write a thank-you letter. Sending this letter will remind the interviewer that you are serious about wanting the job.

Address your letter to the main person who interviewed you. Be sure to spell the person's name correctly. Get a business card for correct spelling. In your letter, restate your interest in the job and briefly say why you are the right person for the job. Thank the interviewer for his or her time. Write and mail the thank-you letter immediately after the interview. The employer will be impressed with your quick follow-up.

Here is an example of a thank-you letter written after an interview:

> Rachel Lee
> 120 Park Street
> Harris, New York 90021
> (313) 555-1111
>
> Linda Tilly, Librarian
> Harris Public Library
> 21 Green Street
> Harris, New York 90021
>
> September 4, 2004
>
> Dear Ms. Tilly,
>
> Thank you for the time you spent interviewing me yesterday. I enjoyed learning about the job responsibilities of a library technician. I believe the library offers an important service to the community. I also believe that my love of books and my attention to detail qualify me for the position. I would be proud to be on your staff.
>
> I look forward to hearing from you soon.
>
> Sincerely,
> *Rachel Lee*
> Rachel Lee

Career Trend

Many interviewers believe that sending thank-you letters through e-mail is acceptable. The e-mail letter should be written in the same style as a letter sent through regular mail.

If You Are Offered a Job

The job interview is over. You have sent a thank-you letter. Now, you receive a telephone call from the interviewer. The job is yours if you want it.

Before you accept the job, you should discuss with the interviewer the yearly or hourly salary and benefits the job offers, such as health plans and vacation time. You should also ask when the job will start. If the salary and benefits are what you are looking for, then accept the job. If, however, the salary and benefits are not what you hoped for, negotiate, or discuss, with the interviewer these amounts. If you both then reach an agreement, thank the interviewer and find out when and where you should report to work.

If You Are Not Offered a Job

You receive a letter stating that you are not being offered the job. What do you do? The most important thing to do is to get information from the interviewer about why you did not get the job.

Call the interviewer when you are not feeling sad or angry. Give the interviewer your name. Remind him or her that you had interviewed for the job but that you were turned down. Then, politely ask what you could have done differently to get the job. Afterward, thank the interviewer and ask him or her to keep you in mind for future jobs. Use this information to prepare for your next job interview.

Rachel Lee, for example, was not offered the job as the library technician. The librarian sent Rachel a letter saying that someone else had been offered the job. Rachel waited 2 days so that the disappointment could not be heard in her voice. Then, she called the librarian. The following conversation is between Rachel and the interviewer.

Career Fact

If you are not contacted within a few days of the date that the interviewer told you, then telephone the interviewer and ask about your standing for the job.

Rachel: Ms. Tilly, this is Rachel Lee. I just received your letter saying that I was not chosen for the library technician job. I wondered if you could answer a few questions that would help me in my future job search.

Ms. Tilly: Sure, Rachel.

Rachel: How could I have done better during the interview?

Ms. Tilly: You interviewed quite well. However, the person I chose had done volunteer work in her school library. Also, I did notice that you were disappointed that you would not be working with people much. I really had the sense that you would be happier working more with people.

Rachel: You're probably right. Well, thank you again, Ms. Tilly. Please keep me in mind if a job comes up that you think is a good match for me.

Ms. Tilly: I will, Rachel. Good luck.

From this talk, Rachel learned that, like herself, Ms. Tilly was not sure that Rachel would enjoy being a library technician. Rachel also learned that volunteer experience could have improved her chances of getting the job. Rachel can use the information she has received to help her during a future job interview.

Remember
You learned in Chapter 1 that volunteer work can get you started in a career.

Some interviewers do not write or return telephone calls telling job seekers that they have not been chosen. If you are not contacted, do not be discouraged. Do not let the disappointment you feel stop you from doing well on other job interviews.

✓ Check Your Understanding

Write your answers in complete sentences.

1. What are three ways to practice for a job interview?

2. How should you dress for a job interview?

3. What should you do after a job interview?

Learn More About It

BUILDING SELF-CONFIDENCE

It is the day before an important swim meet. A champion swimmer sits quietly by the pool. He sees himself growing taller, his arms and legs stretching. Now, he pictures himself diving into the pool. His swimming strokes are perfect. He passes the other swimmers easily. He wins the competition.

The swimmer is doing what many successful people do. He is picturing his success. Picturing success helps to build self-confidence. It is a technique, or method, you can practice to prepare yourself for interviews.

Many people use this technique. Businesspeople picture themselves talking in front of a group of people. Athletes picture themselves playing at their best. Actors and actresses picture themselves giving their best performances.

To picture your success in a job interview, close your eyes. Take a deep breath. See yourself relaxed. See yourself smiling. Hear your strong, clear voice. Listen to your thoughtful, well-prepared answers. Now, picture the handshake and the nod of the interviewer. Hear the interviewer say, "The job is yours."

CRITICAL THINKING Why would picturing success help you succeed in job interviews?

JOB DESCRIPTION
Library Technician

Job Summary
A library technician works in a library. He or she organizes and manages books and other printed resources. He or she also handles the technology found in a library, such as an electronic catalog of books, CD-ROMs, the Internet, and audiovisual equipment.

A library technician can work in a public library, school library, or large company. Work hours can vary. Some library technicians may work regular hours while others may work evening hours or on weekends.

Work Activities
A library technician may do any or all of the following activities:

- Assist librarians in running libraries.
- Enter and manage information in a library's computer system.
- Help library users find information using computers.
- Sort and shelve library material.
- Check materials in and out of the library.
- Issue new library cards to users.
- Track down missing materials.
- Teach children library skills.

Education/Training Requirements
Requirements can vary from a high school diploma to a college degree. Some colleges and vocational schools offer degrees in library technology or library-related studies. Some employers will train employees who have very little experience.

Think About It

How do you think improvements in technology would affect a library technician?

Chapter

22 ▷ Review

Summary

- The purpose of a job interview is to help both the employer and the job seeker make a decision. The employer decides who is the best person for the job. The job seeker uses the interview to convince the employer that he or she is the best person for the job. The job seeker also uses the interview to decide whether the job is right for him or her.

- To prepare for an interview, a job seeker should 1) research the company, 2) write questions that he or she might be asked during the interview, 3) write answers to those questions, and 4) think of questions to ask.

- Before going on a job interview, a job seeker should practice asking and answering questions. He or she should pay attention to appearance and speech during practice sessions for the interview.

- During an interview, a job seeker should have a good attitude, be alert, and be polite. Looking neat and arriving on time are very important.

- After a job interview, a job seeker should follow up immediately with a thank-you letter to the interviewer.

- If a job seeker is turned down for a job, he or she should contact the interviewer. The job seeker should ask what he or she could improve upon in order to prepare for other job interviews.

annual report
job interview
mission
public relations department

Vocabulary Review

Complete each sentence with a term from the list.

1. A meeting between a job seeker and an interviewer is called a _____.

2. A company's purpose is called its _____.

3. A book or booklet published yearly that describes a company and its finances is called an _____.

4. The department in the company responsible for giving out information about a company is called the _____.

Chapter Quiz

Write your answers in complete sentences.

1. What is the purpose of a job interview to an interviewer?

2. What is the purpose of a job interview to a job seeker?

3. How should a job seeker prepare for an interview?

4. Why is it important to be on time for an interview?

5. How should a job seeker sit during an interview?

6. When should a job seeker send a thank-you letter?

CRITICAL THINKING

7. A job interviewer asks you to discuss one of your weaknesses. Write what you would say. Also, tell how you would make up for your weakness.

8. Suppose you are turned down for a job. The employer says you did not have enough experience. How can you make the most of this information?

Career Portfolio Project

Picture yourself as an interviewer. Write a list of qualities that you would look for in a job seeker. Consider dress, behavior, and personality. Now, picture yourself as a job seeker. Respond to the list that you wrote. Explain how you, as a job seeker, could satisfy every item on the list.

Unit 4 **Review**

Choose the letter of the best answer to each question.

1. What is the purpose of a career plan?
   A. It outlines what you want to achieve with a career.
   B. It identifies your strengths.
   C. It identifies your weaknesses.
   D. It lists all the jobs you have had.

2. How can an internship give you valuable job experience?
   A. It can help you make new friends.
   B. It provides on-the-job learning and training.
   C. It can teach you computer skills.
   D. It provides information about career trends.

3. Why do employers like workers with positive attitudes?
   A. They often seem to enjoy their work more than other workers.
   B. They think things will work out right.
   C. They handle problems well.
   D. all of the above

4. How can networking help you find a job?
   A. It helps you understand why school is important.
   B. It puts you in contact with people who can pass on job information to you.
   C. It gives you a chance to use your people skills.
   D. all of the above

5. What is the purpose of a résumé?
   A. It helps you choose a career.
   B. It shows your abilities in sports.
   C. It can get you a job interview.
   D. It includes complaints about other jobs you have had.

6. Why should you write a thank-you letter after a job interview?
   A. to make a good impression after the interview
   B. to ask for another interview
   C. to pressure the company into hiring you
   D. to provide more details about yourself

Critical Thinking
Explain how staying in school can help you plan your career.

Unit 5

Success in Your Career

Before You Read

In this unit, you will learn how to be a success on the job and how to change your career plans as you grow and change.

Before you start reading, ask yourself these questions:

1. How can my attitudes affect my success at work?

2. Why is good teamwork important to success on the job?

3. What kinds of events can cause me to change my career plans?

Some types of businesses, such as banks, offer training programs for new employees. These programs teach how to treat customers properly.

Learning Objectives

- Explain what you can do to mentally prepare yourself for a new job.

- List ways to learn new job skills and remember information.

- Describe income taxes, job benefits, and safety on the job.

- Explain why some industries or businesses have unions.

Chapter 23 > Starting a Job

Words to Know

employee handbook	a document that gives workers important information about the rules and policies, or ways of doing things, in a company
peer mentor	a person who has the same job responsibilities as another but is more experienced and can offer advice about the job
job aid	any device that can help a worker remember important information
W-4 form	a form that determines the taxes taken from a worker's paycheck
net income	money earned minus the amount withheld in taxes
W-2 form	a yearly statement of wages and taxes sent by a business to a worker
tax return	a report to the government that shows how much a worker has earned, paid in taxes, and either owes in taxes or is due in a tax refund
job benefits	anything given to workers other than wages, such as vacation pay, sick pay, health insurance, and a pension

Lauren came home with her first paycheck. She did not look happy. Read the conversation below between Lauren and her father.

"What's wrong, Lauren?" her father asked. "I thought you would be excited about getting your first paycheck."

Lauren frowned. "Well, I am, Dad. But I'm not making as much money as I thought."

Lauren's father studied her paycheck. Then, it became clear to him. "The company has taken out taxes. You have to pay them. Paying taxes is part of working."

Being Prepared for the World of Work

Lauren started working without knowing much about taxes. She did not know that most employers take out, or deduct, taxes from paychecks. Knowing the realities of work can help you prepare for your new job.

Your First Weeks at a New Job

Beginning a new job can be stressful. Many people worry about whether they will get along with their co-workers. They are not sure about how they will handle their job duties. They are afraid of asking simple questions or failing at their job. These feelings are natural. However, there are things you can do to make a new job less stressful.

- **Understand exactly what you are supposed to do.** If you are confused about what is expected of you, talk to your manager. Ask questions until you know exactly what to do. Do not wait until you make a mistake.

- **Make a commitment to do tasks well.** Make a promise to yourself that you will always try to do your best. Do not rush through new tasks. Everyone has a "learning curve." This term means that a task takes longer when you are first learning how to do it. Explain to anyone who is impatient that you are new and just learning the job.

- **Look for recognition from others.** Many companies are very good about rewarding their employees. They give "Employee of the Month" awards. Other companies give merit raises, which are raises for work well done. However, sometimes you will have to ask your manager, "How am I doing?" Do this a few weeks after you have been at the job. Also, get feedback from your co-workers or customers.

- **Think of your work as valuable to the company and to yourself.** Start your new job with a positive attitude. At times, you may feel that your job is not "important." However, the success of a company depends on all of its workers.

- **Look for ways to grow.** At some point, you will probably become comfortable in your job. However, do not become too comfortable. You may lose your desire to do well. Always look for ways to be creative. Volunteer for new duties. Suggest ways the work could be done better.

✓ **Check Your Understanding**

Write your answers in complete sentences.

1. Why is it stressful to start a new job?

2. What is a learning curve?

3. How can you grow in a job?

Career Fact

Most kinds of work require problem-solving and decision-making skills. For problem solving, first analyze the problem. Then, think of possible solutions and choose the best one. For decision-making, understand the needs. Then, look at possible plans of action.

Training on the Job

Most companies provide their workers with some training for their jobs. Jenna, for example, became a customer service representative for a bank after she graduated from high school. Before beginning her job, Jenna spent two weeks in a classroom. There, she learned how to use the bank's computers. She also learned how to treat customers properly and how to solve problems.

Evan found a job as a warehouse worker for an office supply company. His main duties were to pack and ship supplies. Evan learned his job from another worker. He watched and helped the other worker for a day and asked questions. When he was unsure of what to do, Evan went back to his co-worker for advice. Often, a manager came by to check on Evan's work.

Remember
Following someone on a job to see what he or she does is called *job shadowing.*

Other Resources on the Job

On the day they begin jobs, new employees are often given an employee handbook. An **employee handbook** tells workers important information about the rules and policies, or ways of doing things, in a company. It may include information about sick, holiday, and vacation pay and other benefits. You should read your handbook carefully.

Did You Know ?

Many companies offer an orientation, or welcome, session for groups of new employees. This session often provides information about company policies. The session may also include a tour of the job site.

There are a number of resources you can turn to in order to learn your job responsibilities. You read about training in classrooms. Another form of training is through peer mentors. **Peer mentors** are co-workers who have the same or similar responsibilities that you have. They offer help and advice to new employees. Of course, your manager will also help you understand your responsibilities. Accept any help that is offered to you and ask questions when you do not understand something.

A memorandum, also known as a memo, is a note sent from one worker to another worker or group of workers. Memos can be very helpful for doing your job. Sometimes, a memo will give the date, time, and location of a meeting. It can also contain an important policy change. Always try to promptly answer all memos that require an answer.

Another important job resource is the work schedule. Companies may post work schedules for different shifts each week. Work schedules tell which employees are working at what times.

Some companies provide a variety of job aids. A **job aid** is anything that can help a worker remember important information.

An example of a job aid is a sign that says: "Wear your safety equipment at all times." Another job aid is a wall calendar that shows a project schedule. Lists of postal rates and product prices are also job aids.

Work and Taxes

By law, both businesses and workers must pay taxes to federal, state, and local governments. In return, these governments provide certain services, such as police protection and public schooling. Your employer will deduct, or take out, money from your paychecks to pay taxes. On the following pages you will learn how the tax process usually works.

STEP 1   When a company hires an employee, the employee fills out a W-4 form, part of which is shown below. A **W-4 form** determines the taxes withheld, or taken out of, a worker's paycheck.

The information you write on your W-4 form will affect the amount of taxes withheld from your salary.

Using Technology

One important job aid is a calendar program, found on most e-mail systems. Calendar programs can help a person schedule meetings and send out reminders to employees of meeting times. Workers can also enter their own schedules into a calendar program for others to check.

STEP 2 A company pays its worker after withholding taxes owed to federal, state, and local governments. The company might also take out money for a retirement plan or health insurance. Attached to the worker's paycheck is a paycheck stub, like the one shown below.

The paycheck stub gives the details of earnings and taxes. **Net income** is what employees sometimes call "take-home pay." On the paycheck stub below it is called "Net Pay." It is the total income earned minus the amount withheld.

Grant's Grocery Store

EMPLOYEE NUMBER	CURRENT HOURS			CURRENT				
	REGULAR	OVERTIME	Y.T.D. NET	F.I.T.	F.I.C.A.	STATE TAX	LOCAL TAX
12345	20|00	|00	170|60	18|00	9|00	6|00	1|70

CURRENT EARNINGS			YEAR TO DATE				
REGULAR	OVERTIME	SPECIAL	Y.T.D. GROSS	F.I.T.	F.I.C.A.	STATE TAX	LOCAL TAX
120|00	|00	|00	240|00	36|00	18|00	12|00	3|40

CHECK NO.	DESCRIPTION	AMOUNT	DESCRIPTION	AMOUNT	TOTAL DEDUCTIONS
082349					
ENDING DATE					34|70
01|14|05					**NET PAY**
CHECK DATE					
01|21|05	AUTHORIZED DEDUCTIONS AND SPECIAL PAY ELEMENTS				85|30

STATEMENT OF EARNINGS AND DEDUCTIONS • DETACH AND RETAIN FOR YOUR RECORDS

A paycheck stub contains a lot of information. Review it carefully when you get paid.

STEP 3 At the end of each year, the company sends every worker a W-2 form, such as the one shown on page 313. A **W-2 form** is a statement that shows the amount of money a worker earned during the past year. It also shows the amount of taxes that have been withheld from the worker's paychecks. All workers need their W-2 forms when reporting their taxes to the government. This process is discussed in Step 4.

a Control number			OMB No. 1545-0008	Safe, accurate, FAST! Use IRS *e~file*	Visit the IRS website at www.irs.gov.

b Employer identification number 123-45-6789		1 Wages, tips, other compensation 12,723.36	2 Federal income tax withheld 856.11

c Employer's name, address, and ZIP code	3 Social security wages .00	4 Social security tax withheld .00
	5 Medicare wages and tips 13,755.00	6 Medicare tax withheld 199.45
	7 Social security tips .00	8 Allocated tips .00

d Employee's social security number 123-45-6789	9 Advance EIC payment .00	10 Dependent care benefits .00

e Employee's first name and initial Last name Lorraine Anderson 138 Lyonsville Rd Los Angeles, CA 90024	11 Nonqualified plans	12a See instructions for box 12
	13 Statutory employee ☐ Retirement plan ☒ Third-party sick pay ☐	12b
	14 Other DCP-CAS 1,031.64	12c
		12d

f Employee's address and ZIP code

15 State Employer's state ID number CA| 95-1234567	16 State wages, tips, etc. 12,929.79	17 State income tax 200.98	18 Local wages, tips, etc.	19 Local income tax	20 Locality name

Form **W-2** Wage and Tax Statement   **2004**   Department of the Treasury—Internal Revenue Service

Copy B—To Be Filed With Employee's FEDERAL Tax Return.
This information is being furnished to the Internal Revenue Service.

The W-2 form includes the total amount of income a worker earned during a year and the taxes that were withheld.

STEP 4   Each year, by April 15, all workers must send in a report to the government called a **tax return**. The report states how much the worker earned in the previous year and how much he or she paid in taxes. For example, a person who worked in 2004, would have to send in a tax return by April 15, 2005. If the company withheld too much in taxes, the worker will receive a tax refund. If the company withheld too little, the worker has to pay the taxes that are due.

The tax laws in the United States can change from year to year. The government agency that enforces tax laws is called the Internal Revenue Service (IRS). The IRS offers free information on taxes and filling out tax returns. You can visit their Web site at www.irs.gov.

Did You Know

The United States has a "graduated tax system." The more money you earn, the higher the percentage of taxes you must pay. However, the percentage can never go above 35 percent.

Learn More About It

PAYCHECK STUB VOCABULARY

Here are some abbreviations and terms that you may find on paycheck stubs and tax forms.

Abbreviations and Terms	What It Means
F.I.C.A.	Federal Insurance Contribution Act; also known as Social Security tax; provides income to people who are retired or unable to work
F.I.T.	Federal income tax
Gross pay	Total amount of money earned in pay period
Local	Local taxes, such as those paid to a city or county
Net pay	Actual pay after all withholdings or deductions have been taken out
Overtime (OT)	Hours or pay above the usual rate
Pay period	Period that the paycheck is for
Regular	Hours or pay at the usual rate
Ret.	Retirement fund, such as a pension
State	State taxes
Y.T.D.	Year-to-date

CRITICAL THINKING Why do you think paycheck stubs contain so much information?

Job Benefits

Earlier in this chapter, you read that many employers offer job benefits to their employees. **Job benefits** include anything given to workers other than wages, such as health insurance, vacation and sick pay, retirement plans, and pensions.

On page 315 you will read descriptions of some common job benefits offered by companies.

Health Insurance

Usually, a company and its employees each pay a certain amount of money for health insurance every pay period. When the employee goes to a doctor or hospital, all or part of each bill is paid by the health insurance plan. Sometimes, an employee's family can be included in the insurance plan too. Insurance plans vary in cost and services provided. Some companies also provide prescription drug plans and dental and vision insurance.

Sick and Vacation Pay

Most companies allow employees a certain number of paid sick days per year. Many companies offer paid vacation time in addition to holidays like Memorial Day. An example of vacation time is two weeks of vacation the first year of employment. Additional days or weeks are given with added years of service.

Pension or Retirement Plan

Some companies withhold a certain amount of money from each qualifying employee's paycheck. This money is put toward the employee's retirement plan. When the employee retires or leaves the company, he or she gets the money back in one check or in monthly payments. Many companies also offer retirement savings plans, such as a 401K program. In a 401K program, a company matches funds saved by an employee for a certain period of time.

Job Safety

In 1970, the federal government passed a law called the Occupational Safety and Health Act. This law requires all employers to provide a safe and healthful workplace. Workers must be provided with safe equipment, protective clothing when needed, and education about safety practices.

Write About It

Make a list of the different kinds of benefits that you need, such as life, health, or dental insurance. Then, number the items in your list in order of their importance to you.

Career Trend

Workplace safety is becoming a popular career field. Some occupations within this area include safety training specialists, environmental health specialists, emergency management specialists, health safety technicians, and safety inspectors.

Did You Know ?

The Bureau of Labor Statistics says that 25 percent of all on-the-job injuries occur during the first 6 months of employment.

The Occupational Safety and Health Administration (OSHA) was formed to inspect companies and enforce safety laws. Still, more than 14,000 Americans die from on-the-job accidents every year.

What does that mean to you? It means you have the right to a safe work environment. You also have to take some responsibility for your own safety. If you are a new worker, enroll in any safety classes offered by the company. If you work around chemicals, poisons, or dangerous machinery, ask how they can be handled safely. If a company offers you hard hats or other safety equipment, use them.

Unions

Career Fact

In 2003, about 13 percent of all wage and salary workers belonged to unions. That number was lower than in previous years.

Some workplaces require employees to join a trade union. You learned about trade unions in Chapter 13. Trade unions exist for many kinds of workers. The purpose of trade unions is to improve wages and working conditions for workers. Becoming a member of a trade union means that you will have to pay union dues. The dues are used to support the trade union and the work it does.

Some businesses are "union shops." If you work in a union shop, you must join the trade union soon after you start working. In states that have right-to-work laws, workers, in general, do not have to belong to trade unions. However, employees in some industries are not protected by the right-to-work laws of any state.

✓ Check Your Understanding

Write your answers in complete sentences.

1. What is a W-4 form?

2. What are four different benefits companies offer?

JOB DESCRIPTION
Bank Teller

Job Summary
A bank teller works in a bank. He or she is responsible for much of the business that takes place in a bank. A bank teller spends most of the day dealing with customers. Bank tellers are the people customers usually speak with inside the bank.

Bank tellers spend a lot of time working on computers. Work hours can vary. Most bank tellers work about 40 hours per week. Some night and weekend work may be required, depending on when the bank is open. Full-time and part-time positions are available.

Work Activities
A bank teller may do any or all of the following activities:

- Cash checks and make deposits for customers.

- Accept credit card payments from customers.

- Check that deposit slips are accurate.

- Check customers' accounts.

- Count cash very carefully.

- Keep a record of all cash given to him or her each day.

- Use computers to record deposits and withdrawals.

Education/Training Requirements
Most bank tellers are required to have at least a high school diploma. Some employers do not require any previous work experience and will train employees who have very little experience. Additional requirements include good math, communication, and computer skills.

Think About It
Why is it important for a bank teller to have good communication skills?

Chapter

23 ▷ Review

Summary

- Workers should start a new job with a positive attitude. They should learn their duties, always try to do their best, look for feedback from co-workers or customers, and try to grow in the job.

- Most companies provide new workers with some training. Workers can also learn through peer mentors, employee handbooks, and job aids.

- Workers should learn about taxes. Employers withhold federal, state, and local taxes from employees' paychecks on a regular basis.

- Most companies offer a variety of job benefits. Some common benefits are health insurance, dental insurance, sick and vacation pay, and pension or retirement plans.

- All workers have the right to a safe work environment. Employers should provide safety equipment, protective clothing when needed, and education about safety practices.

- Labor unions exist for many types of workers.

employee handbook
job aid
net income
peer mentor
W-2 form

Vocabulary Review

Complete each sentence with a term from the list.

1. Money earned minus the amount withheld in taxes is called _____.

2. A _____ is a yearly wage and tax statement sent by a business to an employee.

3. A person who has similar job responsibilities as another but is more experienced and can offer advice about the job is called a _____.

4. Any device that can help a worker remember important information is called a _____.

5. The rules and policies of a company can be found in the _____.

Chapter Quiz

Write your answers in complete sentences.

1. How can starting a new job be stressful?

2. What are some things a worker can do to learn on the job?

3. What kind of information do employee handbooks contain?

4. What are some examples of job aids?

5. By what date must income earners file their yearly tax returns?

6. What is the job of OSHA?

CRITICAL THINKING

7. Why should you not rush through tasks when you are new at a job?

8. Can you think of two job aids that might benefit a bank teller?

Career Portfolio Project

Some of the most important qualities you can bring to a new job are being loyal, dependable, flexible, prompt, a team player, and a creative thinker. Employers also like people who show leadership qualities. Choose three of the qualities mentioned that you think you have. Write about situations in which you have shown these qualities. When asked about yourself at an interview, you can respond with what you have written. Finally, choose two of the qualities that you are not sure that you have. Make a plan for how you could develop these qualities in yourself.

Being a success in your career usually involves getting along with the people you work with.

Learning Objectives

- Explain the importance of work ethics.
- Explain the benefits of working as a team.
- Describe laws that give workers the right to fair treatment.
- Understand your right to privacy in a workplace.

Chapter 24 ▷ Working With People

Words to Know

co-worker	any person you work with, including your manager
work ethics	the values and ways of behaving that are important in a work environment
teamwork	the efforts of a group, called a team, to achieve a common goal
consensus	an opinion or a position reached by a group as a whole
minority	a group of people that makes up less than 50 percent of the population of an area
discrimination	unfair treatment because of one's race, skin color, religion, sex, age, or disability
terminate	to fire an employee
sexual harassment	any unwelcome or inappropriate sexual behavior

Luis had been hired to work on a road crew. His friend Eric had helped him get the job. One day after work, Eric gave Luis a ride home. When Luis got into the car, he noticed a power drill on the backseat.

"Isn't that the power drill we used at work today?" Luis asked Eric.

"It sure is," Eric replied. "I'm going to borrow it."

"Did you ask the boss? Mr. Torrez said that all the tools had to be locked up at night."

"Relax," Eric said, winking. "I'll return it soon. He'll never know that it's gone."

Luis knew that Eric's attitude and actions were wrong. However, he was not sure what to do about it.

Getting Along With Co-Workers

Career Fact

It is important to treat your co-workers with respect. Be polite and ready to help. Be a good listener. If you are honest and respectful toward others, they will probably be honest and respectful toward you.

A big part of being successful in any job is getting along with co-workers. A **co-worker** is any person you work with, including your manager. The workers in most companies work together as a team. They try to get along well with each other. Team members share the same goals: to make the company or organization they work for a success and their own lives richer.

This chapter is about how to handle problems with co-workers, such as the one facing Luis. It is also about how to stop problems from occurring in the first place.

Making Good Work Decisions

Ethics are principles that guide behavior. Ethics are based on generally accepted ideas of right and wrong. **Work ethics** are values and ways of behaving that are important in a work environment. There are work ethics that apply to most work situations. An example of a work ethic is to always try to do your best.

Another work ethic is to respect your manager's authority. It is the job of managers to oversee their employees' work. When your manager asks you to perform a task, you must try to follow his or her directions. Complaining or insisting on doing things your own way will only create bad feelings.

Write About It

Make a list of ethical behavior you think should be practiced in the workplace. For each item on your list, provide a sentence explaining why you have included it.

Workers should also respect company property. Some employees use company telephones to make many personal calls. Like Eric, they think it is okay to use a company's tools, office supplies, or other equipment for personal use. This behavior, however, is dishonest. Eric, for example, acted dishonestly in taking the tool without getting permission. Luis must convince Eric to return the equipment. If Eric refuses, then Luis must decide whether or not to tell his boss, Mr. Torrez, about it.

Teamwork

At a workplace, teams, or groups of people, often work together. **Teamwork** is the efforts of a team to reach a common goal. Being a good team member is another workplace ethic.

Alexis, a new art teacher at a preschool, learned the value of teamwork. Her job was to do art projects with the children. Alexis had some great ideas for projects. However, the children did not listen to her.

The principal saw that Alexis was having problems. She assigned a volunteer to help Alexis. The volunteer, Jim, had a lot of experience working with children. However, Alexis did not want to work with a volunteer. Jim was 74 years old. "What can he do for me?" she thought to herself.

Jim soon showed her. His calm and friendly manner attracted the children. However, he was firm with them when they misbehaved. Alexis started changing how she handled the children. Soon, they began listening to Alexis, too.

Alexis finally realized how helpful Jim was. "I'm really glad that you're here," she said. "I'd be a failure without you."

Jim shook his head. "You really know how to get students excited about art. All I do is help them to calm down. The fact is, we are a great team."

That day, Alexis realized that each of them had certain strengths. By combining their strengths, they could be more productive and have fun, too.

Communication is a key to good teamwork. Good team members let others know what they are doing at all times. The team discusses important issues together. Team members come to a consensus about how to work out problems. A **consensus** is an opinion reached by a group as a whole.

> **Did You Know?**
> A good team member avoids negative attitudes. He or she respects the opinions and appreciates the contributions of others.

> **Remember**
> Good communications skills are important to develop while you are in school. These skills include reading, speaking, and writing.

More and more companies today are setting up teams in the workplace. These teams are usually made up of people from different parts of the company. In 2004, about one third of American businesses with fifty or more employees had at least half of their employees working in teams.

Valuing Differences

Being a good team member will become even more important in the future. The U.S. workforce is changing. Women are playing a greater role than ever before. Minorities are taking new leadership roles in business and government. A **minority** is a group of people that makes up less than 50 percent of the population of an area. With the help of technology, disabled Americans are now able to work in many different jobs, too.

As a young worker entering the workforce, you will need to learn how to value your co-workers' differences. You should recognize the special strengths that each person brings to the workplace.

✓ **Check Your Understanding**

Write your answers in complete sentences.

1. What are work ethics?

2. Why should you always try to do your best?

3. How can teamwork help people be more productive?

Your Right to Fair Treatment

Eduardo works hard every day. He works overtime whenever his manager asks him to. Eduardo likes his co-workers and is well respected by them. He is the most skilled worker in the group.

When a management position became available, Eduardo applied for the job. He had all the qualifications. Then, Eduardo learned that someone with less experience was offered the job.

Eduardo is one of a few Latino people who work for the company. He thinks that he did not get the promotion because of his cultural background.

Employers are required by law to treat all workers fairly. The Civil Rights Act of 1964 stated that no employer may practice **discrimination** in the workplace. That is, employers may not use race, skin color, religion, sex, or national origin as a reason to hire or fire a person. Another word for *fire* is **terminate**. Later laws have also made it illegal to discriminate based on a person's age or physical disability. In addition, employers cannot refuse to promote employees for reasons of discrimination.

Another important right that workers have by law is the right not to face sexual harassment. **Sexual harassment** is any unwelcome or inappropriate sexual behavior.

What exactly is sexual harassment? Suppose Joan's manager asks her for a date. Joan politely turns him down. A week later, Joan's manager tells her that the company is doing poorly. He might have to let some of the office workers go. He tells Joan that if she goes out with him, he will see that she keeps her job.

This kind of unwelcome pressure is one example of sexual harassment. Making unwanted sexual comments or touching someone in certain ways are also examples of sexual harassment.

What should a worker who believes that he or she has been sexually harassed or discriminated against do? First, the worker should keep careful written records of what is said or done to him or her. The written record should include dates and times as well as the names of other workers who witnessed any inappropriate actions. Then, the worker should go to the appropriate department in the company to report these actions.

Career Fact

The federal Equal Pay Act of 1963 made it illegal to pay unequal wages to men and women who do nearly equal work in the same company.

Did You Know ?

In large companies, workers can make complaints to their human resources department or to their union. Quite often, a company or union will have a way of handling such complaints.

Did You Know ?

The EEOC received about 84,000 discrimination complaints in 2002. About 22,000 of these cases were eventually settled.

Eduardo, the worker that you read about earlier, could go to the appropriate department in the company. He could also take his complaint directly to the Equal Employment Opportunity Commission, or EEOC. This federal agency investigates charges of discrimination against employers. If the EEOC finds the charges to be true, it will try to reach an agreement between the employee and employer. If no settlement is reached, the EEOC may bring charges against the employer in a federal district court. In addition, a worker can file a lawsuit against his or her employer. However, this action takes time, energy, and money.

The Americans with Disabilities Act, or ADA, is a law that was passed in 1990. Under this law, employers cannot discriminate against people with disabilities. Employers with 15 or more employees must also provide equipment for disabled workers to perform their jobs. Many workplaces have wheelchair ramps, special computer keyboards, headsets, and special restroom areas set up for disabled workers.

Certain employers are required to provide disabled workers with equipment, such as special computer keyboards, to do their jobs.

Privacy in the Workplace

The Supreme Court has defined privacy as a person's right to control the spread of information about himself or herself. However, privacy is not directly protected by the U.S. Constitution. The Fourth Amendment of the Constitution protects privacy rights only when the government is involved.

Most Americans believe that a person has a right to privacy, even while at work. As a result, 24 states have passed laws that try to protect a person's right to privacy in the workplace. However, these laws do not fully protect workers' privacy. As a result, employers can gather some information about their workers.

Employers have the ability to check on their employees to make sure that they are being honest and productive. Special software programs and equipment allow employers to read e-mail messages and personal computer files of employees, listen to telephone conversations, and monitor Internet usage. The amount of time employees spend away from their computers can also be known to their employers.

In addition, when they believe that workers are acting unethically, some employers use hidden cameras to watch their employees. These cameras can be installed in public areas, locker rooms, and even restrooms.

Unions and other groups that support workers are working to get stronger laws passed that protect workers' privacy. Some groups are trying to get federal laws passed that would punish employers for invading employee privacy. However, employers will work against these laws because they need ways to make sure employees are productive. The debate over privacy in the workplace will continue for years to come.

Using Technology

Workplace Fairness is a nonprofit organization that provides workers with information about many issues, including employee rights. The organization's Web site is www.workplacefairness.org.

Career Fact

Employers own their company's e-mail and telephone systems. They can review the contents of these systems at any time. Most e-mail and telephone systems save deleted e-mails and voice-mail messages even after an employee has deleted them.

There are many privacy issues for the federal and state governments to deal with in the future. Keep yourself informed about them and how you can protect your privacy in the workplace.

✓ Check Your Understanding

Write your answers in complete sentences.

1. What is one example of discrimination?

2. What are two ways an employee can fight a case of discrimination?

3. What was the purpose of the ADA?

Learn More About It

DRUG TESTING

An important privacy issue today is testing employees for the use of illegal drugs. Using illegal drugs can affect a worker's performance. It can also endanger the safety of the worker and other people around him or her. In some industries, taking a drug test when applying for a job is common. You may be asked to take a drug test even after you have been working in a job for a while.

Workplace drug testing has increased almost 300 percent from the early 1990s. However, many people believe that drug testing is unfair, is often inaccurate, and is not known to stop drug use. They believe that drug tests invade a person's privacy and are embarrassing. Sometimes, another person is asked to watch an employee take a certain type of test to prove that the sample is not changed in any way.

Some people are against drug testing because it can also reveal many physical and medical conditions. It can show an employer that an employee is likely to inherit certain diseases. It can also reveal that a woman is pregnant. In addition, there can be mistakes in reading the test results. These mistakes can cause someone to be unfairly fired or not be hired in the first place.

CRITICAL THINKING Do you think job candidates should have to take a drug test?

JOB DESCRIPTION
Paralegal

Job Summary
A paralegal is responsible for helping lawyers prepare for court cases. He or she helps lawyers with legal paperwork. A paralegal usually works in a law office or government office.

Paralegals spend most of their day at a desk. They also spend a lot of time doing research. Paralegals usually work a 40-hour work week. Overtime hours are sometimes required. Full-time and part-time positions are available. Sometimes, paralegals are hired temporarily to help out during busy times of the year.

Job Activities
A paralegal may do any or all of the following activities:

- Help lawyers prepare for trials and meetings by doing research and writing reports.

- Organize and track clients' files.

- Investigate the facts of a case for lawyers.

- Maintain office financial records.

- Manage other employees in the office.

Education/Training Requirements
Education requirements range from a high school diploma to a college degree. Most employers require formal paralegal training in a paralegal program. These programs are offered at colleges, community colleges, and business schools. Additional requirements include good computer skills, good organizational skills, and good writing skills.

Think About It
Why do you think it is important for paralegals to have good computer skills?

Summary

- Success in the workplace involves getting along with co-workers.

- All workers should follow work ethics. For example, they should always try their best, respect authority, respect company property, and treat co-workers with respect.

- Employees can benefit from good teamwork. They should value each other's strengths and differences. They should combine their strengths to be more successful.

- Employers are required by law to treat workers fairly. Laws forbid discrimination in the workplace on the basis of race, skin color, age, religion, sex, national origin, or disabilities. An employee who feels he or she has been discriminated against can speak to his or her human resources department, a union, or the EEOC. An employee can also file a lawsuit against his or her employer.

- There is little privacy in today's workplace. Employers can monitor their employees' activities to make sure that they are being honest and productive.

consensus
co-workers
sexual harassment
teamwork
terminate

Vocabulary Review
Complete each sentence with a term from the list.

1. Communication is a key to good _____.

2. When you reach a _____, you come to an agreement with a group of people.

3. Making inappropriate sexual comments is a type of _____.

4. Your _____ include the people you work for and the people you work with.

5. Another word for ending someone's employment is to _____ him or her.

Chapter Quiz

Write your answers in complete sentences.

1. What are two work ethics?

2. What is a manager's job in relation to those employees who work for him or her?

3. What is one benefit of working as a team?

4. What are two areas in which an employer cannot practice discrimination?

5. What is the EEOC?

6. What are three ways an employee may be monitored in the workplace?

CRITICAL THINKING

7. How would written records help a worker who feels that he or she is being discriminated against?

8. What other parts of your life are influenced by ethics?

Career Portfolio Project

You have learned in this chapter how important teamwork is to success on the job. Think of a work situation in your chosen career in which you might be part of a team. What is the goal of that team? What is your job on that team? Write a few paragraphs about the strengths you bring to the team and how, together with the rest of the team, you will accomplish your goal.

A job review is an opportunity for a manager and an employee to exchange ideas about the employee's job performance.

Learning Objectives

- Explain the purpose of a job review.
- Tell what a performance standard is.
- Describe three things that can affect job performance.
- List three opportunities to explore during job reviews.

Chapter 25

Using the Job Review as a Learning Tool

Words to Know

job review	an assessment of an employee by an employer
probation	a trial period
performance standard	a guideline that describes an acceptable level of achievement for one part of a job
entry-level job	a job that is appropriate for someone who has had little experience
seniority	the number of years working in a company in relation to other employees

Read the conversation below to find out about one of the first hurdles you will face in a job:

"My boss at the travel agency said we need to talk today," Leah told her friend Melanie. "I've only been there for three months! Could she want to fire me already? I know that I don't work as fast as my co-workers. But I thought I was doing okay."

"You must be having your three-month job review," Melanie said. "A **job review** is an assessment of your work by your employer. Nearly everybody has job reviews. Relax!"

But Leah was still worried. "What happens during a job review?"

"Your boss will review your work so far. It's nothing to worry about. You might want to ask her, though, if she has any ideas about how you could do things faster."

How Job Reviews Work

Career Trend

Many companies today do not use a job review for giving raises, promotions, or bonuses. Instead, job reviews are used to promote employee growth and development.

Did You Know ?

After the first job review, an evaluation is usually done every four months, six months, or once a year.

In many companies, a new employee is on probation for about three months. **Probation** is a trial period. It is a time to see if the job and the worker fit. After this period is over, the employee is given a job review.

A job review is an evaluation, or a judgment, of the work performed by an employee. It is a tool that can help a person learn how to improve in his or her career. A job review is sometimes called a performance review or performance appraisal. Often, an employer will use a form, such as the one on page 335, to rate employees during a job review.

During a job review, an employer comments on how well job-related tasks have been performed. Often an employer will use performance standards to judge an employee. A **performance standard** is a guideline. It describes what is an acceptable level of achievement.

During her first three months at her job, Leah had a perfect attendance record. So, she received praise for that part of her job. She met and went beyond the company's performance standard. However, she was slow in getting customers their airline tickets. In that job area, Leah was informed that she did not meet the performance standard.

A performance standard is measurable. On Leah's review form, her perfect attendance was rated "Exceeds Standards." Her on time ticketing procedures were rated "Needs Improvement." Measurable performance standards help employees to know how well they have performed certain parts of their jobs.

High ratings for performance standards are achievable. Each performance standard can be met. In Leah's case, the more experienced travel agents were able to issue tickets quickly. Leah knew that she should be able to do the same someday.

Escape Away Travel Job Review Form			
Employee: Leah Sorento **Supervisor:** Adrianne Murphy		**Position:** Travel agent **Review:** 3-month	
Performance Standard	**Needs Improvement**	**Meets Standards**	**Exceeds Standards**
Attendance			X
Attitude			X
Relationship with customers			X
Ticketing procedures			
on time	X		
accurate		X	
Computer skills		X	
Relationship with co-workers		X	
Relationship with manager		X	
Meets training requirements		X	

Employers use forms to help them review employee job performance.

Using the Job Review Process

The job review can be a useful tool. How do you make it work for you? Begin by asking your manager what the performance standards are. Know exactly what is expected of you. Once you know the standards, you can work toward meeting them. Every once in a while, ask your manager what you are doing well and where you could improve. Do not wait until a job review to ask about your performance.

When the time comes for your job review, however, you will need to prepare a day or two in advance. Make a list of the things you want to talk about. If you have done something well on the job, remind your boss about it. If you have made mistakes, be prepared to talk about why they happened. Let your boss know that you are evaluating yourself on the job.

Write About It

Do a "performance appraisal" of how you are doing in school this year. List your school subjects as well as general attitude and attendance. Indicate for each item whether you "Need to Improve," "Are Doing OK," or "Are Doing Great." Then, write a plan of action on how to improve your performance.

✓ Check Your Understanding

Write your answers in complete sentences.

1. What are two ways in which a job review can help you?

2. Why is it important for a performance standard to be measurable?

3. Why is it a good idea to know the performance standards before you begin a job?

Dealing With Ratings in a Job Review

Often, during a job review, the manager will review with the employee each item on the form. The manager will explain the employee's ratings and how he or she earned them.

If you are meeting or going beyond a company's performance standards, you are doing very well. However, remember that a job review is often the first time you will find out in what areas you are not performing well. Listen to what your manager has to say. Think about the areas in which your performance is weak. Following are three main reasons why employees do not meet performance standards:

1. Lack of skills or knowledge

If you are not meeting performance standards on a job, show your boss what you are doing and how you are doing it. He or she may be able to show you how to perform better or direct you to a peer mentor.

Leah had never been shown the fastest way to get tickets for her customers. All of her co-workers used a shortcut that she did not know about. In this case, it will be easy for her to improve her performance. She can find someone who will tell her the shortcut.

Using Technology

Another way to prepare yourself for a job review is by reading some job review forms. Many companies have forms you can download for free from the Internet. Use a search engine and type in the key words *performance appraisal*.

Remember

A peer mentor is a person who has the same job responsibilities as another, but who is more experienced and can offer advice about the job.

2. Something is wrong in the work environment.

There are many things in the work environment that can hurt performance. Noise, co-workers who distract you from your work, difficult customers, and poor equipment are just some of them.

Leah has a slow computer. As a result, it takes her a long time to order airline tickets for customers. In this case, Leah's manager can either change the performance standard or get Leah a new computer.

3. Lack of motivation

People need to be recognized for their work. They need to know that their work is of value. If Leah feels a lack of motivation, she should discuss this issue with her manager during her job review.

Exploring New Opportunities in the Job Review

Job reviews can also be a time to explore new opportunities within the company. If you feel that the challenge is gone from your job, you may wish to ask your manager for some new responsibilities.

New opportunities come in many forms. Jorge is a police officer. He has been patrolling his neighborhood for 20 years. He enjoys his work, but he is always looking for new challenges on the job. Over the years, he has served on different task forces. A task force is a temporary group formed for a specific goal or operation. During his work on these task forces, Jorge has done fundraising and has trained new officers. He received these assignments by talking with his captain during job reviews. When opportunities came up, the captain asked Jorge if he was interested.

If you find yourself wanting new challenges on the job, let your manager know. Like Jorge, you may make important contributions to your company as well as make yourself more valuable to the company.

During a job review, you can also ask your manager about career paths. Career paths outline, or map, how a person could advance or change jobs in a company to earn more or do something more challenging. Career paths were discussed in more detail in Chapter 1.

A career path for travel agents in Leah's company is as follows: Inexperienced travel agents work in entry-level jobs. An **entry-level job** is a job for someone who has had little experience. Most new travel agents handle family vacations and local travel. Agents must work at this level for at least two years before they can be promoted. Then, agents can either become business travel agents or sales agents. Business travel agents arrange travel for large companies. Sales agents try to bring in new business for the company. Both positions earn about the same salary.

Did You Know ?

Career paths are found mostly in large companies or organizations. Often, the organization will have charts that show the steps in a typical career path.

An experienced travel agent may choose to specialize in business travel or sales.

A business travel agent can become a sales agent. The reverse is also true. This change is called a lateral transfer. A lateral transfer happens when an employee moves to a different department or position but stays at the same business level and salary. The benefits to this type of move are the new challenges and the opportunity to learn more about the business or company.

Finally, a business travel agent or sales agent can become a team manager. The team manager is in charge of a group of agents. This position is the highest level a person can reach in Leah's company.

Managers usually help employees along a career path. They direct employees to further training. They also help them get promotions. Use the job review to let your goals be known. Most managers will appreciate your desire to advance and learn new things.

Remember
A promotion is a job change that moves a person to a higher position or level in a company.

Getting Promoted

Employees are usually promoted only after they have worked for a company for a certain amount of time. An employee's level of seniority within the company is also important. **Seniority** refers to the number of years working in a company in relation to other employees. The more seniority an employee has, the more likely he or she is to be considered for a promotion. Employers also look at an employee's attitude and overall performance.

To move up in a company, always try to take on new challenges. Brainstorm to come up with new ideas. These ideas could be about how to do a job more efficiently. They could be new product or marketing ideas. They could be suggestions for new technologies to use in the office. Present these new ideas to your managers. Even if the ideas are not used, your manager will know that you are thinking.

Career Fact

Education also affects promotions. Some positions require more education. An employee must get that education in order to be promoted.

Finally, make sure your manager knows that you enjoy your job and plan to stay with the company. During job reviews, mention your interest in being promoted. Your positive attitude can get your manager to start thinking of you in new ways.

✓ Check Your Understanding

Write your answers in complete sentences.

1. What are the three main reasons why employees do not meet performance standards?
2. What is a career path?
3. What are three things you will need to have in order to be promoted at a company?

Learn More About It

NEW TYPES OF JOB REVIEWS

Traditional job reviews make some managers and their employees' uncomfortable. Employees are often rated by a single person, their manager. The manager tells the employee how he or she is performing. However, the manager may not be objective or well informed.

Other kinds of job reviews have become popular in recent years. These reviews may provide a more balanced view of the employees' work. Two types of job reviews used often today are peer reviews and self-reviews. Businesses often combine these types of reviews with the more traditional review.

In a peer review, co-workers are asked to evaluate an employee's work. In self-reviews, employees rate themselves in a number of areas. There is often a form to complete. Self-reviews involve the employee more in the review process. They also allow managers to act more like counselors than judges. Sometimes, in a self review, the employee is asked to set goals for himself or herself.

CRITICAL THINKING How does a self-review involve the employee more in the process?

JOB DESCRIPTION
Meeting Planner

Job Summary

A meeting planner is responsible for planning events for executives or companies. These events might be meetings, conferences, company picnics, or fundraisers. A meeting planner may work for a small company or large corporation. He or she may also own his or her own business.

Meeting planners usually work in an office when they are in the planning stages. They often have to spend time at the meeting site before the meeting. Meeting planners usually work about 40 hours a week. They may have to work additional hours, such as when the meeting or event is taking place. Full-time and part-time positions are usually available.

Job Activities

A meeting planner may do any or all of the following activities:

- Select the site for an event and make a budget for costs.
- Make travel plans for those people attending the event.
- Arrange for speakers and other kinds of entertainment.
- Choose the menu for the event.
- Reserve any audio and video equipment that is needed.
- Help clean up after the event.

Education/Training Requirements

Education requirements vary from a high school diploma to a college degree. Most employers require college courses in business or communications. Some employers will train employees who have very little experience. Additional requirements include good communications skills and good computer skills.

Think About It

Why would a meeting planner have to work during and even after a meeting or an event?

Chapter

25 ▷ Review

Summary

- Job reviews are evaluations. They can help employees improve their performance in their careers.

- Most companies have standards by which they judge an employee's performance. A good performance standard can be measured and achieved.

- Employees should know what the performance standards are before they begin their jobs. Then, they can work toward meeting these standards. Employees should take an active role in the job review process. They should be prepared to answer and ask questions.

- When an employee does not meet performance standards, the manager and employee should talk about why. It could be due to a lack of skills or knowledge, something wrong in the work environment, or a lack of motivation. Once the reason is known, the manager and employee should work to correct it.

- Job reviews are a good time to explore new opportunities. The employee can ask about extra assignments, career paths, lateral transfers, and promotions.

entry-level job
job review
performance standard
probation
seniority

Vocabulary Review

Complete each sentence with a term from the list.

1. Most companies have a trial period at work known as _____.

2. The number of years you are working for a company in relation to other employees is called _____.

3. The type of job a beginner is most likely to get is an _____.

4. A _____ is a guideline that indicates an acceptable level of achievement for that part of the job.

5. An evaluation of an employee by an employer is called a _____.

Chapter Quiz

Write your answers in complete sentences.

1. What does it mean to evaluate something?

2. How often do job reviews generally occur?

3. What do employers use to judge an employee's performance?

4. What should you do if your job seems too easy and is no longer challenging?

5. What are the benefits of a lateral transfer?

6. What are two ways to move up in a company?

CRITICAL THINKING

7. How is a career path like a map?

8. Why are companies more likely to promote someone who has seniority?

Career Portfolio Project

Think about a career you are interested in. What kinds of activities will you do in a typical day on the job? How will you be rated on these activities?

Create a performance appraisal form. This form should be based on the job you have chosen and its duties. List at least five performance standards. Keep in mind that performance standards must be measurable and achievable.

Changing with the times includes continuing to learn and trying new things throughout your life.

Learning Objectives

- Show how personal choices and unplanned events can affect career plans.
- Describe how changing human needs can affect career plans.
- List five ways to continue lifelong learning.
- Review the career-planning process.

Chapter 26 ▷ Changing With the Times

Words to Know

obsolete	no longer in use
severance	a sum of money often given to employees who are terminated under certain circumstances; it is usually based on length of employment
outplacement	a professional group that helps terminated employees cope with job loss and find new jobs
unemployment compensation	money an employee collects from the state government while he or she is out of work
self-actualization	a state of development that is reached when a person achieves his or her goals

In high school, Logan dreamed of being a professional news photographer. He took art and photography classes in school. He spent most weekends looking for subjects to photograph. After Logan graduated, he decided to travel for a while.

Eventually, Logan settled in Atlanta, Georgia. There, he sold some of his photographs. Logan also got a job in a camera store. For six nights a week, he worked in the store. During the day, he took trips outside of the city to take photographs. Logan also tried to sell his photographs to newspaper and magazine editors.

Three years later, Logan was still working nights in the camera shop. He had also fallen in love and wanted to get married. His life was changing in a big way. Read his conversation with his best friend Samuel on page 346.

"Karen and I are getting married next month. We'd like to have at least three children," Logan told Samuel.

"Sounds great," said Samuel. "So, why do you look like something's bothering you?"

"Marriage is going to be a big change for me. I'm not sure that my career path is going to work out," Logan told Samuel.

"I thought you loved photography," Samuel answered.

"I do love photography," Logan said, "and I still like to travel. But traveling so much means I'd have to be away from home a lot. I don't really want that now. I want to spend time with Karen and start a family. But that's not going to be easy to do if I keep working in the camera store at night and traveling during the day."

Being Prepared for Change

In Unit 1 of this book, you read how important it is in today's world to be flexible. Technology, world events, and changing demographics all influence the job market. For example, your company may close its factory if what it makes becomes **obsolete**, or no longer in use. Most products eventually become outdated in design, style, or construction. Newer designs and technologies replace these products. The owners of a business may decide to move a factory to another country where labor costs are cheaper. Such factors require workers to revise their career plans.

There are other factors that can also affect people's career plans. These other factors are personal choices, unplanned events, and changing needs. This chapter is about how to prepare for most of these changes.

Remember
Demographics refer to certain facts about a population, such as average age or family size.

Personal Choices and Unplanned Events

When Logan was in high school, he made a career plan. His long-term goal was to be a photographer. While trying to sell his photographs, Logan took a job working in a camera store. However, when he decided to marry, his career plans changed.

As you grow older, you will make personal choices that could change your life. Unplanned events can also change your life. In either case, you must be prepared to revise your career plan. The following situations are a few choices and events that you may experience:

Marriage

Getting married can cause you to change your career plan. Logan, for example, did not want to travel as much once he got married. He did not want to work nights, either. As a result, Logan went back to school for some technical training. He soon got a job with a magazine publisher in its art department. He helped to design the magazine's pages and also did some photography research. If you decide to marry, you will need to review your career plan with your partner.

Children

Having children can cause parents to make very difficult choices. Children are a major responsibility. They require lots of attention and love. Sometimes, parents have to choose between their careers and spending time with their children. Some parents give up their jobs or find other jobs that will allow them to spend more time with their children.

Divorce

Unfortunately, some marriages end in divorce. When people get divorced, they might have to make changes that affect their lives and their careers. Some people go back to school or take courses to learn skills that will help them get new jobs after a divorce.

Career Trend

Retail sales is a good career to consider during a period of change. It requires little experience, and there are usually many jobs available. Some young people work in retail sales part time to help pay for school. Older people often work in retail sales after retiring from another kind of work. People of all ages work in retail sales while looking for work in other fields.

Did You Know ?

It costs about $10,000 to $20,000 a year to raise a child under the age of 18.

Career Fact

The Social Security Disability Insurance program (SSDI) provides income and support services to workers with a medical condition that prevents them from working. SSDI is the largest federal disability insurer. Most private companies also offer some form of disability insurance.

Sickness or Disability

No one plans on becoming ill or having a disabling accident. However, thousands of people are injured or become ill each year, sometimes as a result of their jobs. Thousands more become ill or disabled because of events that are not job related. Whenever a sickness or disability occurs, people must revise their career plans.

Losing Your Job

People lose their jobs for many reasons. You learned in Chapter 2 that jobs are often lost during a slowdown in the economy. Other times, a change in the business, such as one business buying another, may lead to jobs lost.

Being terminated can be very upsetting in many ways. Suddenly, your source of income is gone. However, nearly everyone loses his or her job at least once in his or her career. Most people eventually get over the feelings of distress and move on. They find new jobs, sometimes in new industries.

If you are terminated from a job, make certain that you understand the reason for your termination. Also, ask the company for letters of reference. A good letter of reference can help improve your chances of getting another job.

Severance is a sum of money given to employees who are terminated under certain conditions. The amount of money is usually based on length of employment. Severance packages may also include outplacement services as well as temporary continuation of medical insurance. When using **outplacement**, the company pays for an outside group to help terminated employees find new jobs. Counseling services, computers, telephones, fax machines, and career resource libraries are often available at the outplacement site to help employees research and find new jobs.

If you are terminated, keep a record of the events that occurred in connection with your job loss. This record will help you fill out unemployment compensation forms. **Unemployment compensation** is money you collect from the state government while you are out of work. You can also use your records to help you follow up any legal action if you think that you were fired because of discrimination.

Every state has an agency that provides temporary benefits to most terminated workers. The state unemployment compensation system is like an insurance policy. Your employer pays fees each month into a state fund. If you lose your job through no fault of your own, you can apply to receive money from this fund. Unemployment benefits may last for six months or may be extended even longer. It depends on the state and on current law.

Using Technology

Each state has its own system for handling unemployment benefit claims. On the Internet, at www.doleta.gov, you can find links to the agency in your state. You can also find more information about the laws in your state concerning unemployment benefits.

Learn More About It

EMPLOYEES-AT-WILL PRINCIPLE

In most of the United States, nongovernment and nonunion employees are employed "at will." This term means that your employer can terminate you at any time without notice or reason, as long as the cause is not discrimination. This action can happen even if you performed well on the job.

Most countries in Europe have laws that prevent employers from terminating workers without "just cause." In the United States, only a few places have these laws. Because of employment-at-will, most U.S. workers are not protected against being terminated even if they did not do anything wrong.

Union employees are not employees at will. Unions have rules stating when and how employees may be terminated. An employer must have just cause to terminate a union member's employment. A union member can also challenge the reasons for his or her termination.

CRITICAL THINKING How does the employees-at-will principle threaten job security?

Our Changing Needs

As people become older, their values and needs change. In the 1950s and 1960s, a psychologist named Dr. Abraham Maslow had an idea about how people and their careers change with age.

Maslow said that people have five basic human needs. These needs are illustrated in the diagram on page 351. We attempt to satisfy these needs in both personal and professional ways. Maslow ranked these needs according to importance. He said that we start by satisfying our need for survival. Survival is our first and most basic need. Then, we work to each higher level of need. When we reach the top, we have reached our goals. At any time, something may cause us to slip down or climb farther up the ranking of needs. Some of us may never reach the top.

Maslow believed that our first need in life is simply to survive. We are most concerned with having food, shelter, clothing, and good health. To meet this need, we will take any job as long as it gives us the income we need to live. Once our need to survive is satisfied, we look for security and safety. During this stage, we may look for a job with a more steady income.

After we feel safe and secure, we then develop a need to belong. We want satisfying and lasting relationships with people. During this time, we may start a family. Professionally, we may improve relations with co-workers. We may also choose to do volunteer work in our community.

Once we feel a sense of belonging, we try to satisfy our need for esteem. We want respect from others, and we want to respect ourselves. We are more self-assured about who we are and what we want. At this time in our lives, we may feel ready to start our own business, or, we may try to get a big promotion.

Maslow's Five Basic Needs

Finally, we are able to work toward self-actualization. Maslow invented this term in 1968. It is the highest level in his ranking of needs. **Self-actualization** is the state of development reached when a person achieves all of his or her goals. At this stage, we should feel both fulfilled and happy.

Maslow's ideas are only one view of how our needs and values change. The most important thing is to be aware of how your needs change as you grow older or have different life experiences. This knowledge will help you to revise your career plans throughout your life.

✓ **Check Your Understanding**

Write your answers in complete sentences.

1. What is an example of a personal choice that could affect your career?

2. What is an example of an unplanned event that could affect your career?

3. What did Maslow believe?

Write About It
Abraham Maslow said that there are two things necessary for self-actualization. One is self-exploration, and the other is action. "The deeper the self-exploration," he said, "the closer one comes to self-actualization." Write a brief paragraph about what you think Maslow meant.

Lifelong Learning

Career Trend

Adult learning programs are quickly increasing in number. This is partly because of our aging population. Many older people have a lot of leisure time. In addition to opportunities for adults to learn, there are many part-time jobs teaching adults.

One of the most important things we can do to prepare for change is to practice lifelong learning. Lifelong learning means being aware of how you are changing and growing. It also means being aware of the world around you and how it is changing. Adding new skills or sharpening old ones is part of lifelong learning, too. Here are five things you can do to practice lifelong learning:

1. **Stay aware of what is happening in the world.**

   Read newspapers and magazines. Search the Internet. Listen to the news on radio and television. Learn what is happening in your local area, in the country, and in the world. In terms of your career, you might want to learn which industries in your area are growing. Such knowledge can better prepare you for job opportunities.

2. **Keep up any outside interests or hobbies.**

   Take language lessons or cooking classes. Play in a community band. Be physically active. Make exercise or sports a regular part of your life.

   As you grow older and your needs change, your hobbies may turn into a second career. Magda had a career in nursing. Her hobby was studying family histories. She traced her own family history back more than 300 years. After 20 years, Magda left nursing to start a business helping others to trace their family trees.

3. **Join professional associations in your job field.**

   Attend meetings to learn what others are doing that is new and interesting. Sometimes, professional associations hold national conferences to share ideas and information.

Continue learning by attending professional meetings.

4. **Continue your education.**

   Take classes at a community college, a four-year college, or a university. Find out whether teachers at some of these places will let you audit classes for free. To audit means to listen to or attend a class without actually enrolling in it. You do not get credit when you audit classes. However, it is a good way to learn something new.

5. **Be active in your community.**

   Volunteer. You will learn more about people and the world around you. You will also feel great about giving something to a cause you believe in. If you find something you really enjoy doing, it may become a second career.

Reviewing the Career-Planning Process

The average person changes jobs many times in his or her lifetime. Most people even change careers several times. Each time you change jobs or careers, work through some or all of the career-planning process.

Suppose that you are 40 years old. You have been doing the same kind of work for 20 years. Things that once interested you no longer do. What do you do? Go back to Step 1 of the career-planning process and start again. Soon, you will begin to feel excited. You will have more energy. Follow through on what you decide, even if it means getting more education. You will not regret the effort.

Here is a quick review of the career-planning process:

STEP 1   **Look at the big picture of career trends and the job market.**

STEP 2   **Assess yourself and your lifestyle choices.**

STEP 3   **Explore careers.**

STEP 4   **Build a foundation for your career.**

STEP 5   **Get hired.**

STEP 6   **Be successful in your career.**

STEP 7   **Continue to learn and change your plans as needed.**

You Make the Difference

As you go off into the world of work, always remember that you have something worthwhile to give to the world. You have strengths that can be turned into successes. However, it is up to you to make things happen. Use the information in this book and the resources around you. Learn from your experiences, good and bad. Good luck!

✓ Check Your Understanding

Write your answers in complete sentences.

1. How can you engage in lifelong learning?

2. How might keeping up an outside interest or a hobby help you in the future?

JOB DESCRIPTION
Retail Salesperson

Job Summary
A retail salesperson is hired by a store to help customers find what they are looking for. He or she may help customers with clothing, appliances, or many other products. Retail salespeople must be well informed about the products they sell.

Most retail salespeople work in retail stores. They do not usually travel. They often have to stand for long periods of time. They usually have to work evenings and weekends. They may have to work additional hours during holidays. Full-time and part-time positions are available.

Job Activities
A retail salesperson may do any or all of the following activities:

- Help customers find a product they are looking for.
- Show customers the features of a product.
- Ring up and bag or wrap purchases for customers.
- Take returns or exchanges from customers.
- Stock shelves in the store with products.
- Do inventory checks.
- Arrange for delivery of a product to a customer.

Education/Training Requirements
Requirements usually include a high school diploma. Employees of large stores may attend formal training programs. New employees usually receive on-the-job training. Additional requirements include good communications skills and good math skills.

Think About It

What kinds of training do you think take place in a retail sales training program?

Summary

- Many things can cause us to revise our career plans. Some of these are factors that affect the job market: technology, world events, and the changing population. Others are personal choices, unplanned events, and human needs.

- Some of the personal choices that could affect careers have to do with marriage and children. Unplanned events such as sickness, accidents, or divorce can also affect careers.

- Changing human needs can also affect our career plans. Dr. Abraham Maslow said there are five basic human needs: survival, security and safety, a sense of belonging, esteem, and self-actualization. With each need, we may seek different things from our professional or personal lives.

- There are many ways to continue learning. We can keep up on the news. We can take adult education classes. We can pursue hobbies. We can join professional associations. We can also volunteer our time and become involved in our communities.

- As you grow and change, you should re-evaluate your career situation. Refer back to the career-planning process in this book to do that.

obsolete

outplacement

self-actualization

severance

Vocabulary Review

Complete each sentence with a term from the list.

1. Providing career counseling and computers with Internet access are examples of _____ services.

2. The state of development reached when a person achieves his or her personal goals was named _____ by Dr. Abraham Maslow.

3. A sum of money based on length of employment and given to terminated employees is called _____ .

4. To become _____ is to become no longer useful.

Chapter Quiz

Write your answers in complete sentences.

1. Name three personal choices that can cause us to revise our career plans.

2. What are two unplanned events that could cause a need for a career change?

3. What is unemployment compensation?

4. What is the most basic human need according to Dr. Abraham Maslow?

5. What is at the top of Maslow's ranking of needs?

6. What is the first step in the career-planning process?

CRITICAL THINKING

7. Which do you think changes a person's career plan more—a personal choice or an unplanned event? Why?

8. Why is volunteering part of lifelong learning?

Career Portfolio Project

By now you should be a career expert! You should be prepared to move on to the next step in your career planning, whatever step that might be. To help you remember what you learned in this book, write a review of the book. Discuss how the book is organized and what subjects it covers. Reread the table of contents for help.

Write about three or four of the most useful things that you learned from the book. If you can, mention one or two things that were not covered in the book that you want to learn about. You might also discuss topics that were discussed briefly. Tell how you could find out more about those things.

Unit 5 Review

Choose the letter of the best answer to each question.

1. To overcome stress, what should you do when you start a new job?
   A. Arrive early, leave late, and do not talk to anyone.
   B. Do not answer any questions.
   C. Be clear about what you are supposed to do.
   D. Make telephone calls to all of your friends.

2. What are W-2 and W-4 forms used for?
   A. paying taxes
   B. applying for jobs in law and public safety
   C. working overtime
   D. getting job promotions

3. What are work ethics based on?
   A. the career you choose
   B. right and wrong ways of behaving in a workplace
   C. how to treat disabled workers
   D. controlling the spread of information about a person

4. Which of the following is not a discrimination issue in the workplace?
   A. sexual harassment against women
   B. not hiring handicapped people
   C. denying someone a job because of skin color or religion
   D. privacy in the workplace

5. Which of the following will help you get a promotion?
   A. You have been at the company for some time.
   B. You have performed well on the job.
   C. You have the right education.
   D. All of the above

6. Which of the following is an example of lifelong learning?
   A. changing to a new career
   B. having children
   C. being physically fit
   D. planning a career

Critical Thinking

What are your biggest concerns about starting a new job or being a success on the job? How do you plan to cope with these concerns?

Glossary

A

accounts receivable clerk a person who keeps track of the bills that have or have not been paid (p. 76)

agricultural inspector a person who inspects farms and the crops and animals raised on farms to make sure that farmers follow laws on health and safety (p. 158)

air traffic controller a person who manages the movement of airplanes in and around an airport (p. 226)

alumni students who have graduated from a school; former students (p. 273)

annual report a book or booklet published yearly that describes a company and its finances (p. 293)

apprenticeship an on-the-job training program in which a skilled worker teaches someone, called an apprentice, a trade or craft (p. 52)

apprenticeship program a special type of program in which a student learns skills on the job and also in a classroom (p. 175)

aptitude a natural ability to learn something or to do something well (p. 35)

assembler a factory worker who puts together the pieces that make up a product (p. 172)

assistant a person who helps another person who holds a higher-level job (p. 61)

athlete a person who is trained to play a certain sport (p. 184)

attendant

attendant a person who serves or helps another (p. 45)

attitude a way of acting, thinking, or feeling that shows a person's true nature (p. 255)

automotive service technician a person who uses technology to inspect, repair, and maintain cars or light trucks (p. 213)

B

billing clerk a person who records bills and sends them to customers (p. 76)

blind ad an ad in which the name of the hiring company is not given (p. 270)

bonus an amount of money awarded to a person who sells a certain amount or does an outstanding job (p. 147)

bookkeeper a person who keeps records on how much money a business spends and makes (p. 76)

bricklayer a skilled worker who builds walls, fireplaces, patios, or walkways with brick; also called a brickmason or blockmason (p. 171)

C

candidate a person seeking employment (p. 280)

career a chosen field of work in which you try to advance over time (p. 4)

career cluster groups of careers that are related to each other based on a similar industry or business (p. 60)

career counselor a trained professional who helps people with their career searches (p. 34)

career ladder a series of related jobs within a career that leads to greater responsibility and a higher position or level (p. 8)

career objective one step toward meeting a long-term career goal (p. 243)

career plan an outline of what a person wants to achieve with a career, including details of ways to reach a career goal and a timeline (p. 239)

carpenter a skilled worker who builds structures by cutting and putting together wood and other materials (p. 171)

certification a process that shows that an individual has met certain requirements to do something (p. 118)

civil servant a person who works for the government (p. 102)

civil service the system that is used to hire people for government jobs (p. 102)

clerical relating to office work (p. 76)

commission a fee paid to a salesperson for selling goods or services, usually a percentage of the selling price (p. 147)

communications skill a skill that involves sharing information (p. 258)

computer programmer a person who writes software programs that computers follow in order to perform their functions (p. 212)

computer software engineer a person who designs, develops, and tests the computer programs that enable computers to perform their functions (p. 212)

computer support specialist a person who helps people solve problems with their computers (p. 212)

consensus an opinion or a position reached by a group as a whole (p. 323)

correctional officer a person who works in a prison as a guard (p. 128)

cosmetologist a person who helps people to look neat and well-groomed (p. 115)

cover letter a short letter to an employer that is included with a résumé (p. 286)

co-worker any person you work with, including your manager (p. 322)

crane operator a person who is licensed to operate a vehicle that lifts large objects (p. 227)

curator a person who works with objects in a museum or wildlife in a zoo, aquarium, or nature center (p. 90)

customer service representative a person who handles customers' questions, requests, or complaints in person, by telephone, or through the Internet (p. 143)

cyclical unemployment what happens when people are out of work due to a slowdown in the economy (p. 20)

D

data information (p. 40)

data entry keyer a person who types information into a computer or updates information already stored in a computer (p. 213)

demographics certain facts about a population (p. 22)

dental assistant a person who helps dentists care for patients (p. 199)

dental hygienist a person who cleans and takes x-rays of teeth (p. 199)

depression a very long, severe period of recession (p. 20)

dietetic technician a person who helps a dietition plan, prepare, and manage food programs (p. 114)

dietitian a person who plans and manages food programs for healthy eating (p. 114)

directory a published resource that lists information for a certain area or subject (p. 270)

discrimination unfair treatment because of one's race, skin color, religion, sex, age, or disability (p. 325)

E

emergency dispatch operator a person who answers and handles emergency calls (p. 128)

emergency medical technician (EMT) a person who treats people who need immediate medical care before they get to a hospital (p. 198)

employee handbook a document that gives workers important information about the rules and policies, or ways of doing things, in a company (p. 310)

employment having a job (p. 4)

enlist to join (p. 102)

entrepreneur a person who organizes and runs a business (p. 149)

entry-level job a job that is appropriate for someone who has had little experience (p. 338)

environmental activist a person who works to change laws and attitudes about the environment (p. 159)

executive a person who helps run a business (p. 53)

F

feedback a reaction from someone about what you have done or how you have performed at something (p. 255)

fire inspector a person who examines buildings to make sure that they are safe from fires (p. 129)

fire investigator a person who gathers facts to determine the cause of a fire (p. 129)

floral designer a person who creates flower arrangements using live, dried, or plastic flowers (p. 185)

forester a person who works to keep a healthy balance between wildlife, plant life, and water quality in forests (p. 158)

G

goods things that can be seen, touched, bought, and sold (p. 19)

government the way a country, state, or city is organized and managed (p. 102)

H

hand packer a person who prepares items for shipment by hand (p. 227)

home health aide a person who cares for sick, injured, or older people in their homes (p. 200)

human resources department the people in a section of a business who interview job applicants and handle employee records; also called a personnel department (p. 280)

I

informational interview a question-and-answer session between a person who is interested in a career or job and a person who has that career or job (p. 63)

internship an on-the-job learning and training experience (p. 245)

ironworker a skilled worker who works with the steel that will become the framework for large structures (p. 171)

J

job any activity done in exchange for money or other payment (p. 4)

job aid any device that can help a worker remember important information (p. 310)

job application a form that a worker fills out when applying for a job (p. 4)

job benefits anything given to workers other than wages, such as vacation pay, sick pay, health insurance, and a pension (p. 314)

job interview a meeting between someone looking for a job and someone wanting to hire a person for a job (p. 292)

job prospect a future possibility of employment (p. 266)

job review an assessment of an employee by an employer (p. 333)

job shadowing going to a workplace to learn about the daily activities of a person who does the job every day by following that person on the job (p. 248)

job sharing a situation in which two people share the responsibilities of a single job (p. 54)

journeyman a person who has mastered his or her trade (p. 175)

L

language arts skill a communications skill using writing, reading, or speaking (p. 258)

leisure free time used for rest or recreation (p. 51)

librarian a person who works with materials and people in a library (p. 90)

license a legal document that gives a person permission to do something (p. 118)

licensed practical nurse (LPN) a person who has completed a training program in caring for patients (p. 198)

line installer a person who sets up electrical wires and cables to provide customers with electricity, telephone, or cable network services (p. 213)

livestock animals raised on farms (p. 158)

M

machinist a factory worker who uses tools or machines to make metal parts (p. 172)

manufacture to make goods with machines, usually in a factory (p. 21)

manufacturing the name of the industry that makes things, especially by using machines (p. 172)

mental health assistant a person who helps people suffering from mental illness (p. 199)

mentor an experienced person who helps and advises a person with less experience (p. 246)

military personnel the people who work in the armed forces (p. 102)

minority a group of people that makes up less than 50 percent of the population of an area (p. 324)

mission purpose (p. 292)

museum educator a person who helps people to learn about a museum's objects (p. 90)

N

navigate to steer, or control the direction of, something (p. 226)

net income money earned minus the amount withheld in taxes (p. 312)

networking being in touch with a wide variety of people, called contacts, who can pass along information on job opportunities to you (p. 268)

nursing aide a hospital worker who helps care for patients (p. 198)

O

obsolete no longer in use (p. 346)

occupation another term for career (p. 4)

outplacement a professional group that helps terminated employees cope with job loss and find new jobs (p. 348)

overtime the amount of time worked in addition to the normal 40 hours in a business week (p. 93)

P

park ranger a person who works to protect the natural resources in national or state parks (p. 102)

part-time worker a person who works less than 35 hours in a business week (p. 93)

payroll clerk a person who makes sure that paychecks are correct and delivered on time (p. 76)

peer mentor a person who has the same job responsibilities as another but is more experienced and can offer advice about the job (p. 310)

pension a regular payment given to a retired person for work that he or she performed; usually given by a former employer (p. 7)

performance standard a guideline that describes an acceptable level of achievement for one part of a job (p. 334)

personality traits the different ways a person behaves; characteristics (p. 38)

personnel agency a business that helps people find either temporary work, staff jobs, or both (p. 51)

pharmacy technician a person who helps fill prescriptions for medical drugs (p. 201)

pilot a person who controls, or flies, an airplane (p. 226)

positive self-talk replacing negative thoughts with positive ones (p. 255)

pre-employment tests exams given by possible employers that may test your skills, your personality, or your attitudes (p. 255)

prioritize to rank in order of importance, or priority (p. 47)

probation a trial period (p. 334)

procrastinate to put off things without a good reason (p. 256)

production the act of making something (p. 7)

professional association an organization whose members all have the same career or occupation (p. 65)

proficiency being able to do something well (p. 259)

promotion a job change that moves a person to a higher position or level in a company (p. 8)

proofread to carefully read written material and mark any corrections needed (p. 281)

protégé a person who is guided or helped by a more experienced person (p. 246)

public relations department a department in a company that is responsible for giving out information about the company (p. 293)

R

receptionist a person who receives customers or visitors in an office (p. 76)

recession a period when the production of goods and services decreases for 6 months or more (p. 20)

recommendation a positive statement that tells that a person is qualified for a job (p. 245)

recruiting specialist a person who provides information to people about joining the armed forces (p. 103)

referee a person who watches the plays during sporting events, such as football or basketball, to make sure that players follow the rules (p. 184)

reference the name of a person who will provide a statement that describes another person's character or job responsibilities (p. 245)

registered nurse (RN) a nurse who has completed a two- or four-year program in patient care (p. 203)

research to carefully read and study facts about a certain subject (p. 63)

resource something that can be used for support or help (p. 4)

résumé a written statement of a worker's job goals, experience, and education (p. 280)

retail sales the selling of goods or services directly to customers (p. 142)

retirement when someone leaves a job or career after many years (p. 6)

S

salary the payment a person regularly receives for work (p. 5)

sales representative a person who works to sell the products that a company makes (p. 143)

scout a person who identifies the most talented athletes in a sport (p. 184)

security guard a person who protects stores and businesses from illegal activities, such as robbery (p. 128)

self-actualization a state of development that is reached when a person achieves his or her goals (p. 351)

self-assessment figuring out your strengths and interests (p. 33)

self-esteem self-respect (p. 33)

self-image how you feel about yourself (p. 255)

seniority the number of years working in a company in relation to other employees (p. 339)

services paid work done to help others, such as teaching or waiting on tables (p. 19)

set designer a person who builds and paints sets, or furniture and scenery, for plays, movies, or television shows (p. 185)

severance a sum of money often given to employees who are terminated under certain circumstances; it is usually based on length of employment (p. 348)

sexual harassment any unwelcome or inappropriate sexual behavior (p. 325)

ship engineer a person who maintains the engines, boilers, and other machinery on a ship (p. 227)

shipping and receiving clerk a person who tracks goods that are received and goods that are shipped to other places (p. 77)

skill an ability to do something well, usually because you have practiced it (p. 32)

Social Security number a set of numbers assigned to each citizen of the United States by the federal government for tax purposes (p. 281)

social worker a person who helps people to meet their needs by providing counseling and arranging other services (p. 114)

software program a set of instructions that tells a computer what to do (p. 212)

specialist a person who works in and knows a lot about one field (p. 61)

stevedore a person who loads and unloads ships (p. 227)

stock clerk a person who keeps track of the goods in stockrooms or warehouses (p. 76)

T

tax return a report to the government that shows how much a worker has earned, paid in taxes, and either owes in taxes or is due in a tax refund (p. 313)

teacher assistant a person who helps a teacher (p. 90)

teamwork the efforts of a group, called a team, to achieve a common goal (p. 323)

technician a person who has training in technology in a certain field (p. 60)

technology the use of science to create new or better products (p. 7)

telemarketer a person who sells products or services over the telephone (p. 143)

terminate to fire an employee (p. 325)

time management learning to use time well (p. 256)

tool and die maker a skilled worker who makes parts for machines that are used to make metal products (p. 172)

tractor-trailer truck driver a person who is licensed to drive a large truck used for transporting goods (p. 226)

trade an occupation that requires certain skills (p. 170)

trade magazine a magazine that contains articles about a particular industry (p. 270)

trade union an organization of trade workers whose main goal is to protect the working conditions and wages of members of the organization (p. 176)

transportation the movement of people or goods from one place to another (p. 226)

U

umpire a person who watches the plays during baseball and other games to make sure that players follow the rules (p. 184)

unemployment compensation money an employee collects from the state government while he or she is out of work (p. 349)

unemployment rate the percentage, or fraction, of people in the labor force who are looking for work but who have not found jobs (p. 19)

V

veterinarian an animal doctor, also called a vet (p. 199)

veterinary assistant a person who helps veterinarians in caring for animals (p. 199)

vocational school a school in which students are trained in specific jobs or trades (p. 52)

W

W-2 form a yearly statement of wages and taxes sent by a business to a worker (p. 312)

W-4 form a form that determines the taxes taken from a worker's paycheck (p. 311)

wastewater treatment operator a person who operates equipment that cleans and treats wastewater from sewers and certain types of businesses (p. 158)

Web developer a person who designs or creates Web sites for the Internet, also called a Web designer (p. 213)

work environment all the things that surround and affect a person at work (p. 50)

work ethics the values and ways of behaving that are important in a work environment (p. 322)

working conditions how things are at a job, such as the number of hours worked in a week (p. 7)

X

x-ray technician a person who takes x-rays of a patient's body; also called a radiologic technician (p. 198)

Index

G

General Aptitude Test
Battery (GATB), 35
Goods, 17, 19–20
Government, 101, 102
Government careers,
100–109
associations for, 108
job trends in, 104
learn more about,
106–107
lifestyles of people who
have, 105–106
strengths of people who
have, 104–105
Great Depression, 20
*Guide for Occupational
Exploration*, 64

H

Hairdressers, 114
Hand packers, 225, 227
Hard skills, 37, 254
Healthcare careers, 196–207
associations for, 206
job trends in, 200
learn more about, 204
lifestyles of people who
have, 202
strengths of people who
have, 200–201
Health insurance, 315
Heating and air
conditioning technicians,
214, 216
Help wanted ads, 268,
270–271, 272
High school, careers and,
254
Home health aides, 13, 197,
200
Human resources
departments, 279, 280

Human services careers,
112–123
associations for, 122
job trends in, 115–116
learn more about, 120
lifestyles of people who
have, 118–119
strengths of people who
have, 116–117

I

Illustrators, 186, 189
Information, writing for,
205
Informational interviews,
59, 63, 66–67, 268
Information clerks, 76, 77,
80
Instructors, 184, 185, 187,
188–189
Interests, 37
Internal Revenue Service
(IRS), 313
Internships, 239, 245–246
Interview. *See* Informational
interviews; Job interviews
Ironworkers, 169, 171

J

Job(s), 3, 4
applying for, 278–287
first weeks on, 308–309
starting, 306–317
training on, 309–310
types of, 60–62
Job aids, 307, 310–311
Job applications, 3, 4,
281–282
Job benefits, 307, 314–315
Job interviews, 33, 280, 291,
292–301
Job offers, 298–299
Job openings, 4, 267–268

Job prospects, 265
Job reviews, 332–341
Job search, 264–275
Job security, 7
Job Service, 273
Job shadowing, 239, 248,
309
Job sharing, 45, 54
Jobs Rated Almanac, 12
Job training programs, 4
Journeyman, 169, 175

K

Karate instructors, 193

L

Labor force, 19
Language arts skills, 253,
258
Law and public safety
careers, 126–137
associations for, 136
job trends in, 129–130
learn more about,
134–135
lifestyles of people who
have, 132–133
strengths of people who
have, 130–131
Leisure, 45, 51
Librarians, 89, 90, 92, 94
Library technicians, 301
Licensed practical nurses
(LPNs), 197, 198, 203
Licenses, 113, 118
Lifelong learning, 352–353
Lifestyle, 44–55
Line installers, 211, 213,
214, 216, 217
Livestock, 157, 158
Long-term care, 115
Long-term goals, setting,
242

Photography Credits

All photographs © Pearson Learning Group unless otherwise noted.

Cover: *t.l.* © George Hall/Corbis, *m.* © Greg Pease/Stone/Getty Images, *b.l.* © PhotoDisc/Getty Images, Page 2: © Syracuse Newspapers/Carl Single/The Image Works Incorporated, 6: © Tony Freeman/PhotoEdit, 16: © Spencer Grant/PhotoEdit, 20: © Brown Brothers, 30: © Tony Freeman/PhotoEdit, 35: © Cleve Bryant/PhotoEdit, 44: © Jim West/The Image Works Incorporated, 52: © Michael Newman/PhotoEdit, 58: © DK Images, 61: © Robert Brenner/PhotoEdit, 74: © Lon C. Diehl/PhotoEdit, 78: © PhotoEdit, 81: © Digital Vision/Getty Images, 88: © Jim Cummins/Taxi/Getty Images, 92: Matt Rainey/The Star-Ledger, 100: © Peter Turnley/Corbis, 105: © Tom Prettyman/PhotoEdit, 112: © Michael Newman/PhotoEdit, 119: © David Pollack/Corbis, 126: © Gordon M. Sachs, 133: © Tom Carter/PhotoEdit, 140: © Michael Newman/PhotoEdit, 147: PhotoDisc Red/Getty Images, Inc., 156: © Marc Edwards/Peter Arnold, Inc., 159: © Terry Brandt/Grant Heilman Photography, Inc., 168: © Paul A. Souders/Corbis, 172: © Michael Newman/PhotoEdit, 175: © A. Ramey/PhotoEdit, 182: © Tom Stewart/Corbis, 188: © Cindy Charles/PhotoEdit, 196: © Gabe Palmer/Corbis, 199: © Robin L. Sachs/PhotoEdit, 201: © Spencer Grant/PhotoEdit, 210: © J. Coletti/Stock Boston, 213: © Morton Beebe/Corbis, 224: © David Butow/Corbis Saba, 227: © Jeff Greenberg/PhotoEdit, 238: © Michael Newman/PhotoEdit, 247: © Tony Freeman/PhotoEdit, 252: © Tom Stewart/Corbis, 258: © Tom Carter/PhotoEdit, 264: © Spencer Grant/PhotoEdit, 271: © V.C.L./Taxi/Getty Images, 278: © Robert Brenner/PhotoEdit, 290: © Dennis MacDonald/PhotoEdit, 295: © Dwayne Newton/PhotoEdit, 306: © John Riley/Stone/Getty Images, 312–313: Internal Revenue Service, 320: © Bruce Ayres/Stone/Getty Images, 326: © Owen Franken/Corbis, 338: © Gabe Palmer/Corbis, 344: © Micheal Newman/PhotoEdit, 353: © Fisher/Thatcher/Stone/Getty Images.